# Steps to Independence

D1016409

# Steps to Independence

## Teaching Everyday Skills to Children with Special Needs
### Third Edition

By

**Bruce L. Baker, Ph.D.**
*Professor of Psychology*
*University of California, Los Angeles*

and

**Alan J. Brightman, Ph.D.**
*Manager*
*Worldwide Disability Solutions Group*
*Apple Computer, Inc.*

with

Jan B. Blacher, Ph.D.
Louis J. Heifetz, Ph.D.
Stephen P. Hinshaw, Ph.D.

and

Diane M. Murphy, R.N.

·P A U L·H·
BROOKES
PUBLISHING C?

Baltimore • London • Toronto • Sydney

**Paul H. Brookes Publishing Co.**
Post Office Box 10624
Baltimore, MD 21285-0624

www.brookespublishing.com

Copyright © 1997 by Paul H. Brookes Publishing Co., Inc.
All rights reserved.

Typeset by Brushwood Graphics, Inc., Baltimore, Maryland.
Manufactured in the United States of America by
The Maple Press Company, York, Pennsylvania.

**Third printing, November 2000.**

Illustrations by Michael Cassaro.

**Library of Congress Cataloging-in-Publication Data**
Baker, Bruce L.
    Steps to independence : teaching everyday skills to children
with special needs / Bruce L. Baker, Alan J. Brightman ; with
Jan B. Blacher . . . [et al.] ; [illustrations by Michael Cassaro] —
3rd ed.
        p.   cm.
    Originally published as a series of 9 manuals, which are now
rev. and combined into one volume.
    Includes index.
    ISBN 1-55766-268-1
    1. Mentally handicapped children—Life skills guides.
2. Mentally handicapped children—Education.   3. Special
education—Parent participation.   4. Parents of handicapped
children.  I. Brightman, Alan.  II. Blacher, Jan.  III. Title.
HV891.B16      1997
649'.152–dc20
                                                    96–26889
                                                       CIP

British Library Cataloguing-in-Publication data are available from
the British Library.

# Contents

vi ✐ Contents

# Acknowledgments

This book has a very long and rich history, with many people who deserve our gratitude. We thank Dr. Michael Begab and the National Institute of Child Health and Human Development; in 1971 they began to support our efforts to develop training manuals for parents of children with special needs. We thank our colleagues in the Read Project at Harvard University who spent many hours in the early 1970s zipping zippers and sweeping floors to determine how a host of everyday skills might best be taught. We also thank the staff and parents of Camp Freedom, an educational residential camp for children with special needs that we directed during the 1970s. We thank these individuals for having taught us so much and for having given such useful feedback on the manuals. We thank Ann Wendel at Research Press for believing in the manuals and publishing them, beginning in 1975. We thank the many staff and parents who were involved in the UCLA Project for Developmental Disabilities during the 1980s for their input. Since the 1970s, when we first began publishing the Steps to Independence series, we have received positive comments and useful suggestions from hundreds of parents and teachers, and to them, too, we are grateful.

With the support and guidance of Melissa Behm of Paul H. Brookes Publishing Co., we revised the manuals in 1989 and combined them into one book for parents and teachers of children with special needs. During that same year, we published a monograph with the American Association on Mental Retardation (Parent Training and Developmental Disabilities), summarizing research done with these materials. Now we have revised again. We especially acknowledge the feedback we received from Mary Beth Sullivan, from the Brookes staff, and from anonymous reviewers retained by Brookes. We also gratefully acknowledge the contributions made to the manuals on which this book is based by our former co-authors, Louis J. Heifetz, Diane M. Murphy, Stephen P. Hinshaw, and Jan B. Blacher.

*Bruce L. Baker*
*Alan J. Brightman*

# Section I

# Basics of
# Teaching

# Chapter 1

# Setting Out

Maybe more than anything else, this is a book about *expectations*. Both for you and for your child.

Not many years ago, children with special needs were almost automatically associated with failure and frustration. Kids with labels were viewed as kids who *couldn't*. Despite the frequently heroic efforts of parents and of special education teachers to demonstrate how much these children could, in fact, learn, the prevailing "wisdom" all too often counseled not to expect too much. How many parents had to listen to some version of the phrase "He'll only go *so far*"? And all because these children had a label that other children didn't carry.

Parents, too, had a label that caused others to view them with different expectations. They were *parents*. Which meant that they weren't professionals. Which meant that what they knew about their child—never mind what they were capable of *doing* with their child—was of little value in making sound educational decisions for that child. They were simply parents, people who "took care" of their children while others made decisions about their children's educational futures.

## Great Expectations

Times, thankfully, have changed. Since the 1960s, we have witnessed not only the passage of historic legislation but also, as a result, a dramatic adjustment in expectations for children with special needs—and in expectations for their parents. Children with labels, today, are seen as children who *can*. They can learn. They can interact productively with their nonlabeled peers. They can be expected to participate more fully in all aspects of society. And their parents are seen as partners in ensuring that many options—educational, recreational, and vocational—will be available to them.

3

It is truly a new era for children with special needs, an era in which parents and professionals determine together, with positive expectations, the educational course of each child. It is an era, too, in which the roles of parents and professionals require them to reconsider their individual responsibilities. Who decides what a child will learn? And who takes action to see that the learning happens? Simply stated, this new era for children with special needs requires parents to reexamine what it means to be a parent and requires teachers to reexamine what it means to be a teacher.

# Parent Roles

There is no one "correct" approach to reexamining roles. Teaching is a natural part of being a parent. Virtually every time you interact with your child you are teaching him or her something—whether you realize it or not. Many parents of children with special needs have decided to become more intentional teachers. Some parents have taken it upon themselves to learn how to conduct daily teaching sessions in their home. Other parents, after considering their full range of responsibilities at work and at home, have realistically decided that an everyday teaching role would be impractical. Their teaching will have to take advantage of opportunities that present themselves throughout the day or on the weekend. In either case, the child gains, particularly when the parents have participated actively with their child's teachers in shaping an individualized education program (IEP).

# Good Teaching

One of our basic assumptions in writing this book was that, no matter what decisions you may have made about your role as a teacher, you will be better able to fulfill that role if you understand, firsthand, what good teaching is all about. Put another way, once you know how to teach your child a skill—from beginning to end—and once you know how to manage behavior problems, then you'll be much more valuable to (and valued by) others in your child's educational world. A related assumption is that the only way to learn about good skill teaching is to do good skill teaching. Even once. So, however busy your life is, we urge you to find some time, somehow, during which you will teach your child a new skill. It won't take you that long, and, like most parents, you'll probably be delighted at how good you are at it. But, more important, you'll be much better prepared to be a partner on your child's educational team.

It won't take you that long, we said. Sometimes days. Sometimes weeks. But think of it this way. Think of all the time you already spend

with your child—time during which you're likely doing many things for her that she might be able to do independently. By urging you to try teaching, we're not suggesting that you find additional time to spend with your child. We're simply suggesting that you take some of the time you already spend and direct it toward what we believe will be a rewarding and long-lasting experience for you both.

# Philosophies and Fads

"OK," you might say. "Teaching certainly makes sense. But there seem to be a lot of ways to go about this. What's the approach in this book, and how do I know whether it will work?" Good questions. The special education field has more than its share of different approaches, each with vocal proponents. It is very difficult to be an informed consumer, to separate the philosophies about education for people with mental retardation from sound evidence about what works.

Because we desperately want to help children with mental retardation and related disabilities, we are particularly vulnerable to philosophies and fads of the moment. Some of these will be found to have merit and will survive to become the common practices of tomorrow. Others will fade, to be replaced by a new fad. For example, a philosophy that is guiding some educators' thinking today is *full inclusion*—the proposition that all children with special needs should be educated entirely in general classrooms. What do you think? This is an extreme outgrowth of earlier philosophies, such as *inclusion, mainstreaming,* and *normalization,* which argued that opportunities for children with special needs should be as close as possible to those for typically developing children. These earlier ideas turned out not to be passing fads but perspectives that have become widely accepted, not so much because they were demonstrated to "work," but because they seemed to many of us to be the right thing to do.

Other philosophies and fads do not fare so well. Remember patterning? Megavitamin therapy? Additive-free diets? Each of these offered new hope to parents and absorbed immeasurable time and money, only to finally be discarded from the weight of scientific studies and professional opinion. The same kind of thing seems to be occurring in the 1990s with "facilitated communication." This is a method whereby a "facilitator" gently guides a person with autism to purportedly express ideas or inner thoughts heretofore unspoken. Too good to be true? Well, it looks like the answer is yes. Repeated scientific investigations are finding that, in their studies, it is the "facilitator," albeit inadvertently, who is producing or shaping the output. How is a parent to know? It has been helpful that many professional organizations, weighing the evidence, have cautioned consumers about facilitated communication.

So, as we said: Good questions. Be assured that the teaching techniques in this book are based on principles of behavior change that educators have known for some time. They have been derived from thousands of published studies of effective teaching as well as from the shared experiences of countless parents and teachers. These behavioral teaching principles have become an integral part of effective school programs.

Although most educators would generally agree with the broad teaching principles we employ, there is one point with which some will disagree. Some educators argue that teaching should always be done informally, in the child's natural environment and within ongoing play and living activities. Other educators point out the benefits of separate designated teaching sessions where the teacher repeatedly practices a skill with the child. Our opinion is . . . well, it depends. There is good evidence that both approaches are successful, and a blend of the two approaches is likely best for most children. You will decide how closely to follow the specific teaching programs that we suggest and how much to adapt them to provide teaching moments throughout your child's day.

## You're the Expert

A final point before we—and you—get started. It's an obvious point, perhaps, but one that hundreds of parents reminded us could not be made too often. Though you may be the parent or teacher of a child with special needs, you are unlike any other parent or teacher of such children. You are uniquely you. You have your own dreams and visions, your own wants and needs. And in one essential way, you have a kind of information that no one else could possibly have: You know your child—or your classroom—more intimately than anyone else.

We ask, therefore, as you begin this book, that you don't think at all about trying to change who you are. Rather, add to what is uniquely you a new set of skills and, perhaps, a new way of looking at your child, to become an even more substantial partner in building his educational future. Much of what we say here may not seem all that new to you. For instance, you may have already successfully used a version of the techniques described here with other children. It is our hope, though, that this book will help you to enlarge upon these experiences so that you can do what you are doing even better. Remember: Keep your expectations high—for both you and your child.

## Using This Book

This book is intended to be used actively—to be written in, thought about, discussed with other parents or colleagues. The content ranges

from broad teaching principles to highly specific teaching suggestions. You will likely skip around some, using the parts of the book that suit your needs and your child's needs best. The chapters in Section I cover the basics of teaching and should be read first.

When you have finished Section I, turn to any chapter in Section II that is of interest. These chapters address teaching skills in specific areas. The first four chapters in Section II examine basic skills for the young child: Get Ready Skills (Chapter 8), Self-Help Skills (Chapter 9), Toilet Training (Chapter 10), and Play Skills (Chapter 11). The next three chapters cover more advanced skills that lead the child to greater independence: Self-Care Skills (Chapter 12), Home-Care Skills (Chapter 13), and Information Skills (Chapter 14). Chapter 15, Plugging into the Personal Computer Revolution, is new to this edition. Here we look briefly at exciting new opportunities for a child with special needs to acquire information, with greater promise for independence than we could have dreamed of in the not-too-distant past.

Section III provides an expanded consideration of ways to think about and manage child behavior problems, including Behavior Problems (Chapter 16) and Initiating a Behavior Management Program (Chapter 17). The appendices serve as reference guides when you begin to teach specific skills. They include specific suggestions for teaching get ready skills (Appendix A); an inventory for assessing a child's self-help skills (Appendix B); and specific, detailed programs for teaching a number of self-help skills (Appendix C), play skills (Appendix D), and information skills (Appendix E).

Chapter 2 gets you started on the road to becoming a successful skills teacher. But before jumping in, let's take a moment to look at one parent who's already been traveling that road for some time. The teaching program you're about to glimpse will, on the surface, seem fairly simple. But the strategies behind it were carefully developed and practiced in ways that you'll learn about in the following chapters.

---

## ✐ Billy's Bed

On Wednesday morning, Billy woke up to find that something new had been added to the list on the wall. There, at the bottom, was a picture of a bed neatly made. And he knew right away what this meant.

The list was, in fact, Billy's list. He and Mom had put it together a while ago. It had begun with just two pictures; now it had grown to look like this:

| Billy | Sun. | Mon. | Tue. | Wed. | Thu. | Fri. | Sat. |
|-------|------|------|------|------|------|------|------|
| 🧼 | ✓ | ✓ | ✓ | | | | |
| 🪥 | ✓ | | ✓ | | | | |
| (comb) | ✓ | ✓ | ✓ | | | | |
| (shirt) | | ✓ | ✓ | | | | |
| (shoe) | ✓ | ✓ | ✓ | | | | |
| (bed) | | | | | | | |

And now bedmaking. He hadn't ever done this before, but last night he and Mom agreed that he would try.

"How are you doing, Billy? Breakfast is almost ready."

Billy looked up at the list again. Washing hands and face and brushing teeth were no longer a problem—they were, by now, an easy way to get checks. Getting dressed, though, still depended on what Mom laid out for him the night before. Jerseys and sweaters, for example, were easy. But shirts with small buttons were still hard, and sometimes he needed help with them.

As Billy continued to work his way down the list, Mrs. Jackson went to his room and began straightening out the bed. By the time Billy returned from the bathroom, the bed was almost completely made; all that remained was to pull the bedspread up from where she had left it folded about halfway down.

Dressed now and ready to go, Billy asked Mom for the morning check marks.

"Looks like you got them all today, didn't you?" Mrs. Jackson began to check off each accomplishment with exaggerated inspection. "Now what about the shoes? Oh yes . . . ." Another red check on the list. "Five more checks this morning, Billy. How many did we agree upon for you to go bowling this Friday?"

"Twenty, right?" he asked.

"Twenty it is. But look at this. There's no check yet next to the new bed picture on the list. Shall we try that before breakfast, too?"

Billy suddenly became less cheerful—his usual and predictable withdrawal from something new. "Aw, I'm hungry."

Mrs. Jackson had learned to be gently insistent and to remind Billy of the reward. "Come on, Billy, it'll just take a minute and you'll get another check. Billy, watch what I do."

Since the bed was practically all made anyway—Mrs. Jackson had made sure of that—it required only *one simple motion* to get the bedspread up over the pillow. "Billy, watch what I do." After demonstrating this motion slowly, she brought the bedspread back to where it had been and encouraged Billy to try the same.

"It did look pretty easy," Bill thought to himself. "OK, Billy, you try. Pull it over the pillow. Good. See, you get another check. Tomorrow we'll do a little more bedmaking, OK?"

"OK."

Billy had indeed finished making his own bed, and for that he deserved his check. He earned it as he earned them all!

Chapter **2**

# Targeting a Skill

There are many children like the Billy we just described. For some, the challenge may not be learning how to make a bed, but how to tie a hair ribbon, catch a ball, or "go potty." For others, even carrying out skills already mastered is an unpredictable affair. In either case, there never seems to be a lack of challenges.

In later chapters, we consider ways to motivate your child to perform those skills he may have already learned but will not always do. For now, let's concentrate only on the challenge of teaching new skills. Your first task will be to select the one new skill that you will begin to teach.

## Guidelines to Consider When Choosing a Target Skill

### What Skills Are You Now Doing for Your Child?

First, *observe your child's typical day* and, in the spaces that follow, make a list of some of the self-help skills that *you now do for him* and that you might want to teach him to do for himself. Your list might include skills such as tying his shoes, making his bed, washing his hair, putting his toys or clothes away, bathing him, or cutting his meat. Is he completely toilet trained? If not, add toileting skills to your list.

You might also add to your list some household chores that you think your child is ready to learn, such as emptying wastebaskets, setting the table, raking leaves, or sweeping. What about play? Are there toys and games you'd like to see him master? Could he learn to play better with other children? By himself?

11

_____

_____

_____

_____

_____

You cannot teach all . . . *wait a minute!* Did you make your list? If not, please do it now. The rest of this section will be much more valuable to you if you stop for a moment now to list some of the skills you'd like your child to learn.

You cannot teach all of these at once, so here are three considerations in targeting a skill to begin teaching.

## Which Skills Does Your Child Want to Learn?

You will want to observe your child carefully to see what she might want to learn next. Perhaps she will tell you. Perhaps she will show you by attempting a skill on her own, like trying to spread peanut butter with a knife, or trying to tie her shoes, or maybe trying to shoot baskets with the other kids.

## Which Skills Is Your Child Ready to Learn?

Keep in mind that as a child grows and develops, some skills naturally happen before others. Sitting, for example, comes before walking. Eating with a fork comes before cutting with a knife. When choosing a target skill, therefore, consider what your child can already do and what he might be ready to learn next.

Note, for example, the chart on Billy's wall (see Chapter 1). In small ways, each skill Billy learned provided him with a better basis for learning the others. Learning to wash his hands and face made brushing his teeth that much easier to master: He was more at home in the bathroom, he had learned how to turn the water on and off, and he knew what it meant to "rinse." Search for clues in what your child already does, and enjoys doing, that might help you select an appropriate target skill.

Look at the list of skills you have just made. Are there some skills that your child seems almost ready to learn—in which he makes an effort to do the task and can do parts of it already?

## Which Skills Do You Want to Teach?

You will, of course, want to begin with a skill that you feel is important for your child to learn now. Perhaps there is one area in which a lack of skills causes the greatest problem for the entire family. For example, your son's inability to feed himself at mealtime might mean that the family can never sit down to eat together. Or your daughter's inability to dress herself in the morning may mean that you have no time left to spend with the other children before they leave for school.

Circle one skill on your list that you will target to teach first. Keep this skill in mind as you read the remaining chapters in Section I. It will be easier for you if you choose a self-help or play skill. Toilet training and information skills are more difficult to teach and should wait until you've taught a self-help or play skill.

Skill to teach  _____

**Please:** Do not read further until you have written down a skill. (Don't worry, you can always change your mind.) You may not be used to writing directly in a book, but that's really the only way to effectively use this one.

# Chapter 3

# Establishing Steps

---

### Learning Progresses in Gradual Steps

"Count me out of this hand, guys. I've got to help Richie get ready for bed."

"Hey, Herb, last time we were here for poker you were starting to teach him to take a shower. Can he do it yet?"

"Well, yes and no. I mean he can get himself undressed and he can turn on the water, but he still needs help in getting the temperature right. Now he's learning to lather himself. He already knew how to wash his face and hands, now we're teaching him to do his stomach, chest, and legs. When he's been rinsed, he can dry himself perfectly. We taught him that first."

"You know, Herb, you're even beginning to sound like a teacher. I ask a simple question and . . . . Let's hope Herb doesn't start thinking that carefully about the card game or we'll all be broke."

---

Herb's answer might have been confusing to someone who viewed taking a shower as one complete skill that a child either can or cannot do. Yet when we consider a skill to be simple, it is because we have already learned to perform each of the separate actions that combine to make it up.

# Proceed in Small Steps

To build up a skill, you must *first break it down into steps* that are small enough to be easily managed by your child. Being aware of this one simple fact, and thereby viewing each learning task from the child's point of view, begins to guarantee successful teaching.

If we recall the list on Billy's wall, it is clear that Billy and Mrs. Jackson had worked together on a number of self-help skills. Having done that, Mrs. Jackson could rather easily tackle the task of making a bed. She seems to have a kind of special ability that magically guarantees immediate and continual success. But if we explore Mrs. Jackson's approach a little further, it becomes clear that this special ability is not magical at all, but is based on a simple strategy of observing behavior and teaching in gradual steps. So let's explore.

As Mrs. Jackson saw it, making a bed is not one big skill, but a complex chain of many separate steps connected in a logical order. No one had to tell her what these steps are. She had only to make a bed—*slowly*—keeping track of what she did and in what order.

She had, of course, made a bed many times before, and it was always a quick, routine activity. Yet the first time she performed this exercise—going slowly, keeping track of separate actions — she was amazed at the number of links in the chain.

Who would have imagined that there were so many steps in as simple and automatic a skill as making a bed? Billy would have! For it is precisely his inability to arrange these steps in their correct order that would prevent him from succeeding.

By carefully listing the steps in making a bed, Mrs. Jackson developed a program for teaching this skill. She broke the skill down into separate, specific, and simple actions, which then provided her with a guide for teaching. To Mrs. Jackson, the breakdown looked like this:

Making the bed-

1. Pull top sheet up as far as it will go.

   Tug at both sides to smooth out wrinkles.

2. Pull blanket up and smooth out wrinkles.

3. Fold blanket and sheet back together.

4. Pull spread up and smooth out.

5. Fold spread back.

6. Put pillow on.

7. Bring spread up over pillow.

Take the skill you have chosen to teach and try to break it down into small steps. Don't just think about it. Get a shoe, a ball, a tricycle, a bathtub, or whatever and actually *do it!* List the steps below:

The separate steps that make up a skill form your basic teaching program. The program you developed by listing the steps you took might look different from our program. That's fine. There is certainly not just one correct way to teach a skill.

***Wait a minute.*** Did you really do it? If you did, *take a break.* You've earned it. But if you didn't, *please do.* It will make the rest of this section much clearer.

You now have a list of steps. This tells what needs to be taught, but does not yet describe how to teach. The main rule is *to teach gradually.* Begin with the step just after those your child can do and only proceed to the next step when your child is ready. A frequent mistake in teaching is to demand too much too soon. If you are careful to break a skill down into all of its many steps, you will then be able to teach your child a little at a time. (Note that Mrs. Jackson began by teaching the last step first. This is a teaching method called *backward chaining* and is described in Chapter 9.)

The next four chapters describe several other guidelines for ensuring success in teaching. Follow these and add to them those qualities that make you someone special to your child.

Remember, your goal is not to become like Mrs. Jackson or like us, but to build on who you already are to become a better teacher for your child. Your eventual teaching style will be yours alone, and that's what will make it work.

# Chapter 4

# Picking Rewards

When we stop to think of it, why would Billy (see Chapter 1), or any child, want to learn bedmaking—or anything? For a child with special needs, learning has rarely happened easily. There have been confusing demands, awkward materials, and often the same unhappy result: failure. With failure the expected outcome, it is no wonder that your child may not be eager to learn a new skill. The fun of succeeding that motivates many children is often unknown to the special child. So, although there is much he'd like to be able to do, it is safer for him to relax in a routine where you will do things for him.

Throughout this book, we describe small but important ways to change your child's world so that failure and frustration are replaced by success and satisfaction. But just because you are ready to teach bedmaking or riding a tricycle does not mean your child will be eager to learn. It may just look to her like another failure in the making. You will thus need to find added incentives to draw her into the teaching session, to make her willing to try what you ask. *You will need rewards.*

## Rewards for Learning

When we stop to consider what makes us behave as we do, we can usually figure out what motivates us. Often we act in a certain way because it pays off in one way or another: in money (paychecks), the approval of others (praise, smiles), the promise of good things to come (vacations), or the pleasant and private feeling of a job well done. All of these outcomes represent rewards for performance. Whenever they occur, we generally look forward to their recurrence, and we learn how to behave to make sure this happens. Your child's behavior is motivated in exactly the same way.

The important relationship between rewards and behaviors can be easily understood as follows: *Behavior that is followed by a reward is much more likely to happen again.*

---

### &#x2619; Praise and Prizes

" . . . 23, 24, 25! Very nice, Rosa. You brushed your hair! Now here's the hair ribbon."

Rosa peeked at herself in the mirror as her cousin Alicia fastened the bright yellow ribbon in her hair. Rosa had brushed her hair all by herself—just like Alicia!

"Rosa, show your mother how pretty you look."

Mrs. dePaz was surprised. "Now why will she brush her hair for you and not for me? I ask, coax, sometimes even plead with her . . . ."

Alicia smiled. "Well, I don't know. But I do know she likes praise—and loves hair ribbons."

---

When we perform well, we are pleased by the recognition and praise from those we respect. When our behavior leads to something pleasant for us, we are more likely to perform it again. *This is the nature and purpose of rewards.*

Rosa brushed her hair because she liked Alicia's praise, and she especially liked the hair ribbon reward. These positive ways of encouraging good behavior are more effective than the negative kind of coaxing and yelling that no one enjoys. Most important, with rewards as the expected outcome, the child looks forward to once again performing well.

But what exactly does the effective teacher reward? In the teaching situation a child will behave in one of four general ways. He may

1. Do nothing (not pay attention, gaze out the window)
2. Do something other than the task (yell *no,* cry, leave the room)
3. Make some attempt at the task (not perfect, but a try)
4. Perform the task successfully

Both of the last two are good behaviors (desirable) and should be rewarded as soon as they happen. The first two, however, are not good behaviors (undesirable) and should not, therefore, be rewarded at all. Sounds simple, right? Yet one of the most common mistakes is to reward, in one way or another, *all* of the above behaviors in the teaching session. The reason for this lies in not fully understanding the purpose and use of rewards. Let's look at the different kinds of rewards and how they can be used, and misused, in the teaching session.

# Types of Rewards

## Attention

The most important reward you can give your child is your attention—and you can give it in a variety of ways. Smiles, hugs, kisses, clapping, cheering, and praise are just some of the kinds of attention you can give in the teaching session. There's nothing like a pat on the back and an excited "Nice try!" to let your child know he's doing well.

Because your enthusiastic attention is such a powerful reward, and because it can so effectively increase the behavior it follows, you need to be careful to use attention wisely. After all, yelling, criticizing, and coaxing are also forms of attention, aren't they? They're not as pleasant as cheers and smiles, but they do show your child that you're paying attention to him, and for this reason they could easily be seen as rewards. Like all rewards, they may increase the likelihood of your child's behavior—undesirable as it may be.

What do you suppose would happen, then, if your child decided not to cooperate in the teaching session and you began to scold him? Or coax him? Or plead with him?

That's right. Since you rewarded his refusal to cooperate, you should expect him to continue to refuse and to be more likely to refuse in the future. Since he's getting so much of your attention for *not performing,* why should he start performing now?

That's why we urge you to use your attention wisely in the teaching session. When your child succeeds at a task or makes a good try, jump in right away with enthusiastic praise and whatever other kinds of attention feel genuine and natural. When your child discovers how easily he can get your positive attention, he will be much more likely to continue doing what you ask. And the teaching time will be pleasant for both of you.

## Snacks

Snack rewards are very small portions of food or drink. These can be the treats that most children like: small pieces of cookie, granola, a sip of juice, or a grape.

Use whatever snack you know your child enjoys, and switch to a different one if she seems to tire of it after a while. Better still, have a combination of her favorite snacks on hand while you teach. Use your snack rewards when your child is hungry and thirsty and, therefore, most likely to want them. Finally, always accompany the snacks with praise.

As soon as your child is successful or makes a good try in the teaching session, give her the snack *immediately* (coupled, of course, with your praise). In some cases, parents find it quickest and easiest to pop the snack directly into their child's mouth. Use very small bites so that your child doesn't have to chew for more than a few seconds and so that she doesn't get full too soon.

Each time your child begins a new (and therefore slightly more difficult) step in the teaching program, give her a snack reward for every success. Once you see that she is beginning to master the step, give her a snack only after two complete successes and, later, after three or more.

Before you continue to the next step, your child should be doing the newly learned step with your attention as her only reward. Save the snacks for when they're needed most, for when the task again gets a little difficult. But never save or stop your praise.

---

### &#x00D8; Food for Thought

Some parents don't like the idea of using snack rewards because "it's too much like animal training" or because "she seems to do fine without them." You will, of course, need to decide for yourself. Our advice, though, is to consider your child as you make that decision.

The best teachers make their decisions according to what helps their students learn most effectively (as opposed to deciding on the basis of what they, themselves, may or may not like). Many children do, in fact, learn with attention as the only reward. But some will learn more quickly when snacks are used. It's worth a try.

---

## Activities

Almost anything your child already enjoys doing can be used as an effective reward in teaching new skills. The list is endless: listening to a record, playing a favorite game, taking a walk, baking cookies, wrestling on the floor, holding a favorite doll, playing with a toy truck, watching television. . . . Using activities like these in the teaching session generally works best with the more advanced child who can wait for a short while for her reward.

Using desired activities to motivate less-desired ones is sometimes called "Grandma's Law." Grandma was always wise enough to say: "First eat your spinach, and then you can have ice cream." That is, *an activity a child likes to do more is a good reward for one she likes to do less.*

Consider this example: Veronica loves to watch TV, especially the cartoons. She doesn't like to exercise much, though, and she's getting a bit overweight. Her older sister decides to teach her to roller-skate. Which is the correct way to follow Grandma's Law?

"First eat your spinach and then you can have your ice cream."

1. "If you roller-skate with me for 15 minutes, then you can watch the cartoons."
2. "OK, you can watch the cartoons, but then you have to roller-skate with me for 15 minutes."

Sure, the correct use of Grandma's Law is number 1: first the less-desired activity, then the more-desired one. If you guessed number 2, you made a common mistake. It may sound nicer—and maybe it delays a small tantrum for a while—but more often than not, it leads to an even bigger tantrum later.

Remember Grandma's Law as a good motivator if you plan to use activity rewards. Like most of what grandmothers say, it makes good sense.

## Tokens

Instead of giving an activity reward each time the child performs a task, parents often like to offer a reward that can be earned over a period of time. To maintain their child's motivation meanwhile, they use tokens.

Tokens can be anything. Like money, they are valuable because of what they can be exchanged for. They bridge the gap between work now and a reward later. You can use checks on a piece of paper, stars, plastic poker chips, or a chart like the one on Billy's bedroom wall (see Chapter 1). Much of the importance of token rewards lies in their trade-in value to the child. In Billy's case, you'll remember, 20 checks (a kind of token reward) were worth a trip to the bowling alley, something his mother knew he wanted to do very much. If tokens are to be effectively employed in your teaching program, your child must be able to trade them in for something that is rewarding for him.

Introducing your child to token rewards is a simple but gradual process. When he performs a desired behavior, give him a token immediately, with praise and a short, to-the-point explanation such as, "Good boy. Here's a token for taking out the trash" (or whatever). The first time this happens, the child probably has no idea what his token is or does; you must demonstrate for him its exchange value by saying something like, "Now, if you give me one token, you can have . . . [a favorite food, perhaps, or a small toy, game, or book]." And, of course, you should give the reward immediately.

---

## &#x24D8; Token Training

No matter what kind of tokens you decide to use—checks on a chart, poker chips, coins—it will take time for your child to learn they are important for him to earn. As we've pointed out, you'll have to start by making **immediate exchanges** of tokens for rewards he'll enjoy. In the beginning, do so in a clear and emphatic way. Praise him for the job he's done and give him the token. Then, immediately have him give you the token as you give him the reward. Tell him what you're doing as you go: "Nice job, Francisco, you washed up without being told! Here's your check [mark check on chart and hand chart to Francisco]. What's the check for? Right—washing on your own. Now, give me the check [have Francisco hand over the check sheet] and look what you get: a cup of juice. Way to go!"

Gradually, have the child "save" the token for longer periods of time (5 minutes; then 10 or 15 minutes; then until the end of the day) before you make the trade for the reward. If necessary, go back to immediate exchanges every so often to keep up his interest in the token system. Remember, a token program is not built in a day!

---

Your child can have the opportunity to earn more than one token each teaching session—and still more throughout the day for other good behaviors outside of the teaching session. Once you have demonstrated the value of tokens to him, you might help him save them—as, for example, Billy was doing in our case study. In this way, you will not have to exchange every token for a small reward as soon as it is earned, but instead you might exchange them for a bigger reward at the end of the day or at the end of the week (or whenever he earns what he was saving for).

Tokens are a very effective type of reward. They are both convenient for you and exciting for your child. But it is necessary to keep the following guidelines in mind.

1. Always specify clearly, and in advance, the desired behavior and the number of tokens to be earned. Your child should never feel that earning tokens is a casual business. Instead, he should know each time what you want him to do, and how many tokens that behavior will earn. *He should never receive a token if he has failed to carry out the agreed-upon behavior* (but be certain it is a task he can do).

2. Make certain that a variety of rewards will be available to your child in exchange for his tokens. You might establish, for example, that a dessert will cost 2 tokens, watching TV 3 tokens, and a pair of roller skates 60 tokens. By varying the kinds of items and activities that tokens can buy, you ensure that their·value as rewards will be maintained.

3. As much as possible, involve your child in selecting both the skill to be learned and the rewards to be earned.

4. Again, always keep your promise. A token program is only as good as your word; make sure that the agreed-upon reward is available when the child has earned it.

## ◎ A Lesson Learned

"When it's that quiet, well, you know they're into something." Mrs. Barnett paused at the children's bedroom door. Laura, her child with special needs, was playing teacher, and Jill, Laura's 2-year-old sister, was enjoying the game of being led through the steps of making a bed.

"Tuck it in. Good girl, Jill. C'mere—other side. Good girl."

It wasn't so long ago that Mrs. Barnett had begun teaching Laura the many steps in bedmaking, and she smiled now to see her gestures and words repeated with such authority.

"Get the pillow. OK, fold this up. Good, Jill."

Laura nodded approvingly and proceeded to the dresser. She took a red star from the box and put it on Jill's piece of paper as Mrs. Barnett had done each day for her. Laura no longer needed the star rewards to motivate her, though the ice-cream cone that five stars earned was still welcome. But while Laura's happy student didn't quite know what it was all about, that star for her was the treasure of the moment: "Mommy, see . . . ."

# Rewards Make Learning Faster and More Fun

When teaching skills to your child, her happiness at mastering the task might be reward enough to keep her interested and trying. In most cases, however, your teaching will go more smoothly if you add your praise; her favorite activities and snacks; and, if appropriate, a system of token rewards.

At first, when learning is difficult and skills are a bit shaky, successes mean more when they are recognized by others. Laura had worked to learn bedmaking in order to receive her mother's praise, as well as yogurt—especially strawberry yogurt. These rewards made Laura more eager to tackle the task and made the success more fun. Later, though, when she had mastered the task, she no longer needed yogurt or even as much praise in order to perform—there were now other rewards. Bedmaking had become fun, a skill to be proud of, to show off, even to teach others.

Before reading the next chapter, write down some rewards that you might use in teaching your child.  We'll start the list.

*Praise* _____     _____

_____     _____

_____     _____

_____     _____

_____     _____

_____     _____

## Take a Break!

# Chapter 5

# Setting the Stage

If there are two empty chairs in the kitchen, chances are you won't sit on the floor. The furniture will have "told" you where to sit. In fact, it is remarkable how much of our behavior is controlled by the physical arrangement of our own worlds. The chairs say, "You can sit here." The stove does not.

A child learning to sweep the floor cannot be expected to concentrate well in a cluttered room, or with the TV on, or with friends playing outside, or with a new ball nearby. The ball, don't forget, says, "Throw me," and it may speak louder than the broom!

No matter how talented an actor may be and no matter how clever his script, his performance will suffer if the stage isn't properly set. If the costumes fit poorly or if the scenery makes it difficult for the actor to move around, the performance will never come off as planned.

It's the same way with teaching.

No matter how carefully you have planned your teaching program on paper, you won't have a successful "performance" unless you **SET THE STAGE** for learning with equal care. Sometimes even the best teaching plan winds up competing with a stage that is *improperly set for learning*. As a result, the child's attention is won over by distracting noises or materials. Your aim is to set a stage that will indicate to your child, as much as possible, what behaviors are to be allowed and expected, and what behaviors are not. Don't put yourself in the frustrating position of trying to tell your child one thing while everything around him is telling him another.

Setting the proper stage for teaching, then, means arranging the situation in advance to simplify the demands of the task and to reduce the likelihood of distractions.

# Setting the Stage for Learning

To set the stage properly for effective learning, you need to answer these three questions before you teach:

1. WHEN is the most appropriate time to teach?
2. WHERE should the teaching take place?
3. WHAT materials will be needed?

## When Is the Most Appropriate Time to Teach?

You should try to set aside 10 or 15 minutes during the day for teaching and plan to teach 3–5 days a week. These are averages. Some children will be able to pay attention for 5 minutes, whereas others can stay involved for 20 minutes or more. With some skills, you can make progress even if you teach only once a week (say, riding a tricycle), whereas for others you must teach every day (say, toilet training).

"All's quiet now, just Susie and me. . ."

There is no one time of day that is best for teaching. Finding the most appropriate time for you depends a great deal on when you can devote all of your attention to your child. This means picking a time when you don't have to be concerned with household matters, a time when the other children are not close by—a time, in short, that's protected for teaching. Think also of your child and be certain that you haven't chosen a time when she is likely to be too tired or hungry.

This may sound impossible at first. How much free time do you have in a day anyway? And how are you supposed to know when a friend might decide to telephone? Of course, no time will be perfect, but take your best shot and make changes as needed.

> 🌰  **Remember**
>
> These guidelines are meant to help you select the most appro-
> priate time of day to work with your child in formal planned
> teaching sessions. This is the time when she will be learning
> new skills.
>
> However, for these new skills to grow and to be enjoyed,
> there are many occasions throughout the day (2 minutes here,
> 10 minutes there) when you or someone else in the family can
> involve the child in incidental, spur-of-the-moment teaching.
> These are important times, too.

## Where Should the Teaching Take Place?

Where you teach will greatly affect how well your child learns. You
should, therefore, carefully decide on one place—his bedroom, the corner
of the living room, the backyard—that is as far away as possible from daily
distractions and interruptions. Nothing should draw your child's attention away from the only two things there that matter: you and your teaching materials. As a result, like many parents, you may find yourself having
to clear away extra toys, the birdcage, the TV—maybe even Uncle Ed.

Once you've decided where you will teach—and after you've taught
there a couple of days to make sure it works well—plan to use that same
location every time. Your child will soon get used to the fact that this is
where she comes to learn.

## What Materials Will Be Needed?

Teaching most skills requires using some materials. Look at these materials from your child's point of view. Are they interesting and pleasant to
look at? Are they easy to hold and to move? Are they too small? Are they
too heavy? Are they safe? Will they break if accidentally dropped? The
goal of the teaching session will determine what specific materials you
will need. But, in general, you should always ask yourself, "Can my child
do what is expected of him with the materials provided, or would a
change in the materials increase his chances for success?"

For example, with play skills a big ball is usually easier to catch, large
beads are easier to string, and an empty wagon is easier to pull. Later you
can advance to tennis balls, smaller beads, or little brother in the wagon.
A three-piece puzzle is easier than a five-piece puzzle, which is easier
than a nine-piece puzzle. Working at a table is easier if the table and chair

are child size. With dressing skills, clothes that are a little too big will be easier to manage at first.

Can you think of ways to set the stage that make the materials more manageable for your child? What, for example, might you do if his coloring paper slips around on the table? Or if the coat rack is too high to reach? Or if the beanbag usually misses the small hole in the cardboard box?

Some children with special needs have more than one physical or sensory disability. If your child has a motor impairment, for example, you know that he won't be able to manipulate some toys or articles of clothing easily. Go ahead and substitute items that you (or his teacher or physical therapist) know he can handle. If your child has a hearing impairment, you can still follow your teaching program—just add manual signs, gestures, or whatever mode of communication works best with *your* child. If your child has a visual impairment, you may want to use materials that are larger, more brightly colored, or braille-embossed. The point here is: *You* know your child best. *You* know his strengths as well as his limitations. Use whatever toys, materials, or type of "stage" that you think will result in the most success.

# A Final Note on Setting the Stage

We realize that what we've been calling your "classroom" is actually a space in your home—not a room in someone else's school. And at home, one learns to expect the unexpected: neighbors calling, noisy children playing by your window, teaching materials that fall apart, headaches.

Incidents like these are annoying as well as distracting, and there's little you can do to prevent them. However, once you've chosen your time, your place, and your materials for teaching, these unexpected interruptions will be few and far between. They may upset a teaching session or two, but they should never upset your plan for teaching.

## Patience

It is difficult to write about how you should "set the stage" for yourself, except to acknowledge that teaching the child with special needs, as you well know, is a slow process. You should approach teaching with optimism, certainly, but also with realism. With patience. Your willingness to proceed gradually and to stick with it—despite your child's minor setbacks and your frustrations—will be his gain.

Chapter

Teaching

Let's review the STEPS we've talked about so far. We've covered:

**S**etting out to teach
**T**argeting a skill to teach
**E**stablishing the separate steps that make up the skill
**P**icking rewards that your child will work for
**S**etting the stage to maximize success

We've come a long way without even starting to teach yet! But being prepared makes all the difference in whether teaching will be fun or a failure for you and your child.

This chapter and the next one get down to the business of:

**T**eaching
**O**bserving progress and troubleshooting

We emphasize in this chapter the two main ingredients of good teaching: instructing your child what you want him to do and rewarding his efforts.

---

 Tell Me, Show Me, Guide Me

**Tell me** something a hundred times and I still may not understand what you want me to do. **Show me** what you mean—demonstrate clearly and slowly—just once or twice and I'll be closer to that goal. But do it with me—put your hand on mine and **guide me** through it—and I'll make it!

---

# Instructing

Think about it. When you teach an infant you do not launch into complicated instructions; you quite naturally demonstrate for her or guide her.

Most of us would readily admit that we, too, would rather be shown than instructed. We recognize how confusing words, especially directions, can sometimes be. For this reason, as we attempt to teach you with words and a few illustrations, we'd like to be there with you to "show you what we mean" and perhaps "do it with you." We would not have to guide or demonstrate for too long. Soon, we could just prompt you with words and before long begin to fade out our assistance altogether.

We can't be there to tell, show, and guide, but you can make your child's task easier by telling, showing, and/or guiding her. How much you use each of these methods depends upon your child's abilities. The child learning basic skills and having a limited understanding of language, for example, is best taught if you emphasize physical guidance.

## Tell: Verbal Directions

Tell your child clearly and simply what to do. When you're teaching, you should know exactly what you want your child to do. However, it is sometimes difficult to put what we want into words a child can follow. Perhaps we can't find the right words to fit our picture of a task. Or perhaps we find too many words and the picture gets lost in a flood of sounds. How can we make the best use of directions to simplify the child's learning task?

Although we know that no two people would give directions in exactly the same way, there are several guidelines you should consider for effective directions.

***Directions should be given slowly and only when your child is paying attention.*** This suggestion may seem obvious, but keep in mind that all of us (on occasion) have delivered a beautifully phrased direction to a wall, a bed, or a bathtub. The child wasn't looking at us. Using your child's name before the instruction always helps to gain her attention. Make sure she is looking at you before you begin—"Rosa, look at me." (Also see Chapter 8.)

*Directions should be simple.* If you have properly arranged the learning situation, no task should take more than one or two sentences to describe. Your instructions should be clear and concise. They should *direct* rather than *distract*. Recall for a moment Mrs. Jackson's directions to Billy (Chapter 1). "Billy, watch what I do." "OK, Billy, you try." "Pull it over the pillow."

What do you suppose might have happened if instead of the above, Mrs. Jackson had said: "OK, Billy, now pay attention. I'm going to do something because I want you to do it after I'm through." "It's your turn now, and I want you to do exactly what I just did; now do you understand what I want you to do?" "Now take it nice and slow and ease it up toward the head of the bed. Wait a minute; not too fast. OK. Now get it over the pillow, get the whole thing over the pillow."

Quite a difference isn't there? Our imaginary (but not uncommon) Mrs. Jackson spent so much time talking that her directions might have easily been lost among the words.

*Directions should use words your child can understand.* Think about what you are saying. Does your child understand the meaning of the words you are using?

"Put the socks in the *second* drawer."

"It's on the *top* of the dresser."

Does she understand all of the concepts: *second, on top of, in, under, right-hand, red, beside, between, behind*? Sometimes you can find an easier word to indicate what you mean. In any case, when your child fails to perform part of a task, ask yourself if he really understood what he was supposed to do.

If your child still does not seem to understand the verbal message, you may have to simplify it further by using other words, or even modifying the demands of the task. Once you have found a certain direction to be successful in a particular task, you should stick with it. Be consistent!

Even the clearest directions are only words after all, and sometimes words are not enough. Along with your verbal directions, you should demonstrate the steps—a procedure we call *modeling*.

## Show: Modeling

Show your child what to do. Modeling is often the best way to help your child understand what you want him to do. To increase the power of your verbal instructions dramatically, add simple and clear *demonstrations*.

This is a natural tendency anyway and takes into account not only your child's listening ability but also his ability to imitate your behavior.

"Do this" . . . as *you* cut with the knife, or *you* stack blocks, or *you* set the spoons to the right of the knives.

Perhaps you will say the directions aloud as you demonstrate: "See, stand at the line and throw the ball. Like this."

Your verbal directions will be much clearer if your child has watched you perform the skill first. You won't model the entire skill—that's too much for him to remember. Model, instead, each step before you ask him to do it. If he is good at learning from such imitation, you can begin to model bigger steps, demonstrating each time only as much as the child can reasonably be expected to do.

**Note:** Keep in mind that modeling is most effective when it is done slowly and with careful exaggeration.

As your child begins to master a task, modeling will become less necessary. You will also be able to fade out verbal directions, gradually diminishing them to cues such as "Now, the bedspread." Eventually you will eliminate both entirely. This fading will be a gradual process, taking days, weeks, or even months, depending on his success.

## Guide: Physical Guidance

Do the task with your child. After telling and showing him, hold his hands and take him through the motions.

At the earliest stages of guiding, you're the one who's actually performing the skill; your child is simply going along for the ride. But after you've guided him through the task two or three times, you should gradually reduce your physical assistance. Let him take more and more responsibility for performing the task on his own. Hold his hand, for example, a little less securely as you guide the puzzle piece to the proper place. When he succeeds, let go of his hand but keep yours close by to move in if he needs help.

If you decide that either showing or guiding, or both, are necessary to help your child succeed, always use them together with your verbal instructions. And use them only for as long as you think he needs them.

When you are teaching your child and you plan to move to a new step in your teaching program, check to see how your child performs the step you are working on. If he can perform it correctly with your verbal instructions *only*, he's ready for the next step. If you still need to show or guide him, he's probably not quite ready for the next step.

Be sure to end each session with a success. If your child is having difficulty with a task, have him perform an easier step—one you know he can do—before stopping.

# Use of Rewards

### Shaping Behavior: Slow and Steady

You should not wait for the desired behavior to spring forth in full bloom before rewarding your child. If you do, you might find yourself waiting for quite a long while. Rather, you should gradually shape his rough attempts and good tries into smooth performances.

When you begin a teaching session, for example, you might first reward your child for simply walking with you to the teaching session, and again for sitting in the chair, and still again for following a simple direction ("Look at me"). After a short while, though, you will no longer give him a snack for coming with you and sitting down; he's already learned to do that. You'll simply praise him—"Nice going, Sam. You're ready to begin"—and save your snacks for his efforts on the next task.

Increase your demands gradually. If yesterday your child needed your assistance to help him put a puzzle piece in place, you would begin on this same step today. You would immediately reward his easy success with snacks and praise. But your goal for today would be for him to do a little more. So during the rest of the session, you would save the snacks for when he succeeds or makes a good try at putting the puzzle piece in with less assistance and then all by himself.

Successful shaping is slow and gradual. To expect overnight changes in your child's behavior is to set yourself up for disappointment. Ask your child to show small improvements in his performance, reward these small improvements appropriately, and gradually make each new task just a little more difficult than the one before. Steady progress will be made. Parents who stick with their teaching programs prove it all the time.

---

## ☼ Shaping

Megan was learning to *attend* and *follow* directions, and the goal of her task was to get a hat from across the room and bring it to her father when he said, "Bring me the hat." The first days of teaching had not gone well. Megan wandered off, sat down, became distracted, dropped the hat, and her father became progressively more upset. The problem, however, was that he was expecting far too much at first. He had not broken the task into small enough steps.

So they began again. Megan's mother stood with Megan and put the hat in her hands. Her father sat just 4 feet away. When he said, "Megan, bring me the hat," his wife gently guided Megan to her father. He took the hat and immediately praised and rewarded her. The next time, her mother didn't guide her all the way. And gradually, the physical guidance was faded to a slight push, and finally to no guidance at all. Then they started Megan a little farther away from her father each time until she could eventually bring the hat from across the room.

We have explored many techniques to get your child's attention and to progressively teach a new skill. We have talked about the need for rewards, and you have selected several rewards to use with your child. Other suggestions about giving rewards are described next. It isn't necessary that you remember all of them now, but it will help if you refer to this section before you begin your teaching.

## Make Certain Your Rewards Are Rewarding

Favorite snacks are less-effective rewards when used right after lunch. Fun toys are certainly less fun when they've just been played with. And there's no point in your child earning checks to go swimming if you're going to go swimming anyway. It is important that your child really want and look forward to the reward. It helps further if he can only get that reward when he has earned it and not at other times. Also, do not decide on a reward that you cannot withhold. For example, if the family is going to the zoo on Saturday, do not offer this as a reward for earning 10  checks, because if your child does not earn them, you would have to take him to the zoo anyway or break your promise to the other children and cancel the trip. Either of these would be unfortunate. Decide on a reward that you are certain you can give or withhold.

## Remember that Success Is a Reward

If a given step in the task proves, with repeated efforts, to be too difficult, you should break the skill into even smaller steps. At the same time, move back to a slightly easier step. Each teaching session should begin with a step already mastered and then move on to new learning. Again, each teaching session should end with success. So, if your child is getting restless or you feel it is time to quit for the day, be sure to give her one last easy task so that she will end with success.

## Give the Reward as Soon as the Child Performs the Desired Behavior

If a delay occurs—for example, 2 minutes—before finding and giving your child what he earned, he may have forgotten what he did to earn it. Worse, in those 2 minutes he may perform other behaviors that you shouldn't be rewarding. So when your child does what you asked of him, always have his reward ready immediately, and fill the seconds that it takes to give it to him with well-deserved praise.

## Learn to Pay No Attention to Certain Unasked-For Behaviors

We don't often think of our occasional yelling or getting up to chase a child around the room as a reward. Yet both of these (and others you can probably think of) are forms of attention to children. And attention, as we have seen, is a very effective reward. Remember the simple strategy: Behaviors followed by rewards are much more likely to be performed again. Save your attention for those behaviors that you want your child to perform in the teaching situation. Let your child learn that if he wants your attention, he won't get it by running around the room or staring out the window. As much as possible, you should remain seated and ignore this behavior, waiting for him to turn his attention back to you. We realize this is often not easy to do. However, your child should only get your attention by doing what you asked.

## Phase Out Rewards

As your child masters a skill, you will often find that you can phase out most of the rewards—tokens, food, activities, and the like. Praise alone and a sense of mastery will most likely maintain his performance, and you can save the other rewards for helping him with the steps of your next program. Phase out rewards gradually by increasing the amount that you ask of him before giving one of the "extra" rewards. For example, when he can completely make his bed and has just done so, you might say, "Good, now let's hang up this coat, and then you can. . . ." And you've begun a new program! Eventually, his bedmaking skill will be a regular part of his routine and should be maintained by your praise and his increased mastery over his world.

Remember, though, that your praise is never an "extra" reward. It should be given *whenever* he is trying to learn or perform a skill.

Chapter 7

# Observing  Progress and Troubleshooting

---

### How Are You Doing?

"Hi, Judy. How are you and Billy doing this morning? It seems you've been teaching him to make his bed for a long time now. I wonder if he's getting anywhere."

"Wait a minute. You don't have to wonder. Just look at this."

"You mean you've actually been keeping a record of how he's doing?"

"Sure. I wanted to know for sure how much his bedmaking was improving. See, he's doing well. In fact, we're both doing well!"

---

Just *how quickly* your child will progress is impossible to predict, for no two children will ever learn in quite the same way and in quite the same amount of time. It is best not to wonder "How long will it take . . . ?" but instead to ask, "Is my child showing progress?" or "Is this program working well?" or "Can he do more of the task this week than he could last week?" To answer any of these questions very well, you will have to keep records. Nearly all the chapters in Sections II and III suggest a type of record keeping. Here we consider what you might do with your observations or records of progress.

As you teach, you will naturally pay close attention to your child's progress. You will notice whether he's gradually doing a little more of the task or doing it more smoothly than he did before. You'll notice when he loses interest in what you're doing and wanders off.

With all that noticing, it's easy to overlook one part of the teaching session, maybe the most important part: you, the teacher.

So, before you get started, let's take a few minutes to notice you. Let's pay particular attention to how you might behave when the teaching session goes well and when . . . well . . . you know. (Good days and bad days are both bound to happen.)

# It's Going Well

If your child is learning, if the two of you are reaching your goal, that's good. We'd love to be there to check out progress and pass along to you some well-deserved words of praise, just as you have praised your child. But you don't need us; you can reward yourself! Sound strange? Why? Just as rewards keep your child going, they can also keep you going.

There are several ways to reward yourself. The most important is what you say to yourself. If your child is showing progress in learning a new skill, congratulate yourself:

"I did great!"

"Hey, I'm a pretty good teacher."

"Congratulations, me!"

What others say is important too. Show other family members what your child has learned to do and make sure they praise both of you. (You can model this by praising them when they teach him something.) Also, you could keep a diary describing skills that you have taught your child; describe each teaching goal to your child's teacher and let him or her know when you've reached it. Words in the diary and encouragement from the teacher are well-earned rewards as well as reminders that you've truly succeeded.

Another way to reward yourself is to choose, right now, something fun that you will buy or do when you reach your goal. Go out for a movie? A hot fudge sundae? Spend a Saturday afternoon without the kids? You know best what will reward you.

Sure, this idea of rewarding yourself sounds a little silly. After all, you are teaching because you are a good parent, and your child's increased skill is a reward in itself. But why not add the hot fudge sundae just this once?

# It's Not Going So Well

When teaching is not going well, don't panic or question whether it's worth the effort. It is. What good teacher doesn't have bad days? Sometimes even two in a row. So when you run into problems in the teaching situation, go easy on yourself. And start to TROUBLESHOOT.

Troubleshooting means problem solving, beginning with the most likely reasons for the problem. Consider this example. If you switch on a lamp and nothing happens, you probably don't shrug your shoulders and walk away; you troubleshoot. You think about what might be the most common reasons for this problem. Your list might look something like this:

1. The lamp isn't plugged in.
2. The bulb isn't screwed in tightly.
3. The bulb is burned out.
4. The circuit breaker is tripped or the fuse is blown.

So when the lamp doesn't light, you don't immediately give up. You don't blame the lamp—"This lamp isn't trying." You don't blame yourself—"I'm not very good at turning on lamps." You troubleshoot.

Now let's look at the kind of troubleshooting you could do while teaching a new skill. Suppose you get a call from a friend who's asking for advice. Her son Sal has mental retardation, and she has been teaching him play skills. She has been teaching Sal to do stacking rings, and it was going pretty well until the last 2 days. Now Sal is more easily distracted. He takes longer to put the rings on, and he runs off during the teaching session.

You should tell your friend that this is not the time to give up or blame anyone; it's time to troubleshoot. Think a minute about what you've read so far. Does it give you any ideas about what your friend might do?

STOP! Really! See if you can come up
with one or two suggestions before you read further.

Of course, there is no way to know for sure what would work for your friend. But you might have asked her questions like these:

∅ Does Sal still like the reward? (Try a new one.)
∅ Did you fade out your help too much? (Return to an easier step.)
∅ Is the session too long? (Have a shorter session and end with success.)
∅ Is he getting bored with the rings? (Use another toy that is at the same level.)

Now if you can give troubleshooting suggestions like these to a friend, you can certainly give them to yourself.

Actually, setbacks along the way are a natural part of teaching. We all have bad days. Try to avoid blaming yourself or blaming your child. Avoid such thoughts as:

"I can't do this."
"I'm not a good teacher."
"She's trying to make me look bad."
"He's impossible."

This kind of "self-talk" will just make you feel bad. Avoid being too critical of yourself. Somewhere there's a parent who'd love to be doing as well as you are.

# Troubleshooting Checklist

When your teaching has problems right from the start or when it begins well but soon runs into problems, review the following Troubleshooting Checklist. As you will see, it summarizes much that we emphasize throughout this book.

## Problems Right from the Start

1. Does your child have the necessary basic skills?
2. Did you choose a skill that suits your child's skill level and interests?

3. Are you first getting her attention?
4. Are the materials easy for her to use?
5. Are you teaching at a good time and place, without distractions?
6. Are you starting with an easy enough step?
7. Are you giving simple, clear directions?
8. Are you helping (showing, guiding) enough?
9. Are you enjoying teaching and praising her for trying?
10. Are you using a reward she likes?

## Problems that Arise After Teaching Has Been Going Well

1. Is this a bad time for you or your child (sickness, unusual stress in your life)?
2. Has your child lost interest in the reward? Is there something else you can use? Are you rewarding often enough?
3. Have you taken too big a step? (Are you fading your help too fast?)
4. Are you going too slowly? Is it becoming boring for her? (Are you not fading your help fast enough?)
5. Is she becoming bored with the toy? Is there another toy that you can use to teach the same thing?
6. Is your session too long, or are you staying too long with the same task?
7. Are you ending sessions with a success, or is she learning that misbehavior will get her out of the task?

### ✐ Bad Days

All problems in teaching cannot be solved by troubleshooting and changing how you teach. Real-life problems get in the way as well. Sometimes it's just a "bad day" for you or for your child. Perhaps you have a headache, or your child has the flu. Perhaps the school field trip left him with too little time and energy to face a puzzle. Perhaps Uncle Joe (with his eight children and four dogs) just dropped in from out of town for a "short stay." OK, these are small problems. These are times to set aside teaching for a few days and come back to it when you are both ready.

But there are big problems too. Perhaps you face major surgery, or have lost a loved one, or are moving to another city. Problems with health, marriage, friends, relatives, job, and finances do not step aside so that you can teach your child.

There will be times—perhaps long times—when teaching will have to be a lower priority. That's just how it is.

But just because you may have to stop teaching for a while doesn't mean you can't start again later. In fact, even when you need to set teaching aside, it's good to have a plan for beginning again (for example, "the first of next month" or "when Uncle Joe leaves").

# Final Comments: Questions and Answers

It is rare for teaching to "go by the book." Children—all children—are simply not built to react only in the ways that we intend for them. It should not surprise you if, as you begin a new program, you discover that things aren't always going smoothly. For us to anticipate and describe every problem that might arise would be an impossible task. Nevertheless, our experience has revealed a number of questions that parents often ask. We have included some of those questions and our answers, although, of course, the list is still incomplete.

Remember, if you are like most parents we know, your biggest question will be whether you are ready to actually begin teaching. The solution to this question is the simplest of all—just begin. By putting into practice what you've now learned, your confidence will soon grow, your child will begin to progress, and *you will be teaching*.

### Can I teach more than one program?

Yes, but at first you should select just one program and get started on that one before you begin a second program. If several family members are helping to teach, this will make it easier to carry out more than one program. As everyone becomes used to the behavioral teaching approach, you will be able to use it throughout the day to teach many skills. But start slowly. The danger in starting too much at once is that you might at some point feel it is too much work and abandon it completely. Start with one program that is easily managed within your current daily schedule.

### My child is learning puzzles at school. Will I confuse him by trying to teach puzzles using this book's approach at home?

Yes, you might, if you and the teacher are making different demands. Your child's teacher should be happy that you are making this effort. Talk with her, show her this book, and make sure that you are both making the same demands on your child. Likewise, if you have taught your child part of a skill and his teacher, or grandmother, or sister, or anyone else continues to do it for him, talk with them about your program and explain what he should be left to do by himself.

## My child can partly put on a pullover shirt, but not the way your program says. Should I start over again and teach her according to the program?

Probably not. First, see if you can devise a program of steps to teach her, starting from what she can already do. There are many ways to teach a skill, and the programs in this book are meant only as suggestions. If, however, the way she does it now seems unusually awkward, and it looks as if she will not be able to learn further steps easily, you might consider starting over. In short, be flexible. Observe your child and keep the behavior modification teaching principles in mind; you will then be able to adapt and create programs that are tailored for your child.

## Does a teaching program have to be carried out every day to be successful?

Consistency is more important in teaching certain *self-help skills*—especially toilet training—than in any other skill area. A child learning to dress or eat is confused if some days you patiently help him to learn while other days you do it for him because you are in a hurry. Of course, there will be occasional days when other family activities take priority, or when your child is sick, or when you, yourself, for whatever reason, do not feel quite up to teaching. Occasional lapses in a program will not mean disaster. But general inconsistency in teaching may make your teaching efforts in the self-help area relatively worthless.

## Isn't what you call "rewarding" just bribery?

No, because bribery means rewarding unethical behavior. In teaching your child, we are concerned with rewarding only good behavior. In fact, all of us work for rewards, whether they be money, praise, respect, or a feeling of a job well done. We will gladly accept rewards for our own "good" behavior, and these rewards make our behavior more predictable and more enjoyable. But if we were to accept rewards for unethical behavior—well, that's bribery!

## My other children do not need food rewards to learn—why should she?

This is a common reaction to the use of food rewards for learning. The answer, as we have seen, is simple: Your daughter's past learning experiences have been very different from those of other children. Therefore, we do her an injustice to insist either that she should want to learn and thus push her, or conclude that she cannot learn and thus do it all for her. Neither premise is fair. In the same way that a child with a physical disability might need to use a crutch to get around (and no one would argue she should do otherwise), so your child needs some "learning crutches" to help her get around in your teaching situations.

## The food rewards really help to motivate him in dressing, but will they always be necessary?

Probably not for dressing. In the beginning, when the task is new and he is uncertain, extra rewards like food are very important. As your son masters a skill, he will likely begin to perform it for your praise alone or even for the satisfaction that comes from doing something well. But expect that *phasing out* food rewards for any given skill will be a slow and gradual process. Although the snack will no longer be needed to motivate dressing, it will still be useful when you begin to teach another skill.

## What should I do when everything seems to be going wrong?

This is typical of a variety of questions that cannot really be answered. Why? Because it is phrased generally and supplies little information. What, for example, does "everything" mean? Remember that if you are to be successful in modifying behavior, you too must observe carefully and be specific.

## What if my child starts crying and pushing the materials away in the middle of the teaching session?

There is no single way to handle a behavior problem. With this behavior, your child is telling you something, and your best response depends on why she is acting up. Consider the following possibilities:

1.  She might be tired. The session may have gone on too long, and you will need to quickly find a task she can easily do. Wait until she has

quieted down a bit, have her do an easy task, reward her, and end the session.

2. She might be frustrated. The step may be too hard for her and, like most special children, she may be ready to quit when failure seems imminent. In this case, you will again wait until she has quieted down a bit, present her with a somewhat easier step, and then proceed with teaching.

3. She might be angry. She might have wanted to do it one way, and you demanded another way. Her reaction might be a direct expression of anger because the task had not gone her way. You would need, then, to wait until she has quieted down a bit before proceeding.

4. She might often respond to demand situations with crying and refusal so that the demands will "go away." If these behaviors are common responses, you should ignore them and at the same time insist that she stay in the teaching session; then continue as soon as possible with your teaching demands.

## What if my child refuses to come with me to the teaching session?

If he is usually cooperative and this happens, don't make an issue of it; you can try the teaching at a time when he is more willing. If refusing is something that he usually does, then first carefully review the teaching program and make sure

1. You are asking something of him you are sure he can do
2. You are using a reward that you know is special to him
3. You are rewarding him often enough

If the teaching program seems correct, then gently but firmly insist that he participate. Ignore his tears and attempts to leave while guiding him through the steps. Keep the sessions very short (a minute or two) and reward him frequently.

## I have been trying to teach my child to take off his pants, but he won't even do the first step. Instead, he cries and tries to run from the room. How can I make him more cooperative?

There are several potential trouble spots you should reveiw. If you are sure that the skill you've chosen is appropriate for your child, then ask yourself these questions:

1.  Is the first step one that he can do easily?
2.  Is he clear about what you want him to do? Are you clear?
3.  Is the reward something he really wants, and are you rewarding him immediately and consistently?

Don't forget, he's new to this teaching program and possibly surprised by the fact that you're no longer doing the whole skill for him. Make it very easy. You will find that backing up or slowing down is often required. Demand even less than your first step requires, and then work up to it gradually.

Be firm and insist he do it, and be ready to reward him immediately. He will become less eager to leave as he discovers that only in the teaching situation will he find his favorite snack.

### Does the same person always have to work on a program with the child, or can different family members switch off?

Other family members can definitely share in teaching, so long as they first spend time with you to understand what you're doing. They should read this book and you should discuss the program altogether. Also, you should observe each other teaching, so that you are doing it in the same way. Teaching is more successful in families where the whole family is familiar with the program and involved in teaching.

# Before You Continue

Now that you've read Section I, you are ready to teach. You may be concerned most about behavior problems and want to go directly to Chapters 16 and 17. That's fine. But we have found that parents are most successful when they teach one or two skills first, before tackling the more difficult task of behavior problem management.

If your child needs to learn the basic "get ready" skills of coming when called, sitting, and paying attention, go to Chapter 8.

If your child can perform most self-help skills, you may want to go to Chapter 12, and then Chapters 13 and 14. These chapters cover more advanced self-care and home-care routines as well as information skills (e.g., telling time).

If your child is still learning self-help and play skills, you will want to go to Chapters 9 (Self-Help Skills), 10 (Toilet Training), and 11 (Play Skills). We recommend beginning with Chapter 9, targeting a self-help skill, and teaching it for a few weeks (unless your child learns it sooner).

While you are teaching this skill, you can read ahead to get an idea of what the other chapters cover.

Then move on to another self-help skill, a play skill, or perhaps the more difficult areas of toilet training or behavior problem management. Read Chapter 15, on the personal computer revolution, as soon as you can. Computer knowledge is changing faster than, well . . . toilet training, and this chapter is sure to provide you with some interesting ideas.

# Section II

## Skill Teaching

# Chapter 8

# Get Ready Skills

Get ready skills—or readiness skills—are the foundation on which self-help and play skills are built. The most basic get ready skills include grasping objects, sitting up, standing, walking, following simple commands, and coordinating eyes and legs, hands, and fingers to work together. These are some of the skills we learn early and almost automatically. Although we're performing them all the time, we do not normally think of them as skills.

Get ready skills (such as standing alone, holding a cup, and coming when called) are the beginnings of many more useful skills (such as walking up and down stairs, eating, and playing simple games). Once learned, they represent a giant step toward the successful accomplishment of other self-help and play skills.

For many children with special needs, these get ready skills do not come easily. They must be intentionally taught before other activities can be mastered. As a child grows and develops, some skills naturally precede others. For example, it would be frustrating and unnecessarily difficult for you to try to teach your child to walk if he cannot yet stand without support. You should begin by teaching him to stand.

You have the best opportunity to teach your child get ready skills. You know your child best. You know what he can do now and what you still must do for him. And your day is full of chances to teach him to do a bit more. You do not need elaborate teaching materials—chairs and stairs, a cup, table, or the floor are the materials of get ready skills.

## &#11050; Pleasant Surprises

Sharon would sit on the floor and rock aimlessly for hours, fiddling with a piece of string or staring at her fingers as they played in the sunlight. Her mother felt unable to do anything about the emptiness of Sharon's days, and her mood usually reflected this. Much later, after she had taught  Sharon to sit at a table and occupy herself with a very simple game (putting small objects into a container), her mother's mood changed. She was more optimistic about being able to teach Sharon.

Surely it's frustrating for both you and your child that you have to help her with so many everyday tasks, and that she is unoccupied for so much of the day. We have found that many parents report a change in their own attitude as they systematically begin to teach their children for brief periods each day. Many are pleasantly surprised to see their children doing things they never imagined possible.

# Paying Attention

Perhaps the most basic get ready skill of all is paying attention. As you read this, you are concentrating on what we have written: You are attending to the manual. You are also able to ignore—not attend to—many other things, like the sounds of traffic or the sight of an interesting magazine on the table. To attend selectively—to one thing at a time—comes naturally for most of us.

For a child with special needs, paying attention to one task for a period of time is difficult. Yet it is the most important skill to learn. The child who squirms uncomfortably in his chair, who constantly looks around the room, or who does not respond to his name cannot really be considered ready to learn.

For a child to learn, he must first attend to the task at hand and not attend to other things. He must look at you, hear what you say, and then be able to follow your instructions.

Consider the following example of one mother's efforts to teach her son to drink from a cup. Several get ready skills are necessary before a child can learn drinking from a cup. In this case example, Danny's mother describes how easily the skill of attending can be overlooked and how she went about correcting the oversight. This account concentrates on the basic skill of attending.

---

### ☙ Teaching Attending

"I'd been trying for a couple of weeks to teach Danny to drink from a cup, but all my efforts had ended in failure, frustration, and sometimes even tears. He would never pay attention to what he was supposed to be doing. His eyes would wander around the room, he wouldn't respond when I called his name, and he would put his hands inside the cup or knock it over.

***Targeting a Get Ready Skill***   "It became very clear that unless Danny first learned to attend to me, it would be very hard, if not impossible, to teach him to drink from that cup. So my goal now became getting Danny to look at me when I said, 'Danny, look at me.'

***Setting the Stage***   "I set a 5-minute period every afternoon when my other two children were in school and I had some free time to devote all my attention to Danny. I cleared the kitchen table of the sugar bowl, place mats, and the morning newspaper so that he wouldn't be distracted. And I brought one of the chairs around so that we would be sitting close and facing each other. I wanted this to become a comfortable routine for him, one that he would come to expect regularly. From then on, there would be a teaching session every afternoon for about 5 minutes in the kitchen.

***Picking a Reward***   "One of the most important parts of my teaching plan for Danny was to find a snack he really liked—something that I could reward him with when he did what I asked. Knowing that he loved sugar-coated dry cereal and raisins, I got a cupful of these treats ready. Although I thought he might not be too thrilled about learning to attend, he was never one to refuse an afternoon snack.

"I began the program on Tuesday. Everything was set—the table was cleared, the chairs were set opposite each other, and the cereal and raisins were ready in a cup. I brought Danny in and sat him down in the chair. When he sat down, I immediately gave him a piece of cereal and praised him: 'Good boy, Danny, you're sitting down.'

"In the beginning, when I said, 'Danny, look at me,' he didn't do anything. I may as well have been talking to myself; he just kept staring out of the window. I tried once again and this time he got up to explore the room. I realized that I had been expecting too much of him and would have to make the demand even easier next time. But first, I had to figure out how to get him back in his chair.

*Shaping* "When, in his wandering, he just happened to head in the direction of the chair, I got up and led him back. 'Danny, sit down,' I said, as I helped him onto the chair. Immediately I gave him a raisin and said, 'Good boy, you're sitting down.'

*Verbal Instructions, Physical Guidance, and Reward* "Once he was back in his seat, I was determined not to make the same mistake again by asking something of him he wasn't yet capable of doing. This time I moved my chair over so we were sitting opposite each other but closer together. Then I bent down so my face was at his eye level. As I slowly brought the cereal up to my face I said, 'Danny, look at me,' and gently held his head so his eyes would meet the cereal. He had no other choice but to look at it, and for the moment he was definitely paying attention to the snack. I rewarded him immediately by putting it in his mouth. 'Good boy, Danny.'

*End with Success* "This was a good time to end the session, even though it had lasted only a few minutes. More important than the length of time was the fact that the session had ended on a successful note. Danny had looked at the snack and, for now, that's all I asked.

*Consistent Teaching, Fading Prompts* "We continued to have a teaching session every day. These lasted only 4 or 5 minutes, with my repeating the command 'Danny, look at me' and rewarding him about half a dozen times. Several afternoons later I began gradually to guide his head less and less. After many sessions I finally got him to look at my face without guiding his head at all. After I got him to make eye contact in this way, I worked on keeping his attention a little bit longer each time by holding on to the reward for a few seconds before giving it to him. Now when I say, 'Danny, look at me,' he really looks!"

Danny's mother had begun successful teaching. When Danny responded to the direction "Danny, look at me," it was much easier for his mother to get his attention, which is necessary in teaching all skills. Of course, it took time, patience, and a consistent daily effort—but you can guess what Danny's mother would answer if you asked, "Was it worth it?" Danny's mother moved on to teach him to drink from a cup, eat with a spoon, and play a simple game of putting clothespins into an open container.

# Teaching Your Child to Pay Attention

Nearly all types of skills require your child to pay attention, either to you, to toys or objects, to other children, or to the rules of a game. So, before you begin teaching other skills, let's look at seven ways to increase your child's attention.

### Stand Near Her

When speaking to your child, make sure she can see you and hear you. Even talking to her from across the room may be too difficult in the beginning.

### Get on Her Level

Position yourself so that she can see your face. That's what you want her to pay attention to. If she is sitting on the floor, squat down so she can see you. If she is sitting at a table, sit facing her. Make it as easy as possible for her to watch your face.

### Call Her Name

One word your child likely recognizes is her name. Before asking her to do something, get her attention by calling her name—then she'll know you are talking to her. Wait until she turns to look at you before continuing. If she doesn't look, say her name again. Use proper names when you can. Understanding pronouns (I, you, me) is more difficult. If she doesn't respond to her name, take her chin in your hand and gently turn her face toward you.

"Jenny, get the ball."
"Give Dad the ball."

## Make Eye Contact

When you say her name and she turns toward you, look her in the eyes. If she is facing you but looking at the floor, she may be paying more attention to the floor than to you. If she doesn't look directly at you, put a finger gently on her chin and guide her to look at you.

## Choose Your Words Carefully

Use simple, familiar words and short sentences. "Come play" tells her in simple, clear terms exactly what you want her to do. It is better than "recess" or "playtime," which may have no meaning for your child.

## Be Consistent

Use the same words for people, places, and things all the time. Father should always be "Daddy" (or whatever you prefer), and not alternately "Papa" one day and "Dad" the next.

## Use Gestures

Your child will more easily understand you and more readily pay attention to you if you accompany your words with helpful gestures.

---

###  Cup Game

Another way to increase your child's ability to pay attention is a variation on the old carnival shell game. The objects of this game are for your child to watch you hide food under one of three cups, to watch while you move the cups, and then to pick up the correct cup on the first try.

**Materials**   Use three paper cups and small food rewards (M&Ms, cookie pieces, grapes).

**Program**   Keep sessions short (5–10 minutes).

Use one cup. Hide an M&M (or other reward) under the cup. Say "Find the candy." Help your child pick up the cup and find the reward. (He gets to eat it when he finds it on the first try.) Move the cup around a little, and help him find the reward. Continue this until you can move the cup and he can find the reward himself. Next, add a second cup. Hide the food under one and move it a bit, keeping the other where it is. When he has mastered this, switch the positions of the two cups. Gradually, make the switches more difficult. Do this by moving the cups faster or more times.

**Note:** Make sure that your child is watching. He should be correct most of the time for this game to be useful. Don't let him guess, or always pick the cup in the same position. If he is missing the rewards, slow the game down. Add a third cup, but at first only move the cup with the reward. Next, move two cups, and then all three—slowly. Gradually make the switches more difficult. Move the cups faster, and include more switches.

***Something Else to Try***    As a variation, you might try having your child be the teacher; let him hide the reward and switch the cups for you. Be excited when you find the reward.

# Teaching Other Get Ready Skills

We have included suggestions for teaching other get ready skills in Appendix A. There are a great many such skills, and your child's teacher or therapist can give you suggestions for other skills to teach in much the same way. The examples we have included are as follows:

## Basic Attention Skills

Looking When Called
Coming When Called
Identifying Objects
Following Simple Directions
Imitating

## Basic Gross Motor Skills

Sitting Down
Standing Up from a Chair
Walking
Going Up and Coming Down Stairs

## Basic Fine Motor Skills and Activities

Pushing, Pulling, Holding, and Turning
Holding and Releasing Objects
Water Play
Putting Objects into Hole in Box
Pinching

You will teach these following the same STEPS TO approach we examined in Chapters 1–7. You might want to look through Appendix A before targeting a get ready skill to teach.

# Chapter 9

# Self-Help Skills

Self-help skills are among the most important behaviors for your child to learn. They include, among others, dressing, grooming, toileting, eating, and bathing—the early skills, the ones we learned without remembering how and the ones we practice now daily and automatically. For a child, mastering the challenges of eating with a fork or buttoning a shirt, for example, are big boosts in self-esteem and giant steps toward independence.

## Setting Out

Your responsibility for teaching is clearer in the self-help skill area than in practically any other skill area. Home, after all, is where the toothbrush is—not to mention the toilet, the closet, the dining room table, and the bathtub. Home is also where clothes go on in the morning, mealtime comes three times a day, and hands are washed before each meal. These already-established routines provide natural and predictable settings in which you can teach and your child can most comfortably learn.

You could spend your days washing and dressing your child, but wouldn't you spend that time better by teaching him to perform these skills himself? This chapter helps you use your time best with your child when helping him to learn more in the areas of eating, grooming, and dressing. After reading it, you should be able to do the following:

1.  Select a self-help skill to begin teaching in short, structured daily sessions.
2.  Recognize the many opportunities that naturally occur throughout the day for less-formal, incidental teaching.

After you have read this chapter, turn to Appendix C for specific skill-teaching programs.

## Benefits to You

As the world becomes more manageable for your child, it can become more comfortable for you. Your extra patience and effort during the early stages of teaching will be well rewarded by the eventual benefits to both of you.

---

### ◈ Young Gentleman

"And here's the hot dog for the young gentleman," said the waitress, smiling.

"Young gentleman," thought Mrs. Ku. How nice that sounded. As she cut Leighton's meat into small bites, she thought back to a few short months ago. The messy table, fumbling to get his meat on the spoon, and then the decision: "We're going to teach him how to eat with a fork. It may take some time, but how much more pleasant dinner will be."

It did take time, of course, and Leighton didn't like the change very much at first. But he learned to handle the fork and was now quite properly stabbing his food.

"How's your hot dog, son?" asked Mr. Ku. He could see how much Leighton enjoyed eating in a restaurant—eating now like Mom and Dad. "We'll have to do this more often, don't you think?"

---

On the one hand, perhaps your child is not ready just yet to learn skills like eating with a fork. Mastery of earlier self-help skills—eating with a spoon, pulling off pants—can still make life a little bit easier for you. On the other hand, your child may have learned many self-help skills already. However . . .

## There Is Always More to Learn

Once big hurdles such as toilet training or major dressing skills are passed, it is easy to overlook the countless little things that you do daily for your child. These may be skills that she could learn to do for herself, like hanging up a coat, tying shoes, or spreading with a knife. Your first task will be to take a close look at your child's day to see what you are doing for her that she could learn to do for herself.

## ✲ More to Learn?

Mrs. Phelps remarked, "This self-help chapter wouldn't apply to Megan. I mean, she's fine in that department."

> She can do everything for herself now!

As we talked in Mrs. Phelps's kitchen, Megan came in from playing in the snow, kicked off her boots, removed her coat, and gave it to her mother to hang up.

"She is completely toilet trained, and she can dress and eat by herself."

Megan said "hi" as she pulled on her shoes and came over for her mother to tie them.

"Do you want a snack, Megan?"

Megan nodded, and Mrs. Phelps got the bread and peanut butter, picked up a knife, and began to fix a sandwich.

"So, as I was saying, her self-help skills are good—she can do everything for herself now."

Many parents have set for themselves the task of teaching self-help skills to children with special needs. Progress is not always smooth for them, and results are not always dramatic. All too often there are unexpected snags and setbacks. When you are ready to begin a new skill, your child might be less enthusiastic about learning than you are about teaching, and despite anyone's best efforts, problems will arise. But, with it all, progress is made. It has been our good fortune to watch many parents succeed.

# Targeting a Skill to Teach

Your first task will be to evaluate your child's current performance of self-help skills. Which skills can he do pretty well, but only with some assistance from you? Which skills can he do only parts of? And which skills can he do none of—yet.

To help you in this evaluation, we have included the Self-Help Checklist (p. 67), listing 30 self-help skills. Go down this list now, indicating for each skill the category that best describes your child's current performance.

Now, the next step is . . . *wait a minute!* Did you fill out the Self-Help Checklist? If not, please stop now and do it, so the rest of this chapter will make sense to you.

The next step is to target a skill to teach. You may want to take another quick look at Chapter 2, where we talked about how to target a skill to teach. Remember, we talked about choosing a skill that your child is ready to learn and wants to learn and that you want to teach.

On your Self-Help Checklist, circle three skills that you will teach next. These are probably all in column 2—skills that your child can do some of but needs to be taught to master. Decide which of these you will teach first. Now write these three skills in the space provided below, with the first skill you have targeted next to number 1.

# Self-Help Skills to Teach

1.   Skill    _____

      Steps    _____

                     _____

                     _____

                     _____

2.   Skill    _____

      Steps    _____

                     _____

                     _____

                     _____

3.   Skill    _____

      Steps    _____

                     _____

                     _____

                     _____

## Self-Help Checklist

Please check the box that most appropriately describes your child's ability to perform the following self-help skills.

| SKILL | NONE | SOME | ALL |
|---|---|---|---|
| 1. Drinking from a cup | ☐ | ☐ | ☐ |
| 2. Eating with a spoon | ☐ | ☐ | ☐ |
| 3. Eating with a fork | ☐ | ☐ | ☐ |
| 4. Spreading with a knife | ☐ | ☐ | ☐ |
| 5. Cutting with a knife | ☐ | ☐ | ☐ |
| 6. Removing pants (does not include unfastening) | ☐ | ☐ | ☐ |
| 7. Putting on pants (does not include fastening) | ☐ | ☐ | ☐ |
| 8. Putting on socks | ☐ | ☐ | ☐ |
| 9. Putting on a pullover shirt | ☐ | ☐ | ☐ |
| 10. Putting on a front-button blouse, shirt, or coat (does not include buttoning) | ☐ | ☐ | ☐ |
| 11. Putting on shoes (does not include tying) | ☐ | ☐ | ☐ |
| 12. Threading a belt | ☐ | ☐ | ☐ |
| 13. Buckling a belt | ☐ | ☐ | ☐ |
| 14. Zipping up | ☐ | ☐ | ☐ |
| 15. Buttoning | ☐ | ☐ | ☐ |
| 16. Starting a zipper | ☐ | ☐ | ☐ |
| 17. Tying shoes | ☐ | ☐ | ☐ |
| 18. Hanging up clothes | ☐ | ☐ | ☐ |
| 19. Drying hands | ☐ | ☐ | ☐ |
| 20. Washing hands | ☐ | ☐ | ☐ |
| 21. Brushing teeth | ☐ | ☐ | ☐ |
| 22. Washing face | ☐ | ☐ | ☐ |
| 23. Bathing—drying | ☐ | ☐ | ☐ |
| 24. Bathing—washing | ☐ | ☐ | ☐ |
| 25. Brushing hair | ☐ | ☐ | ☐ |
| 26. Washing hair | ☐ | ☐ | ☐ |
| 27. Making a bed | ☐ | ☐ | ☐ |
| 28. Setting the table | ☐ | ☐ | ☐ |
| 29. Changing a bed | ☐ | ☐ | ☐ |
| 30. Sweeping | ☐ | ☐ | ☐ |

# Establishing the Steps

Next, you need to carefully take apart the first skill that you have chosen to teach, as we discussed in Chapter 3. Think about all the steps that make up this skill. One way to accomplish this is to actually perform the skill a few times, making note of everything that you do—so go ahead and drink from a cup, zip a zipper, vacuum the house, or take a bath. Another way is to refer to the Self-Help Skills Inventory that you will find in Appendix B. There we cite each of the skills in the Self-Help Checklist, listing under each the steps that make up the skill.

Your list, of course, won't look exactly like our list. For one thing, the number of steps to include is partly an individual decision. For pretty fast learners, we need only a few big steps. For slower learners, it helps to have a lot of smaller steps. For another thing, we don't know how best to adapt the standard list of steps to your child. But you do.

So, from your list of steps and our list of steps, determine the list that is best for your child. **Write the steps under the first skill that you have chosen to teach.**

At some point, you will need to make lists of steps in the same way for the other two skills that you have targeted. You can do that now or come back to it later.

---

### &#x2040; Small Steps

"R-r-ring." Mrs. Cronin had just begun Keith's daily lesson of putting on a belt when she had to dash for the telephone.

"Keith, try to do it yourself."

Keith picked up the belt and began to fumble with it. Only yesterday he'd done it easily, finished threading it through the last loop after she had completed all the other loops first. But today, his happy success of yesterday was not to be repeated when he tried to do all of it himself. By attempting to move too fast, he'd come to a standstill.

Mrs. Cronin's conversation was interrupted by Keith, belt in hand and practically in tears. She put the phone down for a moment and quickly rethreaded all but the last loop. Sure enough . . . this time he was easily successful.

---

Tears, a tantrum, wandering off—these and many other problem behaviors are not unusual when you are making demands on a child, when you are asking him to do something that you have always done for him. One way to minimize problem behaviors is to keep the task easy.

Your child can only be successful as a learner if you are successful as a teacher. The key to this success is your knowing the many small steps involved in a self-help skill, and proceeding slowly. By gearing your demands in teaching to what you know your child can do, you naturally allow for continual success. Each step requires him to do just slightly more than the one before and with each advance he becomes much more capable.

# Picking a Reward

We talked in Chapter 4 about picking a reward, and you may want to review briefly what we (and you) wrote there. We noted that your attention—in the form of smiles, hugs, praise, whatever—is your child's biggest reward. However, self-help skills usually aren't a whole lot of fun to learn (or teach, for that matter). Your child won't necessarily be motivated to perform well by your attention alone. You certainly should consider using other rewards—snacks, favorite activities.

Think about attention, snack, and activity rewards that your child especially likes, and in the space below write down a few rewards that you will try. Remember to select rewards that are possible to use in teaching self-help skills. Your child, for example, may like lollipops, but if you give her one every time she buttons a button—and have to wait until she finishes before moving to the next button—you may have a longer teaching session than you bargained for.

Rewards to use:

_____

_____

_____

## Exceptions to the Rule

In spite of our suggestions about phasing out rewards after a skill is learned, you might notice that there are some skills your child can already do but that he will not do. In this case, you do not need to teach him the skill, but you will need to use rewards for a while to encourage him to carry it out.

It helps to distinguish between self-care skills and housekeeping skills. Self-care skills, such as dressing, mealtime, and grooming skills, will usually become part of the daily routine once they are learned. These are skills that your child must do (or which you must do for him) to get through the day, and when he has learned them he is likely to continue to do them, perhaps with a few reminders and the promise of praise. Maintaining a check card for these skills is sometimes useful as a reminder. The child may not need the checks to motivate him to do skills, but might miss parts of a routine (getting ready for bed) without a reminder. In this case, he can be taught to give himself a check when each step is done and then to bring the card (with a full column of checks) to you for your praise and perhaps an activity reward (for example, a story at bedtime).

Housekeeping skills, however, are sort of "extra" chores. Most children would be happy to get through the day without making beds, picking up toys, or emptying the wastebaskets. If you want him to participate in the household chores, then, just as other children get an allowance, he should continue to get some form of token reward.

While you may want to increase the amount that he must do for his rewards, it would be unfair and unwise to eliminate the extra rewards altogether. Of course, with housekeeping chores, the check card also serves as a reminder of what to do.

# Setting the Stage

In Chapter 5 we talked about ways to arrange the teaching environment—to "set the stage"—to maximize success. You may want to take another look at what we said there. Let's review the four questions about stage setting, with an eye toward self-help skill teaching.

### When Will You Teach It?

Self-help skills, fortunately, often answer this question for us. The bed is made in the morning, hands are washed before meals, and baths are taken—well, as infrequently as possible if most kids had their way. But you get the point. Unless you are setting aside a longer period for formal teaching—for repeated practice of a skill—you will teach it when it's needed.

### Where Will You Teach It?

Here, too, self-help skills direct us. Toothbrushing and table setting and toileting have their places. With dressing skills, however, you will want to take a look at your child's bedroom, the bathroom, and any other possible space to see where the distractions will be fewest.

### How Will You Reduce Distractions?

Let your mistakes guide you. As you begin teaching, keep an eye out for what distracts your child from the task. Generally, the fewer the noises, people, and interesting items around, the better, so that your child's attention will be focused on what you are doing. During that bathing program, the rubber duckie may have to go.

**What Materials Will You Use?**

The most important point in stage setting for self-help skills is choosing materials that are manageable. With clothes, this often means using something a bit larger. With eating, it may mean making portions a bit smaller.

Watch to see where your child is struggling with the task and try to think of a way to change materials to make it easier. Here are some examples:

✵ Fasten the towel to the rack with a safety pin to prevent it from falling off when drying hands.
✵ Practice putting on socks with Mom's or Dad's athletic socks.
✵ Teach unbuttoning a coat rather than a shirt, because buttons are larger and easier to manage.
✵ Put red and blue tape on faucets to distinguish hot and cold.
✵ Cut the bar of soap in half, so it's easier to handle.

We've included some other ideas in the self-help programs in Appendix C. Talk with other parents, though—you have all discovered tricks that you can share to make learning easier.

 Change the World

Our big world doesn't yield easily to little hands. Children often struggle in an adult world. Setting the stage for success often requires a small change in parts of that world to make them more manageable.

Tyus marches to the table, spoon in hand, ready to eat. His mother anticipates her next teaching step—getting the food on the spoon. She is busy preparing his favorite meal but in a somewhat different manner. His hamburger is now cut in pieces to fit the spoon. The potatoes are mashed and guaranteed not to roll off the spoon. And tonight there will be no soup!

Consider the self-help skill you have chosen to teach your child.

When will you teach it?

_____

_____

Where will you teach?

_____

_____

How will you reduce distractions?

_____

_____

What materials will you use (can these be made more manageable)?

_____

_____

# Teaching

We talked in Chapter 6 about "tell-show-guide," or how to use verbal directions, modeling, and physical guidance in teaching any skill. Take another look at those pages now, because they are very important for self-help skills teaching. Physical guidance might be especially helpful when you are teaching self-help skills that involve the hands, such as cutting with a knife, tying shoes, or tying a bow.

You are almost ready to begin teaching—just one question remains. "Which step do I start with?" Our answer to this question might be unexpected.

### Backward Chaining

Suppose you were in a race that had no rules—just a finish line and a starter to say "Go." Suppose, furthermore, that you wanted to guarantee your success in winning that race. What would you do? After considering a number of inventive possibilities, it is likely that you would decide to start the race right next to the finish line. Then, as soon as the starter said "Go," you'd be finished—and successful. Why not? There were no rules, right?

A teaching strategy called backward chaining views the teaching of a real skill much like the running of the strange race just described, except that your child is the runner and the completion of the task is the finish line. The best way to guarantee success is to start right next to the finish line or, in other words, as near as possible to the completion of the task. Then, as soon as the race begins, your child has only a short distance to go before he reaches the finish line—and success.

Backward chaining is used for teaching skills that are a chain of separate steps, always performed in the same order. Let's take a quick look at how one skill, hand washing, might be taught according to the strategy of backward chaining. Hand washing can be broken down like any skill into many small, manageable steps. But, for the purposes of illustration, let's just break it down into these four:

1. Turning on the water
2. Lathering hands
3. Rinsing hands
4. Turning off the water

Now, what is the finish line in the hand-washing race? Step 4—turning off the water, because this would represent the completion of the task. So, to start your child as close to the finish as possible, what must you do? You must do Steps 1, 2, and 3 for him first, turning on the water, lathering and rinsing his hands for him. You might even have to help him grasp the faucet, too, so that as soon as you say "Go," he could turn the water off and complete the task by himself quickly and easily. The race would be won.

In reality, however, the race cannot remain such a simple one forever; we will want to make the strategy of backward chaining useful for teaching more than just the ends of skills. You've begun by doing practically all of the skill for him, requiring him to do only a little to complete the task. You will continue to teach by doing just a little less for him each time; you'll move the starting line a little farther from the finish line until you eventually get to the beginning.

To return to our four-step hand-washing program, this would require that once your child masters turning off the water, you would begin to have him do some of the rinsing unassisted (Step 3). After he has mastered Step 3, he'd move back to lathering his hands with your help (Step 2), and then to turning on the water (Step 1). Each time he struggles through a new step he then moves into a chain of steps he has already mastered, and it's smooth going to the end.

By following the strategy of backward chaining, your child will win the race every time!

---

### ◈ Last Step First

Mrs. Acevedo used backward chaining when teaching Jessie to take off his coat. She knew that he had already learned several of the final steps of taking off a coat; once it was unbuttoned, he could remove it easily and hang it up. She therefore moved back one more step, requiring that he finish unbuttoning the last button. After he struggled with this new step, he proceeded to the end with the smooth series of steps he had already learned. She had already unbuttoned all of the other buttons and had even started this last one, so the stage was properly set for Jessie's success.

As Jessie learned each step, Mrs. Acevedo moved backward in the teaching sequence, requiring that he do progressively more of the task each time. With each new session came just a little bit of newness and a successively greater amount that was "old hat." More important, Jessie never had to watch his mother finish something that he was only capable of starting.

---

If the principle of backward chaining is carefully followed, once a child starts, he always finishes. Most self-help skills follow this backward chaining strategy. Putting on a shirt, drying hands, eating spaghetti—the list of skills that we think of as one smooth operation is literally endless. In fact, each skill is an ordered chain of separate steps that are best taught by beginning with the last one.

# Observing Progress and Troubleshooting

Teaching self-help skills goes better if you keep a record of your teaching sessions and of your child's progress. You have used the Self-Help Skills Inventory in Appendix B to arrive at steps in your teaching program. One way to keep track of progress is to use these steps as a guide, recording every time you practice a step and how successful your child is. At the end of Appendix B you will find a Progress Chart. The following guidelines will help you to use it:

1. In the left-hand margin of the chart, write down the steps in your teaching program in the order you are going to teach (backward chain). If they don't fit, an alternative is to post your teaching program next to this chart.

2. Write in the date and also the step on which you are working.
3. Place a check mark to indicate each successful attempt your child makes on a step within each teaching session.
4. Place an X for an unsuccessful attempt on a step.
5. At the end of each teaching session, place a circle around the last check mark to indicate a completed session.

---

### ◊ Letting Go

Letting go is not easy, but holding on is not fair. It is up to you to judge when your child should be allowed to struggle on his own, when he has gone far enough with you and must do it without your help. These moments of anxious watching are the most trying times of teaching, but without them learning will never happen.

"Zach, hurry up! Mommy, he's never gonna get his hands dry. I'll go help him, OK?"

"No, let your brother dry his own hands. He's learned to do it by himself."

"Yeah, but you know how hard it is for him. It takes him forever and I'm hungry."

"Oh, you won't starve. Listen, when you wanted to make the salad for dinner, I just let you go ahead and do it, didn't I? And I just stood and watched while you cut up the tomato. . . ."

"Yeah, and that took me forever."

"But you did it, didn't you, and now you'll get faster. Since you've now learned how to use a knife, you just need more practice without my help. Don't you think we should let Zach practice, too, now that he's ready?"

---

**Remember:** Every session should end with a success. Consider, for example, the chart that Billy's mother (way back in Chapter 1) was keeping of his progress (p. 8).

# Progress Chart

Program: **Making the bed**

Number of Attempts

| List of Steps | Date | Step | 1 | 2 | 3 | 4 | 5 | 6 | 7 | 8 | 9 | 10 | 11 | 12 | Notes |
|---|---|---|---|---|---|---|---|---|---|---|---|---|---|---|---|
| 1) Brings spread up over pillow | 10/2 | 1 | Ⓞ | ✓ | ✓ | ✓ | Ⓞ | ✓ | ✓ | Ⓞ | | | | | He put pillow on but didn't do step 1 |
| 2) Puts pillow on the bed | 10/3 | 2 | Ⓞ | ✓ | ✓ | X | ✓ | Ⓞ | | | | | | | |
|  | 10/4 | 2 | Ⓞ | ✓ | ✓ | ✓ | Ⓞ | | | | | | | | |
| 3) Folds spread back | 10/5 | 3 | X | Ⓞ | ✓ | ✓ | ✓ | Ⓞ | | | | | | | Began session with a new step. |
| 4) Pulls spread up and smooths out | 10/6 | 3 | Ⓞ | X | X | ✓ | ✓ | | | | | | | | Forgot to put star on his chart this A.M. |
|  | 10/7 | 4 | Ⓞ | | | | | | | | | | | | |
| 5) Folds blanket and sheet back together | | | | | | | | | | | | | | | |
| 6) Pulls blanket up and smooths out wrinkles | | | | | | | | | | | | | | | |
| 7) Pulls top sheet up and tugs at both sides to smooth out wrinkles | | | | | | | | | | | | | | | |

✓ = successful
X = not successful
Ⓞ = completed session

You can see from our sample chart that Billy's mother held a practice session in addition to the one she held in the morning. Billy was successful with Step 1, but ran into difficulty with Step 2, when he forgot to do Step 1 (which he had already mastered). A reminder by his mom brought success.

As noted in the chart, on October 5th Mom started Billy out on a new step without first having him do a step he already knew. She backed up at once to an easier step. Billy was again successful. The next day Billy was successful with Step 3 when making his bed in the morning, but Mom forgot to give him his well-earned star on his chart. That afternoon Billy was not too excited about his practice session until Mom realized what she had forgotten.

Recording progress is an important part of good teaching. If the type of progress chart we have presented does not seem right for you, make up some other procedure. You might prefer to keep a diary, noting successes as they occur. The important thing is to have a way to periodically check to see if you are making progress. If so, reward yourself—you certainly deserve it. If not, refer back to the troubleshooting section of Chapter 7.

## Behavior Problems

Each child is unique, and each child has her own way of meeting a new teaching situation. However, because the child with special needs has a history of failure, we are certain about one thing: Your child will have some strategy for avoiding that teaching situation. She may cooperate until the first hint of failure, or perhaps you won't even be that lucky. Many children will show virtually no interest in the task, drop the soap, look everywhere but at you, or simply wander off. Others will fly into a rage at the first demand, with enough crying, biting, hitting, and screaming to make teaching seem hardly worthwhile. Some will be less obvious and will look for cute things to do to distract you from teaching.

What you are seeing, partly, is a strategy for making a learning demand go away. In the past, every time these strategies have succeeded in making someone give up trying to teach, the problem behaviors have been strengthened a little bit. Just as a desirable behavior when followed by a reward is more likely to happen again, an undesirable behavior (like screaming or kicking in the teaching situation), when followed by a reward (getting out of the teaching situation), is more likely to happen again.

Our emphasis is to minimize behavior problems by a teaching strategy that makes learning easy and fun. Yet, despite your best efforts, there will still be some problem behavior.

In order to give a clearer presentation of the steps in teaching a skill, we have not talked much about the many behaviors your child will find to interfere with your plans. At times, it may sound as though we are writing about an ideal situation in which your child's behavior problems will not get in the way. They will. We are certain that every parent reading this book will have to adapt the *ideal* teaching approach to the way it *really* is at home.

Chapters 16 and 17 address behavior problems and their management, respectively, at length. We believe, however, that you should work first on teaching skills. Included in Appendix C are program guidelines for teaching the self-help skills that appear in the Self-Help Checklist (p. 67) and the more detailed Self-Help Skills Inventory (Appendix B).

# Chapter 10

# Toilet Training

Let's be honest with each other. You don't need us to tell you that toilet training is among the most important skills your child needs to learn. Nor do we have to tell you that teaching your child how to go to the bathroom isn't much fun. It involves a good deal of your time and a willingness to put up with many frustrations and setbacks along the way. You know this already. Chances are you've already tried one strategy or another to make your child behave in the bathroom "like a big boy (or girl)." Yet the never-ending changing of clothes and the occasional embarrassments still continue. Chances are, too, that your child may be unable to participate in certain programs or activities that have, as their only price of admission, "the completely trained child."

Toilet training simply isn't easy. There are no shortcuts and, frankly, there's very little excitement. Instead, a commitment needs to be made and a set of systematic procedures needs to be followed. This chapter is designed to help you do both.

## Skills Involved in Toileting

Often when we think of toilet training we think of dry, clean pants . . . and little else. In fact, however, the child who is completely trained has learned more than simply how to eliminate in the toilet. Much more. This child can perform each of the following skills:

1.   Recognizing when he has to go
2.   Waiting to eliminate
3.   Entering the bathroom
4.   Pulling pants down

5. Sitting on the toilet
6. Eliminating in the toilet
7. Using toilet paper correctly
8. Pulling pants back up
9. Flushing the toilet
10. Washing hands
11. Drying hands

Your child may already have learned to perform some of these skills and, as you work through your training program, you will want to give him every chance to complete these on his own. Then again, he may not yet know how to do any of these skills, and at this point you shouldn't worry about that.

Your initial goal will be to teach him one skill only: *eliminating in the toilet*. At first you may need to do most or all of the other skills for him. Later, you can gradually begin to teach him the other skills that combine to make up *complete toilet training*.

## Is Your Child Ready?

Your child is ready to learn toilet training if he

1. Can follow simple directions ("Come here, Billy")
2. Can sit in a chair for 5 minutes
3. Can wait at least 1½ hours between elimination times (before beginning urine training)

**Note:** If your child cannot yet follow simple directions or sit for 5 minutes, you should first concentrate on teaching these skills (see Chapter 8).

## Make Your Decision

Whether you have never before tried to toilet train your child, or whether you have tried before but had little success, make the decision right now to learn the approach and stick with it. As many parents have discovered, the end result will prove well worth the effort.

Remember, no one else can toilet train your child for you; it's an around-the-clock task, and your child spends most of his time with you. To be successful, though, you'll have to be consistent. This means enlisting the help of other people with whom your child spends his or her day—a babysitter, neighbors, a teacher, and, of course, other family members.

🌰 **Parent-to-Parent**

Our parent "co-workers" had several important suggestions for us to pass along to you:

Whitney's mother said we could not stress enough that toilet training is a slow and gradual process, with any number of setbacks. "Sometimes you just don't seem to be getting anywhere," she told us, "and it's so easy to convince yourself to quit." Many others agreed with her that the most important message we could relay to you is, simply, "Don't give up!"

Rafael's mother spoke for a number of parents when she recalled how important careful record keeping was for their eventual success. "I was scared of numbers," she remembered, "but over time we became pretty good friends. Record keeping seems like it's going to be a lot more difficult than it actually is . . . and there's no way you can succeed without it."

Finally, Scott's father pointed out how the whole family benefited from being involved in Scott's success. "We did it together, for Scotty and for us. We had to, to make it work."

# Record Keeping

### Recording Eliminations

If your child is already on a good "potty schedule" such that he eliminates in the toilet when you take him regularly and he never has daytime accidents, skip ahead to the section on "Independent Toileting." Otherwise, your *first and most important* step in toilet training your child is to find out his *elimination pattern*—the times each day when he is most likely to wet and/or soil his pants. You can begin a systematic program to train your child only after you know his elimination pattern.

To determine your child's pattern you will keep a record, for 2 weeks, of the times he urinates or has a bowel movement. You will begin toilet training *only* after this 2-week period.

### What to Do for 2 Weeks

1. **Continue** during this 2-week period to handle toileting as you have been. If you have not been bringing your child to the toilet, don't start to do so yet. If you have been bringing your child to the toilet, record

whether he urinates, has a bowel movement, or does not eliminate while sitting there.

2.  **Check** your child when he first gets up in the morning to see if he is dry, or if he has urinated, or has had a bowel movement in his diapers.

3.  **Check** him again 1 hour later, and continue to check him every hour until he goes to bed.

4.  **Record each time** whether he is dry, has urinated, or has had a bowel movement. (We'll talk more about this in a moment.)

5.  **Change** him if he is wet or soiled when you check him. You should do this so you will know whether he has eliminated again in the next hour, and so he will start getting used to being dry.

## How to Keep Your Record

The record-keeping charts in this section are for your use during this 2-week period. We have also included sample charts. After you've completed the rest of this section, copy the blank Elimination Record (p. 83) and write the days of the week across the top. Put it up in the bathroom and begin keeping your records tomorrow.

*Pants Column*   In the column marked *Pants* you will record every hour:

|       |                            |
|-------|----------------------------|
| D     | if he is dry               |
| U     | if he urinated in pants    |
| BM    | if he had a bowel movement |
| U/BM  | if both                    |

Of course, you don't have to wait an entire hour. Anytime you think he is wet, check him, write the time on the chart, and record the results.

*Toilet Column*   If you do put your child on the toilet, record the results in the *Toilet* column in the same way. (Remember, do not start putting him on the toilet yet if you have not already been doing it.)

|       |                                  |
|-------|----------------------------------|
| D     | if he didn't eliminate in the toilet |
| U     | if he urinated in the toilet     |
| BM    | if he had a bowel movement       |
| U/BM  | if both                          |

As you can see, record keeping will take you no more than a minute each hour. Yet this is the **most important** part of your toilet training program.

You may have had experience keeping records before, and feel ready now to begin. Or you may be among the many parents who have never

# Elimination Record

CHILD'S NAME: _____

DATE BEGUN: _____

| Time | Day 1 | | Day 2 | | Day 3 | | Day 4 | | Day 5 | | Day 6 | | Day 7 | |
|---|---|---|---|---|---|---|---|---|---|---|---|---|---|---|
| | Pants | Toilet | Pants | Toilet | Pants | Toilet | Pants | Toilet | Pants | Toilet | Pants | Toilet | Pants | Toilet |
| 7:00 | | | | | | | | | | | | | | |
| 8:00 | | | | | | | | | | | | | | |
| 9:00 | | | | | | | | | | | | | | |
| 10:00 | | | | | | | | | | | | | | |
| 11:00 | | | | | | | | | | | | | | |
| 12:00 | | | | | | | | | | | | | | |
| 1:00 | | | | | | | | | | | | | | |
| 2:00 | | | | | | | | | | | | | | |
| 3:00 | | | | | | | | | | | | | | |
| 4:00 | | | | | | | | | | | | | | |
| 5:00 | | | | | | | | | | | | | | |
| 6:00 | | | | | | | | | | | | | | |
| 7:00 | | | | | | | | | | | | | | |

kept records of behavior before, and expect it to be a difficult and confusing process. We want to make sure that you do not quit before you even begin, so we present several examples here to make record keeping a bit clearer.

## ⌀ Charting

Jeff's mother was very anxious to begin a toilet-training program. When asked about Jeff's elimination pattern, she first described him as "usually wet sometime in midmorning and a couple of times in the afternoon." This was not specific enough, and the 2-week charting period was initiated to gather more exact information. Jeff's mother continued the usual toileting routine, except that she checked Jeff *every hour* and wrote down the results.

Her chart for the first morning looked like this:

| | Day 1 | |
|---|---|---|
| | *Wednesday* | |
| Time | Pants | Toilet |
| 7:00 | U | D |
| 8:00 | D | |
| 9:00 | D | U |
| 10:00 | D | |
| 10:25 | U/BM | |
| 11:00 | D | |

*This is what the chart shows:*

⌀ At 7:00 she had found his pajamas wet with urine (U); she put him on the toilet like she always did, but he didn't go (D).

⌀ At 8:00, 1 hour later, she checked him again and his pants were dry (D). She did not put him on the toilet.

- ✇ At 9:00 he was still dry (D), but he urinated when put on the toilet (U).
- ✇ At 10:00, dry again (D).
- ✇ At 10:25 Jeff wet and soiled his pants (U/BM); his mother saw the signs, but too late to get him to the toilet. She wrote the time down on the chart.
- ✇ At 11:00 he was dry (D).

At the end of 2 weeks, this simple, daily recording of Ds, Us, and BMs had given Jeff's mother the information she needed to begin successful training. There were, of course, several times during the 2-week period when she was busy and forgot to "check"; having the whole family working with her on the toilet-training program was a big help.

Now let's look at a record of one child's elimination pattern for 1 week, from 8:00 A.M. to 12:00 noon. You might be surprised to see how many questions it can answer.

| TIME | Sun. Pants | Sun. Toilet | Mon. Pants | Mon. Toilet | Tues. Pants | Tues. Toilet | Wed. Pants | Wed. Toilet | Thurs. Pants | Thurs. Toilet | Fri. Pants | Fri. Toilet | Sat. Pants | Sat. Toilet |
|---|---|---|---|---|---|---|---|---|---|---|---|---|---|---|
| 8:00 | D | | | D | D | D | | D | u | D | D | | D | |
| 9:00 | BM | u | u | D | u | | u | | u/BM | D | D | u | u | D |
| 10:00 | D | | BM | | BM | u | BM | | BM | | BM | D | BM | |
| 11:00 | u | | D | | D | | D | D | D | | u | D | D | u |
| 12:00 | D | | | u | | u | | u | | u | | u | | u |

Write down your answers:

1. *Where* does she have a bowel movement on Saturday? _____

2. *What time* did she have a bowel movement on Wednesday? _____

3. *How many* bowel movements on Thursday? _____

4. *How many* bowel movements did she have at 9:00? _____

5. *At what time* did she have the most bowel movements? _____

A whole chart looks confusing. But each specific square tells you something that is really quite simple. Check your answers.

**Answers:**

1. Pants
2. 10:00
3. Two
4. Two
5. 10:00

You are now ready to record your own child's elimination pattern. Keep a record for 2 weeks, and during this time read the rest of the chapter so that you will be ready to begin a program.

If you do not keep a consistent record during the next 2 weeks the rest of this chapter will be of no use to you. *Remember that during these 2 weeks there is no such thing as success or failure; you are only trying to see what your child's elimination pattern is so that you can then set up a toileting schedule that makes sense for her.*

In order for the records to show a pattern, you must know what your child does during all the hours she is awake. This means you may have to *send the records* with her to school or to Grandma's and you will have to carefully explain the record-keeping procedure to your family, maybe even to the babysitter. You are the teacher for this program. Others will be helpful if you make clear what they should do, and if they see that you take the program seriously yourself.

# Where to Begin— Bowel or Urine Training?

When first toilet training your child, you should begin with bowel training. However, if 1) your child has all his bowel movements in the toilet and 2) your elimination records show he can wait 1½ hours between urination times, then your child is ready to begin urine training.

**Note:** In some cases a child will already be urine trained but not bowel trained; if this is the case with your child, then proceed with bowel training.

There are many reasons why bowel training comes first. Bowel movements occur less frequently and more systematically than urination. As a result, there are fewer trips to the toilet, and less of your time is needed. Fewer new expectations are placed on your child. More important, each trip to the toilet is more likely to be successful. Also, signs that indicate to you that your child needs to move his bowels are easier to detect (for example, straining, red in the face, quiet, or squatting down).

When bowel training has been accomplished, urine training will follow with little difficulty, as your child will now be familiar with the toileting routine.

When you have 1) kept the 2-weeks' record of your child's elimination pattern and 2) decided whether to begin bowel or urine training, then you are ready to determine his toileting schedule. The following section focuses on how to determine a toileting schedule for bowel training. Even if you are beginning with urine training, you should read this section carefully, since the procedure is almost identical in both cases. After this, we consider the few minor ways this process differs for urine training.

# Determining a Toileting Schedule

1. Take the 2-week elimination records you have kept and circle every BM (preferably in a color that will stand out).
2. For each time period (7:00, 8:00, 9:00, etc.), add across the two pages the number of bowel movements your child has had. Write the total number for each period in the left-hand margin, next to the time to which it refers.

    On pages 88 and 89 are examples of one child's 2-week record with Steps 1 and 2, above, completed. Take some time to understand what these samples show before proceeding.

    For most children, there will be some *pattern* to the elimination. There should be several times during the day when the BMs are most likely, times that have the highest totals for the 2-week period. For example, in the sample charts you've just seen, Alex was most likely to have a BM during one of the following time periods: 9:30 A.M. to 10:00 A.M., 11:30 A.M. to 12:00 noon, or 5:30 P.M. to 6:00 P.M.

**Elimination Record**

CHILD'S NAME: _Alex_
DATE BEGUN: _November 14_

| | Day 1 Wednesday | | Day 2 Thursday | | Day 3 Friday | | Day 4 Saturday | | Day 5 Sunday | | Day 6 Monday | | Day 7 Tuesday | |
|---|---|---|---|---|---|---|---|---|---|---|---|---|---|---|
| Time | Pants | Toilet | Pants | Toilet | Pants | Toilet | Pants | Toilet | Pants | Toilet | Pants | Toilet | Pants | Toilet |
| 7:00 | | | | 7:30 U | | | | | D | U | | | | 7:30 D |
| 8:00 | D | U | D | | U | U | D | U | D | | U | U | D | |
| 9:00 | D (9:30 BM) | | D | | D | | D | | U | | D (9:30 U BM) | | D | |
| 10:00 | D | | U | | D | | (BM) | | D | | D | | U | |
| 11:00 | U | | D | (11:30 BM) | U | | D | U | D | D | D | | D | |
| 12:00 | | | | D | D | | | | (U/BM) | | D | | (BM) | |
| 1:00 | D | | D | | D | | D | | D | | U | | U | |
| 2:00 | D (2:30 U) | | U | | U | | D | | D | | D | | D | |
| 3:00 | D | | D | | D | | D | | U | | D | | U | |
| 4:00 | D | | D | | D (4:30 U) | | U | | D | | U | | D | |
| 5:00 | U | | D | | U | D (5:30 BM) | D | | D (5:30 U) | | D | | U | |
| 6:00 | D | | D | | D | | U | | D | | D (6:30 U) | | D | |
| 7:00 | D | | U | | U | | D | | D | | D | | U | |

3. *If your child has a regular and easily identifiable pattern,* toileting times will be easier to schedule. Fifteen minutes before each of the times he usually has a bowel movement, you should bring your child to the toilet. For Alex, the first toileting time would be 9:15 A.M., the second would be 11:15 A.M., and the third would be 5:15 P.M.

If your child usually has only *one* BM in the morning and if he has a BM the first toileting time, you need not take him again. If he does not eliminate at this time, however, and if he has not soiled between toileting times, you will need to take him to the toilet at the

## Elimination Record

CHILD'S NAME: **Alex**
DATE BEGUN: **November 21**

| Time | Day 1 Wednesday Pants | Toilet | Day 2 Thursday Pants | Toilet | Day 3 Friday Pants | Toilet | Day 4 Saturday Pants | Toilet | Day 5 Sunday Pants | Toilet | Day 6 Monday Pants | Toilet | Day 7 Tuesday Pants | Toilet |
|---|---|---|---|---|---|---|---|---|---|---|---|---|---|---|
| 7:00 | | | | | | | | | | | | | | |
| | | | 7:30 u | u | | | 7:30 D | u | | | | | 7:30 D | u |
| 8:00 | D | u | D | | D | u | D | | D | u | u | u | D | |
| 9:00 | D | | D (9:15 BM) | | D | | D | | D | | D | | D | |
| 10:00 | u | | | D | u | | u | | (BM) 10:30 u | D | D | | u | |
| 11:00 | D | | D | | D | | D | | D | | u | | D | |
| 12:00 | u | | u | | (u/BM) | | u | | D | | D | | u | |
| 1:00 | D | | D | | u | | D | | u | | D | u | D | |
| 2:00 | D (2:30 u) | | u | | D | | D | | D | | D | | D | |
| 3:00 | D | | D | | D | | u | | u | | u | | u | |
| 4:00 | D | | D | | u | | D | | D | | D | | D | |
| 5:00 | u (5:30 BM) | | u | | D | | D (5:30 u) | | u | | D | | D | |
| 6:00 | D | | D | | u | | (BM) | | D | | u | | (BM) | |
| 7:00 | u | | D | | D | | u | | u | | D | | u | |

next scheduled time (for Alex, in our example, this time would be 11:15 A.M.).

Further on, we discuss exactly what you should do at these toileting times. For now, we are only trying to establish a schedule of the best times for toileting. From the 2 weeks of records, we want you to be able to make a statement like: "He usually has a BM about 10:00 in the morning. If not then, it's usually between 11:30 and 12:30. Later in the afternoon, he will sometimes have a second BM between 4:00 and 5:00."

From this kind of statement you can list the best toileting times, which, again, will be 15 minutes before the usual elimination times.

4. *If your child does not have a regular or easily identifiable pattern,* your first toileting time should be 15 minutes before the first time when a BM was recorded. You would then schedule toileting times for every 2 hours after this. If he usually has only one BM a day, you will not toilet him again after he has had a BM.

5. You should now select two to four times during the day that are best for taking your child to the toilet for his Bowel-Training Program. When you have determined your child's toileting times, write them here:

_____

_____

_____

_____

You should carry out toileting at these exact scheduled times for *1 week.* After a week, you should study your records and, if necessary, change the schedule to fit your child's elimination pattern more closely. For example, if he always seems to have a BM 25 minutes after you have toileted him, make your scheduled time 15 minutes later. If he already has had a BM on several days when you go to toilet him, make your scheduled time 15 minutes earlier. **Do not make any changes in your schedule during the first week**; in later weeks you should only adjust your schedule when your records consistently suggest a change. (Do not change your schedule just because his elimination times changed for a day or two.)

The main reason that toilet training fails, when it does, is parents' failure to develop a good toileting schedule and to stick with it. Some people do not see the value in record keeping or do not take the extra time to read these pages carefully and examine their 2-week records for a pattern. Others do this but are not consistent in following the schedule they develop. In either case, toilet training fails and the parents and child both lose. Most parents, however, do succeed, and you can be among them.

Parents find it helpful to get the aid of a spouse or neighbor or older child in determining the best toileting schedule. Perhaps you will find it useful at this point to discuss your toilet-training plans with someone else. In general, it is good to involve someone else in your program so you can talk over progress with him or her.

## Special Note

***Determining a Toileting Schedule for Urine Training***    To determine a toileting schedule for urine training, you should follow the same procedure just outlined for bowel training. Keep in mind the following minor changes:

1. You will circle the *U*s on the 2-week elimination record and add these up.
2. There will be a greater number of times for urination. Select four to eight times during the day when your child is most likely to urinate. No two times should be closer than 1½ hours.
3. Arrange your toileting schedule so that your already-established toileting times for bowel training become part of it.
4. Take him to the toilet at all of the scheduled times.

If you are beginning with urine training, write the best toileting times for your child's urine training here (as determined from the 2-week record).

_____

_____

_____

_____

_____

_____

_____

**Remember:** Determining a schedule is the most important part of toilet training.

# Using Rewards

You may want to refer back to Chapter 4 to review what we have said about rewards, because, as with teaching any skill, rewards are very important for successful toilet training.

At first you should only require your child to do a small step, like sitting on the toilet. You should immediately praise her and give her a raisin, a sip of juice, or whatever reward you have selected. With time your child will no longer need the reward and will be able to sit on the toilet at your request. You should then only reward her after she eliminates.

You should be ready to give your attention and special treat immediately when she eliminates—then quickly remove her from the bathroom so that she will not be eating a snack or playing with a toy for long in the bathroom. Remember, the bathroom is not a playroom.

---

### &#x24D2; Rewards

Mrs. Johnson's bowel training program ran into trouble right from the start: Jamal would not sit on the toilet for longer than 30 seconds. She knew he liked vanilla cookies and praise, but he would never be able to earn them for eliminating in the toilet if he didn't sit there. So the *first* behavior to increase was sitting on the toilet, and we advised that she praise and reward Jamal first for just sitting 30 seconds, then 40 seconds, then 50 seconds, and so on—until he could sit for 5 minutes. When he got up too soon, Mrs. Johnson would dress him and take him out of the bathroom with as little attention as possible and no cookies. Jamal soon learned that the only way he could get her attention—and cookies— was to sit on the toilet.

As Jamal sat on the toilet for longer periods of time, he also began to eliminate in the toilet—for which he immediately received praise and a cookie.

---

# Behavior Problems

To give a clearer presentation of the steps in toilet training, we do not dwell here on the many behaviors your child will find to interfere with your plans. At times, it may sound like we are writing about an ideal situation in which your child's behavior problems will not get in the way. They will.

At the end of this chapter, we discuss some of the most frequent questions asked of us, some of which relate to behavior problems that arise during teaching. In addition, you may want to refer to Chapters 16 and 17, on behavior problems and their management.

# Bowel Training

This section on bowel training has seven parts. Read them all before beginning your child's program.

### Continue the Diapers

This is not yet the time to change to training pants, so keep your child in diapers throughout his bowel-training period. When he soils his diapers, change him in the bathroom, and without making a fuss. Don't scold him, punish him, or even act upset. Change him with as little attention as you can. The attention that children get while being changed—even if it's scolding—is often one reason they continue to soil their diapers. You will want to save your attention for when your child eliminates *in the toilet*.

### Recognize Your Child's Signs

You will be toileting your child on the regular schedule you have determined from his elimination pattern. However, you should also be aware of those other times when he may signal his need to go. Children signal in different ways—straining, quietness, redness of the face, and squatting are typical examples. Learn to recognize your child's signal, and take him to the toilet whenever it occurs. Record every time you toilet him, even if the time is not on the original schedule.

### Set the Stage for Success

You should give your child every chance to perform successfully on the toilet. You have already developed a schedule for toileting her at those times when she is most likely to go. To increase her chances for success even more, follow these guidelines for setting the stage.

***Be Consistent***   Keep your toileting routine as consistent as possible so that your child will come to expect it and be at ease with it. Take her to the toilet *on schedule* and do not change the schedule during the first week. Take her to the same toilet (when possible) and use the same words to make the whole process as predictable as possible.

***Use a Regular Toilet from the Beginning***   If your child is too small, make the seat more comfortable by placing a smaller one over it and by providing her with a box or stool on which she can rest her feet. If you should find it necessary to use a potty chair, keep it in the bathroom and always use it there.

***Avoid Distracting Toys and People***    In the beginning, it is important for your child to learn that the bathroom is not a playroom. She is there for one reason only—to eliminate in the toilet. To help her concentrate on this task, you should remove from the bathroom any toys or games (or people!) that might compete for her attention.

***Avoid Distracting Talk***    You, too, are in the bathroom with your child for a specific reason—to help her attend to the task at hand. Thus, while she is on the toilet, talk to her about what she is supposed to be doing, what the toilet is for, and avoid, at this time, talking about unrelated matters that again might only distract (nursery rhymes, what's for supper, and so on).

---

###  Distractions

Mrs. Charles had taken her 2 weeks of data and determined Julie's elimination pattern. Now, on the second morning of the bowel-training program, with Julie already seated for her 7:15 toileting, both Mr. Charles and Brittany rushed in to use the sink. Immediately Julie was on her feet to join them—unknowingly, Dad and Brittany had distracted her from the task at hand.

For this bowel-training program to be successful, the "morning rush" to the bathroom would have to be worked out more carefully. As it turned out, Dad and Brittany were able to use the bathroom before and after Julie's toileting time (Brittany agreed to get up a few minutes earlier and Dad agreed happily to get up a bit later). With a large family and only one bathroom, however, the scheduling is always difficult and a toilet-training program makes it even more so. Some family cooperation is necessary for success.

---

## Put Your Child on the Toilet

The general bathroom routine is as follows:

1. *Bring your child to the bathroom on schedule or when he signals.* Pull his pants down to below his knees (if he can do all or any part of this task himself, he should be encouraged to do so).

2. *Have him sit on the toilet for 5 minutes.* Stay there with him. Praise him occasionally for sitting. ("That's great! You're sitting on the toilet.") and explain what is expected in a straightforward, nondemanding way.
3. *If he eliminates,* praise him and give him his reward.
4. *If he does not eliminate,* remove him from the toilet and take him out of the bathroom for 10 minutes. Then come back for another 5-minute sitting on the toilet. Again, if he eliminates, praise and reward him.

Of course, you cannot "demand" that your child eliminate in the toilet. This will only make him tense and less likely to succeed. Instead, in the beginning, going to the toilet should be a casual matter, with little required on his part other than to sit.

In the 20-minute period, give your child two 5-minute chances to eliminate, with a 10-minute break in between. This routine avoids the frustration and discomfort of having to sit for long periods of time. Even if he still doesn't eliminate, he has performed part of the task successfully, and at first you should reward him just for sitting.

## Phase Yourself Out of the Bathroom

It is important that you phase yourself out of the bathroom gradually so that your child will get used to staying there by himself. You should begin doing this as soon as your child is able to stay on the toilet without your help and verbal reminders. After you have taken your child into the bathroom, or have put him on the toilet (depending on how much help he needs), stay with him for less and less of the sitting time. Move away *gradually.* At first, pretend to be attending to other things in the bathroom. Then stand in the doorway and, finally, leave the room entirely.

Even though you are "phasing yourself out," you must continue your attention and rewards when he is successful. Come back to praise and reward him, and give him help finishing up when he needs it. When your child consistently eliminates in the toilet, you can begin to phase out rewards as you would with any new skill.

## Keep Records

Record keeping continues throughout the entire bowel-training program. Put a chart on the wall near the toilet. Circle the times you have chosen as your toileting schedule. Every time you take your child to the toilet, write down whether she is dry, wet, or soiled (D, U, BM) and what she does on the toilet (D, U, BM). This chart is the same as you used during the 2-week period, except that now you do not check her every hour.

If you take your child to the toilet (or if she has a BM in her diapers) at other than your scheduled times, record the time and the result on the chart.

Recording progress carefully is just as important as the teaching strategy we have discussed. Keeping a daily record of progress will remind you to regularly carry out the toileting program, as well as help you to see "how it's going."

## Evaluate Progress

By looking at your chart week by week you can answer some important questions.

### Are you toileting him at the best times?

Remember, we suggested that you keep to your original schedule for 1 week and then check to see whether any changes are required. If your child often had a BM in his diaper when you brought him to the toilet at the scheduled time, you should change that time to 15 minutes earlier. If he often soiled shortly after the toileting time, you should schedule a time 15 minutes later.

You might also find that as your child begins to be toilet trained, he will have only one BM a day, and some of the later toileting times can then be dropped out. After making a change in the schedule, always stick to this new schedule *for at least 1 week* before changing it again. Only change it when your records have clearly indicated a change for at least 5 days.

### Are you making progress?

One reward for your teaching efforts is seeing your child learn. Since we sometimes don't see changes too clearly in those skills we teach every day, records of progress will help you to see that he really has learned over the past weeks. Every week you can count from your chart 1) the total number of BMs he has in his diaper and 2) the total number of BMs he has in the toilet. Write these totals down weekly. If the total in diapers is going down and the total in the toilet is going up—*that's progress!*

In this example there was not much progress for the first 4 weeks, and then gradual improvement began. Sometimes progress is faster than this, sometimes much slower. By keeping an accurate record you will be able to see changes that you otherwise might not notice. The progress record is *your* reward!

| | WEEK 1 | WEEK 2 | WEEK 3 | WEEK 4 | WEEK 5 | WEEK 6 | WEEK 7 | WEEK 8 |
|---|---|---|---|---|---|---|---|---|
| BM IN DIAPERS | 7 | 8 | 5 | 5 | 6 | 5 | 4 | 4 |
| BM IN TOILET | 1 | 2 | 2 | 2 | 3 | 4 | 3 | 4 |

# Final Comments

This program is much easier for us to describe than for you to do. It means remembering a schedule and often interrupting something you're doing to toilet your child at the correct time. It means taking diapers off and putting them on twice every toileting time (because of the 5 minutes on, 10 minutes off, 5 minutes on routine) and doing this several times every day. It means continuing to change soiled diapers at other times while trying to greet that task in a "matter-of-fact" way. And, especially, it means being enthusiastic and ready to praise your child for every little step of progress.

You will, of course, be frustrated, disappointed, uncertain, and upset at times. You will have days when other activities make it impossible for you to stick with the schedule. You will feel you're doing something wrong when your child soils his diaper and your schedule didn't "catch him" on time. You will be very tempted to change the schedule often without waiting 1 week. You will—hold it—let's not dwell any longer on possible problems. If you stick with the program despite the fact that it's not easy, *you will succeed.*

## Summary for Bowel Training

*Continue the Diapers*  Keep your child in diapers until you are ready for urine training.

*Recognize Your Child's Signs*  Be aware of times other than the scheduled times for toileting when your child may indicate his need to go.

### Set the Stage for Success

◯ Be consistent.
◯ Use a regular toilet.
◯ Avoid distracting toys and people.
◯ Avoid distracting talk.

### Put Your Child on the Toilet

◯ Bring your child to the toilet on schedule or when he signals.
◯ Have him sit for 5 minutes.
◯ Praise and reward him if he eliminates.
◯ If he does not eliminate, remove him from the bathroom for 10 minutes.
◯ Return him for another 5-minute sitting.

### Phase Yourself Out of the Bathroom

◯ Begin when your child can stay on the toilet for 5 minutes without your assistance and verbal reminders.
◯ Continue to come back and praise and reward him for eliminating ("Good! You're sitting on the toilet!").

### Keep Records

◯ Every time you toilet your child, write down whether he is dry or wet before (D, U, BM) and what he did on the toilet (D, U, BM).
◯ If you take your child to the toilet at other times, then record this also.
◯ Any time your child has a BM in his diapers, record it on your record sheet.

### Evaluate Progress

◯ Determine whether you are toileting him at the right times.
◯ Stay on any new schedule for at least a week before changing.
◯ Count the number of BMs your child has in his diapers and in the toilet and write them down each week.
◯ Finally, don't forget to reward yourself occasionally for sticking with the program!!

# Urine Training

Your child is ready to begin urine training when 1) her BMs occur during the first 5-minute toileting period (so the second 5-minute period is unnecessary) and 2) she has no more than one BM "accident" in her diapers during a typical week.

If you have just completed your 2-week record and have determined a toileting schedule, you are ready to begin. However, if you have been carrying out the bowel-training program and your child has now become ready for urine training, you should do another 2-week record first, just as you did for bowel training. Determine a toileting schedule for urine training and be sure to incorporate the bowel-training toileting times into your new schedule.

With only a few changes, urine training follows the same seven steps as bowel training. So rather than repeat ourselves, we'll just note the ways that urine training differs from what you've already learned.

## Begin Using Training Pants During the Day

Now is the time to take your child out of diapers and rubber pants and switch to training pants during the day. This will add some inconvenience to you at first, as there are bound to be many accidents and puddles. This is a necessary inconvenience, however. From your child's point of view, diapers have always been for wetting. What you are telling her by taking her out of diapers is that those days are over. Training pants are for children who are learning to go in the toilet!

You should continue to keep her in diapers at night, however.

## Put Your Child on the Toilet

For urine training, have her sit on the toilet for 5–10 minutes. If she does not urinate, remove her from the bathroom until the next scheduled time—unless she signals a need to go before then.

---

###  Consistency

Robert's case was typical. There had been times his parents had frantically tried everything to train him and other times when they weren't really doing anything. We don't know how Robert felt after several weeks on our program, but our guess would be: comfortable. Now there was a consistent routine. For example, at 9:30 in the morning, Mom would take him to the toilet. If he was already wet, she wouldn't scold, but just sit him on the toilet anyway. There was nothing in the bathroom to distract him and Mom, every few minutes, reminded him to "go peepee in the toilet."

Mom only made Robert sit there for 5 minutes or so. If he didn't go, she just quietly helped him get dressed again. But when he did go, Mom was really pleased. She would smile and praise him ("Robert, what a big boy!") and even have a cookie or a cracker ready for him. And when Dad or Sis were helping Robert, they would do exactly the same thing—even the cookie! Yes, our guess is that Robert felt pretty comfortable with this program.

## Summary of Urine Training

**Begin Using Training Pants During the Day**   Take your child out of diapers and rubber pants during the day. Continue diapers at night.

**Learn to Recognize Your Child's Signs**   Be aware of times, other than the scheduled times for toileting, when your child may indicate his need to go.

### Set the Stage for Success

- Be consistent.
- Use a regular toilet.
- Avoid distracting toys and people.
- Avoid distracting talk.

### Put Your Child on the Toilet

- Bring your child to the toilet on schedule or when he signals.
- Have him sit for 5–10 minutes.
- Praise him occasionally for sitting.
- If he urinates, *praise* and *reward him immediately.*
- If there's no success, remove him from the bathroom until the next scheduled time for toileting.

### Phase Yourself Out of the Bathroom

- Begin when your child can stay on the toilet for 5 minutes without your assistance and verbal reminders.
- Remember to come back and *praise* and *reward* him for eliminating.

### Keep Records

- Every time you toilet your child, write down whether he is dry or wet before (D, U, BM) and what he did on the toilet (D, U, BM).
- If you take your child to the toilet at other times, note it on your record sheet.

### Evaluate Progress

- Determine whether you are toileting your child at the right times.

❧ Stay on a new schedule for at least a week before changing the times to toilet.

❧ Count the number of times your child has urinated in his pants and in the toilet and write these totals down each week.

❧ Finally, don't forget to reward yourself occasionally for sticking with the program!

# Independent Toileting

### Is Your Child Ready?

You are taking your child to the toilet according to schedule. When she is trained to the point that she does not have more than one accident a week, then she is probably ready to learn to go to the toilet on her own.

If the answer is yes to any of the following, then she is definitely ready.

1. Does she show any signs that she knows she needs to urinate or move her bowels? This may be a word like "BM," "peepee," or "potty," or the manual sign for TOILET. It may be a sound like "mow" or "buh" that is privately meaningful to your child, or maybe just a sudden quietness or "jumpiness" or crossing her legs.
2. Does she ever indicate her need directly to you by tugging on your sleeve, or pointing, or making a sound?
3. Does she ever use the toilet on her own (without your taking her)?

### Learning All the Steps

Remember we said earlier that the completely toilet-trained child can perform a number of skills. The list was as follows:

*Going into the bathroom*

1. Recognizing when he has to go
2. Waiting to eliminate
3. Entering the bathroom

*Independence in the bathroom*

4. Pulling pants down
5. Sitting on the toilet
6. Eliminating in the toilet
7. Using toilet paper correctly
8. Pulling pants back up
9. Flushing the toilet
10. Washing hands
11. Drying hands

Your child can now sit to eliminate in the toilet, and perhaps do some of the other steps. As you can see, if he can do Steps 4 through 11, he is now *independent in the bathroom*. If he cannot do some of these steps by himself, you should teach these next so that after *recognizing when he has to go* and *entering the bathroom,* he will be able to carry through on his own. You have probably been teaching these skills right along, but let's briefly look at some of the steps.

***Pulling Pants Down (Step 4)***   Pulling pants down, as well as pulling them back up and washing and drying hands, are dressing skills your child needs for toileting independence. Read Chapter 9 and refer to the specific program guidelines in Appendix C for the dressing and grooming skills needed in toileting.

***Using Toilet Paper Correctly (Step 7)***   This is perhaps the last step in the toileting routine that any child masters, though you should teach it throughout bowel training. Your child needs to learn to do more than just take a "quick swipe" with toilet paper. You will have to show him how much toilet paper to tear off (more than one sheet, less than the whole roll!). You will also have to monitor the wiping, urging him to slow down, perhaps guiding him and having him repeat the process until he is clean. Since using toilet paper is the least attractive step (of a not especially attractive skill to teach anyway), it would be easy for you and your child to avoid paying it sufficient attention. But don't!

***Pulling Pants Back Up (Step 8)***   Refer back to Step 4. Further skills such as zipping up pants, buttoning or snapping pants, and buckling a belt are necessary for your child to be fully independent in toileting. However, for now these are skills you can help him with after he leaves the bathroom routine. When you decide he is ready to learn these zipping-buttoning-buckling skills, refer to Chapter 9 and Appendix C.

***Flushing the Toilet (Step 9)***   This step is the easiest for your child to learn and the most fun to do. All through bowel and/or urine training you should have him flush the toilet after he has eliminated. It is likely that this will readily become part of the routine, though reminders may be necessary.

***Washing and Drying Hands (Steps 10 and 11)***   You should teach your child these skills, but do not wait for her to master them before you work on Steps 1 through 3: *Going into the bathroom.*

## Establishing a Routine

We should note that your child may well learn each of these separate steps and yet be unable to perform them one after the other in a smooth routine without your repeated prodding. But such a routine is necessary for your child to be truly independent in the bathroom. You will need to gradually fade out your reminders. Wait a bit after she completes a step to see if she will do the next one without a reminder. If she needs a reminder, try asking "What do you do next?" rather than telling her outright. Progressively fade your reminders out of the routine and yourself out of the bathroom.

## True Independence

Once your child is independent in the bathroom, it's time to teach him first to enter the bathroom on his own *and then* to recognize when he needs to go and to hold back until he is on the toilet.

***Teaching Him to Go into the Bathroom***   Stay on each step until
your child can successfully do that step for three to four trips to the bathroom. Then move on to the next step.

1. Take your child almost to the bathroom door and say, "Go to the bathroom" or "Go peepee," or whatever words you consistently use. (It
   will help a great deal to have one word he knows.) Remember to
   *praise and reward* him.
2. Take him partway to the bathroom door and say, "Go to the bathroom." *Praise and reward* him.
3. Point him in the direction of the bathroom and say, "Go to the bathroom." *Praise and reward* him.
4. Say, "Go to the bathroom." *Praise and reward* him.

***Delay Toileting Time: Holding Back Until on the Toilet***   When
the regular toileting time comes along, wait a little before taking your
child to the toilet. Try 10 minutes at first. (The reasoning behind this is
that by toileting your child fairly frequently he may never feel much bladder tension. It is necessary for him to learn that these feelings of tension
are a signal that means "It's time to go to the bathroom." By waiting, you
may be giving your child a chance to experience this tension.)

When you delay, various things may happen:

1. Your child may go directly to the toilet when he feels the tension of a
   full bladder. Great! Praise and reward him.
2. He may come to you, indicating that he knows he needs to use the
   toilet. Also great! Praise him, take him, and reward him for using the
   toilet.
3. He may *begin* to wet or move his bowels in his pants and then come to
   you. That's fine too (at first)—a good beginning. Take him to the bathroom and reward him for finishing in the toilet.
4. He may neither go to the toilet nor come to you nor begin to eliminate. In this case, take him to the toilet as you always have at the end
   of the 10-minute delay, and next time make the delay a little longer,
   say 15 minutes.
5. He may wet or soil his pants during the 10-minute delay period, without coming to you to be taken to the toilet. React in the same way you
   always do when he soils or wets his pants—with as little fuss and attention as possible and without scolding. Continue to try the 10-
   minute delay to give him a chance to recognize a full bladder or rectal
   tension as a signal for using the toilet. If he continues to soil or wet,
   try a shorter delay (5 minutes).

In addition to the regular toileting times, your child may indicate to you a need to go at other times by tugging, pointing, saying a word, or making a sound. When he does, take him to the bathroom and reward him at first whether he eliminates or not. Later, when he is indicating regularly he needs to go, reward him *only* if he eliminates. Whenever your child goes into the bathroom and uses the toilet on his own, praise and reward him.

We often hear from a parent that a child is *completely trained* because he always eliminates on a toileting schedule. The same child's teacher may find him *completely untrained* because she doesn't take him to the toilet on a regular schedule. Neither, of course, is correct. He has learned some of the steps but not all of them. He still must depend on an adult to take him to the toilet. Parents often hesitate to begin to teach independence to the child who goes perfectly on schedule, and we can see why— there will be some accidents again. But the end result is worth it!

## Questions and Answers

It should not surprise you if, as you begin a toileting program, you discover that things aren't always going as smoothly as this chapter envisioned they might. Our experience has revealed a number of questions that parents often ask.

### Does a toileting program have to be carried out every day to be successful?

Consistency is more important in teaching toileting than in any other skill area. A child learning to eliminate on the toilet is confused if some days you patiently toilet him while other days you can't because you're in a hurry. Of course, there will be an occasional day when other family activities take priority, or when your child is sick, or when you, for whatever reason, do not feel quite up to toileting him. An occasional lapse in your toileting program will not spell failure. But a general inconsistency in toileting may prevent a successful teaching effort in the toileting program.

### Does the same person always have to work on the toileting program with the child, or can different family members take turns?

If at all possible, have family members share the task with you. First, they need to spend time with you to understand what you're doing. They should read this chapter, and you should discuss the toileting program together. Also, you should all observe each other, so that you are all doing things the same way and are expecting the same things from your child.

## My child is in a toileting program at school. Will I confuse her by trying to train her using this book's approach at home?

Yes, you might, if you and the teacher are making different demands. Teaching toileting is best done at home, and your child's teacher should be happy that you are making this effort. Talk with her, show her the book, and make sure that you are both making the same demands on your child. Likewise, if you have taught your child some of the steps involved in toileting and her teacher or other family members continue to do these steps for her, talk with them about your program and explain what she should be left to do by herself.

## This chapter says to give my daughter a reward when she eliminates. Does this mean that I give her food while she is still on the toilet?

In the beginning it is important to reward her immediately after she eliminates—while she is still on the toilet. This will make it clear to her exactly what behavior is being rewarded. Later, when she has become successful with eliminating in the toilet, you will want to wait and reward the next behavior your child needs to learn (pulling up pants, washing hands, etc.). Once your child learns a particular behavior it is important to remember to continue praising her for being successful.

## When I put my child on the toilet, he immediately takes interest in the toilet paper—unrolling it and stuffing it into the toilet. Should I take the toilet paper out of the bathroom while I'm toileting him or try to teach him not to play with the toilet paper?

You should remove the toilet paper for now. It is causing a distraction for your child, and it means you have to give him attention for playing with the toilet paper. By saving all your attention for his eliminating in the toilet and by removing the distraction, you are setting the stage to increase the chances for him to be successful in eliminating in the toilet.

## When and how should I teach my son to go to the bathroom standing up?

For most children it is best to begin urine training sitting on the toilet. For boys, straddling the toilet (sitting with his back facing you) makes teaching him to urinate standing up easier, as he will be aware of the differences in eliminating between urine and bowel. When he is successfully able to urinate while straddling the toilet, and he is big enough to reach the toilet standing (a wide stool may be needed), use modeling. Having his dad or brother show him how this is done is the easiest way for your child to learn how to urinate standing up.

## I have been trying to teach my child to have her bowel movements on the toilet, but she won't even sit on the toilet. Instead, she cries, gets off the toilet, and runs from the bathroom. How can I make her be more cooperative?

In general, when a program isn't working, there are several potential trouble spots you should review. If you are sure your child is ready for bowel training, then you should reconsider:

1. Can she sit in other situations for up to 5 minutes without getting up?
2. Is she clear about why she is sitting on the toilet?

In addition, does she often respond to demand situations in the way you have described, so that the demands will "go away"? If this behavior is a common response of hers, you would try to ignore the behavior, giving it no attention. At the same time, insist that she stay on the toilet.

Alternatively, is the reward you are using something she doesn't want? Or could she be testing you to see whether you will give her the reward anyway?

Don't forget she is new to this toileting program and possibly surprised by the fact that you're no longer simply changing her diapers. Make it very easy for her. You will find that backing up or slowing down is often required. Demand even less than your first step (eliminating in the toilet), and work on her cooperation in sitting.

Once you have considered the preceding points and are sure you are demanding something she can do, be firm and insist that she do it. And be ready to reward her immediately. She will become less eager to leave as she discovers that only by cooperating in the toileting situation will she receive her favorite snack.

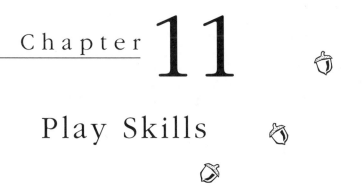

# Chapter 11

## Play Skills

*Someone once asked Louis Armstrong to define jazz. "Man," he answered, "if you gotta ask, you'll never know."*

We could say the same about *play.* It has hundreds of definitions, none more correct than your own. Play, after all, is a subject in which all of us are experts. So why should you learn how to teach play skills? Let us suggest two reasons for teaching play that may not be immediately obvious.

First, the skills your child gains when she learns new ways to play will be useful to her in other areas as well. The child who learns to sit at a table and put together a five-piece puzzle, for example, will be better prepared to learn skills that require her to sit, pay attention, and follow directions. And the child who learns to play a game by herself on the computer may gain some entrance into her older sister's world. When children play, they are doing more than just having fun. A child's play, in fact, is also an important kind of child's work.

Second, the skills and confidence you gain as a teacher will also carry over into other areas. You will become more convinced than ever that your child can be learning at home with you as her teacher.

Of course, the most important reason to teach play is to help your child find more ways to have fun. Play offers countless opportunities to join in with a friend or with other family members and to be a part of what's going on. It provides a time when mistakes are not failures, but just a part of the game.

Then, too, play provides challenges and chances to overcome them. Mastering play activities can help build a feeling of self-confidence and self-worth. Finally, play can fill up empty time. Having appropriate toys available and knowing how to play with them gives your child something to do when there is nothing to do—and that's good for you both!

As we talk about teaching play skills, we follow the same, and by now familiar, STEPS TO approach that we covered in the first seven chapters. In short, you have decided to

**S**et out to teach play, and you will first
**T**arget a play skill or two to teach. Next you will
**E**stablish the separate steps that make up the skill and
**P**ick a reward, although you have already done that. Next you'll
**S**et the stage for teaching and you will be ready to

**T**each. As you go along, you'll
**O**bserve progress, and troubleshoot when things go wrong.

That's it! This chapter reviews STEPS TO with play skill examples and offers some additional suggestions. We have geared the content primarily to the young child with special needs, although the same principles would apply to teaching more-advanced skills to older children. You will want to find play materials that are age-appropriate, however—that are played with by children the same age as your child.

So, if you've decided to try teaching play skills—whether it's your 1st try or your 51st, it's time to get started.

---

###  Jason and Mary Beth

Mrs. Sullivan glances out the window at Mary Beth, who is still playing quietly in the sandbox with her new pail and shovel. As Mrs. Sullivan turns back to her work at the computer, she sees Jason come through the gate and call out: "Hey, Mary Beth, how about playing ball with me? Come on and see if you can catch this."

Mary Beth looks up from her sandbox just as the tennis ball bounces off her shoulder. Jason comes across the yard to get it.

"He's a nice kid," thinks Mrs. Sullivan about her teenage nephew. "He knows Mary Beth has mental retardation and he's always wanting to help her. If he only knew more about teaching. He makes it so hard for her."

Mary Beth has turned back to her pail and shovel. She seems unaware of her visitor, who has just returned from tennis practice.

"What a day I've had, Mary Beth! I must have missed this tennis ball a million times. Maybe I need a bigger ball, huh?"

Mary Beth, still shoveling sand into her pail, glances over at Jason.

"Come on, try to catch the ball." This toss across the sand-box bounces off Mary Beth's just-raised hand.

"That's okay, Mary Beth. You almost caught it. I see you've got a new pail to play with. Hey, you wanna try to catch this ball again?"

This time Mary Beth doesn't even look up.

## Targeting Play Skills to Teach

Jason decided to play catch with Mary Beth because he was a good ball player. If he had thought instead about the *skills Mary Beth was able to perform*, he probably would have decided to play something else with her or to play ball differently.

Of course, that's quite a bit to ask of a young cousin. But the question of your child's skill level is one that you must ask—and answer—before you begin to teach.

How will you decide which play skills make sense to teach your child? It is helpful first to fill out a checklist designed to help you look at your child's current skills. Then, you can select three appropriate new play skills to teach and can set deadlines by which you think these skills can be learned.

## Looking at Your Child's Play Skills

The Play Skills Checklist below presents three categories of skills. In Category A are Basic Play Skills, most of which your child needs to have in order to learn new ways to play. Categories B and C present play activities that your child could enjoy either by herself (Skills for Playing Alone) or with others (Skills for Playing with Others).

Fill out the checklist now. Take your time. Your answers will form the basis for your teaching. You may need to do some of the play activities with your child to see just what she can do.

## Choosing Teaching Goals

The examples used in this chapter assume that your child can already perform the basic play skills listed in Category A of the Play Skills Checklist. If your child has not yet mastered these basic skills, the teaching

---

### Play Skills Checklist

This checklist contains some of the skills involved in many types of play. Place a check in the column to the right of each skill that best indicates your child's current performance level.

|  | 1 Does not do | 2 Does with much help | 3 Does with some help | 4 Does alone |
|---|---|---|---|---|
| CATEGORY A.  BASIC PLAY SKILLS |  |  |  |  |
| Pays attention to someone speaking |  |  |  |  |
| Pays attention to music |  |  |  |  |
| Grasps or holds large toys or objects |  |  |  |  |
| Grasps or holds crayons or pencils |  |  |  |  |
| Pushes, pulls, and turns toys |  |  |  |  |
| Names toys and objects used for play |  |  |  |  |
| Names body parts |  |  |  |  |
| Plays simple hide-and-seek games (peekaboo, hunts for missing toy) |  |  |  |  |
| Follows directions: gives or takes toys |  |  |  |  |

(continued)

| | 1 | 2 | 3 | 4 |
|---|---|---|---|---|
| | Does not do | Does with much help | Does with some help | Does alone |
| Follows directions: opens and closes lids or doors | | | | |
| Follows directions: lines up toys on table or floor | | | | |
| Follows directions: carries toys from place to place | | | | |
| Sits alone for up to 5 minutes | | | | |
| Imitates gestures | | | | |
| CATEGORY B.  SKILLS FOR PLAYING ALONE<br>Sits unattended for 5–10 minutes | | | | |
| Does stacking rings | | | | |
| Builds tower of three blocks | | | | |
| Builds tower of six blocks | | | | |
| Scoops water or beans from one container into another | | | | |
| Drops beads into container | | | | |
| Strings beads | | | | |
| Cuts with scissors | | | | |
| Pastes pictures | | | | |
| Scribbles with crayon on paper | | | | |
| Colors in coloring book, mostly in lines | | | | |
| Does simple noninterlocking puzzles | | | | |
| Does interlocking puzzles, 4–6 pieces | | | | |
| Does interlocking puzzles, 7–15 pieces | | | | |
| Does interlocking puzzles, 16 + pieces | | | | |
| Does color- and shape-matching game (lotto) | | | | |
| Does picture-matching lotto | | | | |
| Plays computer games | | | | |
| CATEGORY C.  SKILLS FOR PLAYING WITH OTHERS<br>Plays bean bag toss in group | | | | |

(continued)

|  | 1<br>Does not do | 2<br>Does with much help | 3<br>Does with some help | 4<br>Does alone |
|---|---|---|---|---|
| Plays bean bag toss |  |  |  |  |
| Throws and catches medium ball within 3 feet |  |  |  |  |
| Throws and catches small ball within 3 feet |  |  |  |  |
| Throws and catches medium ball more than 10 feet |  |  |  |  |
| Throws and catches small ball more than 10 feet |  |  |  |  |
| Kicks ball, as in soccer or kickball games |  |  |  |  |
| Hits ball, as in volleyball |  |  |  |  |
| Hits ball with bat off of tee |  |  |  |  |
| Rides tricycle |  |  |  |  |
| Goes in-line skating |  |  |  |  |
| Swims |  |  |  |  |
| Paints with other children (e.g., two or more children paint large picture) |  |  |  |  |
| Works with clay on project with other children |  |  |  |  |
| Does dramatic play: pretends to be someone else (e.g., Mommy, Superman) |  |  |  |  |
| Dances |  |  |  |  |
| Sings along with other children |  |  |  |  |
| Does simple pantomime |  |  |  |  |
| Does puppet play with others |  |  |  |  |
| Does simple skit with others |  |  |  |  |

strategies in this book still apply, but you will need to select skills to teach from those presented in Chapter 8—Get Ready Skills—and Appendix A.

If your child has mastered basic play skills, identify those skills in Categories B and C where you have checked either column 2 ("much help") or column 3 ("some help"). Select three of these that you will teach your child, endeavoring to pick ones that he will enjoy doing and that you will enjoy teaching.

It's a good idea to discuss your selections with your child's teacher (and, if possible, a physical or occupational therapist). He or she will not only welcome you as a partner in teaching but will also probably have useful suggestions about your child's skill needs. These suggestions may influence your final selection.

In the spaces below, write down just the three skills you've selected (don't worry about the "Deadline" spaces yet; we'll discuss these in a moment). Be as specific as possible about your teaching goal for each one. Each goal should include exactly what action you want your child to do ("catch a ball" rather than "ball playing"), when or under what circumstances you want your child to do the action ("catch a ball when thrown from 3 feet"), and how well you want your child to perform the skill ("catch a ball with no help when thrown from 3 feet"). Including *when* or *how well* you want your child to perform the skill gives you a way to measure your child's progress.

Skill Goal 1: _____

_____

Deadline _____

_____

Skill Goal 2: _____

_____

Deadline _____

Skill Goal 3: _____

_____

Deadline _____

_____

## A Note About Deadlines

You are probably involved in developing your child's individualized education programs (IEPs) at school. In addition to identifying skills to be taught, the IEP also lists deadlines by which each skill will be learned. Of course, these deadlines are always best guesses; your child might learn faster or slower than you and his teacher planned. But having a deadline gives you a useful way to monitor progress.

So return to the three goals you've listed and estimate what you think is a realistic deadline for each one. For example,

Goal: Build a tower of five blocks with my directions.
Deadline: By March 1.

Goal: Ride a tricycle around the block with no help.
Deadline: By the end of summer vacation.

*Wait a minute.* Did you do it? If not, please take a few minutes now to complete the checklist and to select the play skills you'll be teaching.

# Establishing Steps: Your Teaching Program

Children with special needs do not succeed as easily or as often as other children. To your child, the simplest game may seem like an impossible challenge or just another invitation to fail. He may not welcome the chance to try again. And, chances are, you won't be too eager to fail in your teaching again either.

Now that you've chosen three play skills that your child is ready to learn, you need to take three more steps to make sure that your teaching

will lead to success. First, you need to create your teaching program. Then you'll need to pick a reward and set the stage for learning.

Let's assume that you've decided to teach your child to catch a ball. Let's also assume that you can clearly picture what playing catch looks like. To create a successful teaching program, the best thing you can do is to forget that picture. In the earliest stages of teaching, what you and your child will be doing together won't look much like it at all.

Instead, you may be rolling a ball back and forth to each other across a tabletop or along the floor. Or you may simply be placing a ball into his cupped hands and quickly taking it out before he lets it fall. The point is, no matter which skill you decide to teach first, you will have to *return to the basics of that skill* to be sure your child will experience success.

What are the basics? They are all of the separate steps that add up to the smooth performance of a skill, and a list of these small steps will form your teaching program.

Before creating a teaching program for the skill you've chosen, think back to Jason's attempt to play catch with Mary Beth. To Jason, playing catch is obviously a simple skill, something he knows well and probably doesn't even remember learning. To Mary Beth, it's not so simple. She needs to be taught, beginning with the basics.

Let's assume then that Mary Beth's dad decided to help Jason teach Mary Beth how to catch a ball. Mr. Sullivan's teaching program might have looked like this:

*Steps in Ball Catching –*

*Tell her to hold out her hands and –*

*Place ball in her hands.*

*Drop ball into her hands.*

*Flip ball from 1 foot away.*

*Flip ball from 2 feet away.*

*Throw ball from 4 feet away.*

*Throw ball . . .*

Where did these steps come from? How did Mr. Sullivan figure out where to start and where to go next? Most likely, Mary Beth's dad did two things to develop his program: First, he played catch, probably with Jason, to remind himself of all the steps involved; second, he asked himself (and Mrs. Sullivan and Jason) how he might simplify or break down some of these steps even further for Mary Beth.

Look carefully at Mr. Sullivan's list of steps. Notice how it begins with an activity (Mary Beth holding out her hands) that he knew Mary Beth could do. By starting his teaching program with the most basic step, Mr. Sullivan guaranteed that Mary Beth would enjoy some success from the beginning. Notice, too, that the first several steps are ones that place him near Mary Beth, ready to provide whatever help she may need. And notice, finally, how each step on the list builds gradually to the next.

Does this mean that Mr. Sullivan's program is the only teaching program for playing catch? Of course not. If you were to write a teaching program for playing catch, you might include more or fewer steps. For most play skills there is no one correct list of steps. What is important is that your list of steps, your teaching program, begin with a step you know your child can do and contain steps that *progress gradually*. Remember, your child needs to learn each of the play skills step by step, not by leaps and bounds.

In Appendix D, we have already broken down a number of play skills into steps. This might be a good time to take a quick look at them. Also, your child's teacher probably has books or worksheets with some play skills programs already developed (ask him or her to share these with you).

Get ready to teach your child by creating your teaching program for the first play skill you chose. Get a puzzle, scissors, crayon, tricycle, or whatever you need for that activity. And now, do it yourself, when your child's not around. Keep track of the steps involved, and think about where your child will need help.

Make a short list of the steps in this skill. First, write down the GOAL you set (Step 6, below).

CAN DO NOW    Step 1. _____

                  Step 2. _____

                  Step 3. _____

                  Step 4. _____

                  Step 5. _____

GOAL            Step 6. _____

Next, fill in Step 1, the part of the skill that your child can do now. In the teaching session you will begin with this step, so you'll both have a quick success. Now fill in Step 2; make the task a little bit harder by giving a little less help. Now fill in Steps 3–5, each with a little less help from you. (You may find you need more steps.)

If you created your teaching program, TAKE A BREAK.

If not, please do it now. We find that parents who actually carry out the steps and then write them down have more success in teaching.

---

###  Small Steps

Today it was cats. Medium-size cats. Dad would draw one, with Lim showing him where the eyes and nose and mouth should go. Then Lim would color it in.

The little animals in Lim's coloring books were all covered up, practically hidden by the red scribbles that were as much outside the lines as inside. But when Dad and Lim started drawing their own animals together, Lim's artwork began to change.

Dad had begun last week by drawing funny fat cats, so huge that they almost filled up the page. It was just about impossible for Lim to color these cats outside the lines. Now it was medium-size cats, still funny looking but just a little smaller than last week's cats. And most of Lim's coloring was inside the line.

Pretty soon she'd be ready for kittens.

---

# Picking a Reward

You may want to take another look now at our discussion of rewards in Chapter 4. Some play activities, particularly after they are mastered, may be rewarding in and of themselves. Your child may enjoy riding the tricycle, building a tower of blocks, playing tennis, or using the computer—and she'll do these activities without any other reward (except, of course, your enthusiastic attention). At first, though, when a play activity is just another challenge that threatens your child with failure, you will find it helpful to add other rewards.

# Setting the Stage for Teaching

You have increased your chances of success by breaking the play skill down into easy steps. You can further guarantee success by setting the stage well. As we explained in Chapter 5, setting the stage means deciding when and where you will teach and what materials you will use. Think about how you will set the stage to teach the first play skill you have targeted:

1.   When will you teach?   _____

2.   Where will you teach?   _____

3.   What materials will you use?   _____

# Teaching Play: Directing

What will your behavior in a teaching session look like? In simplest form, it should look like this:

> Directing: You try to get your child to perform a task.
> Responding: You respond to his performance.

That's teaching. And repeating this sequence over and over again makes a teaching session. Usually, the more carefully you perform each part of this sequence, the more successful you will be in your teaching.

## Giving Clear Directions

Often a child may seem to be failing at a task when, in fact, he's just not sure what he's supposed to be doing. He's confused by the directions. You know what you want him to do; you just haven't communicated it simply enough.

We have described three ways to get your directions across clearly: Tell him, show him, and guide him. Let's review briefly.

*Tell Him*   The most effective verbal instructions are those that

1.   Begin with your child's name
2.   Are short
3.   Include only words your child understands
4.   Are spoken clearly and firmly

Once you have developed your instruction for any task, don't change it. If your child does not respond immediately to your instruction, repeat it again. Don't add all kinds of "helpful" phrases hoping that these will make your communication clearer. They won't. Most of the time those phrases will provide more distraction than direction.

**Not Like This:**

"OK, hang on tight so you won't fall off, and swing your leg up here."

**Like This:**

"Jason, put your foot on the pedal."

"There are sure a lot of pictures here, aren't there? Where's the one that's similar to this one?"

"Caroline, find the picture that looks like this."

You may find that even the shortest, simplest, and clearest verbal instruction will not, by itself, give your child enough information to perform the task successfully. He may still be confused and need more help to understand what he's supposed to do. You can help him by showing him what you mean and guiding him through the task.

***Show Him***  Show your child what you mean by *modeling* the skill. Get his attention and demonstrate the task for him slowly, with exaggeration, so that he can easily imitate your behavior.

You can also show him by *prompting* with gestures. In other words, talk with your hands. Motion for him to sit down, point to where the puzzle piece goes, and so on. Again, exaggerate your motions.

***Guide Him***   When telling and showing are not enough, put your hand over his hand, or arm, or foot, and physically guide the action. Help him pick up the block, swing the bat, or push down on the pedal. As he learns to do the activity, fade out your physical guidance.

**Remember:** Always end with a success. If necessary, return to an easier step before ending your teaching session.

---

### ⌀  Shaping

"Sal, put the ring on the post."

    Mrs. Verella had placed just one ring, the largest, right next to the stacking post in front of her 4-year old son, Sal. He had done well with this game for the last few days, needing almost no physical guidance. Now, after once guiding him just a bit, Mrs. Verella decided it was time for him to try it with only a prompt.

    Pointing to the ring, she said, "Sal, you do it. Put the ring on the post."

    Sal reached for the ring, fumbled, and let it fall to the floor.

    ·  Mrs. Verella had broken off a piece of chocolate chip cookie, but she couldn't give it to him yet; she knew he could do better than that.

    She put the ring back in front of the post. "Sal, put the ring on the post." Sal looked at the ring and then at his favorite cookie. He grabbed for the ring, held it in both hands, and grinned up at his mother.

    "That's good, Sal," she said, seeing that he was off to a better start this time. "Now, put the ring on the post." She tapped the top of the stacking post with her finger. Still no cookie.

    "That's a boy, Sal. Nice going," she said enthusiastically as his small fingers carried the ring to the top of the post. And almost before the ring slid down, the piece of cookie was in Sal's mouth.

# Teaching Play: Responding

This is where we talk about rewards again—but by now, after reading the earlier chapters, you should be pretty much of an expert on rewards. Let's see. Here's a brief review of main points about rewards—fill in the terms that come to mind:

To motivate your child, you will need to use (1)_____.

A behavior that is followed by a reward is (2)_____ likely to happen again.

One type of reward is your enthusiastic (3)_____, like smiles, hugs, and praise.

You may want to use more tangible rewards. Another type of reward is (4) _____, such as food or drink. These should be given (5) _____ after your child is successful or makes a good try in the teaching session.

Another type of reward is (6)_____, such as playing ball or going for a drive.

Grandma's Law says that a (7)_____ desired activity can be used as a reward following a less-desired activity.

Check marks on a chart, stars, and money are examples of (8)_____ rewards.

Tokens can be earned each day and (9)_____ later for items or activities that your child wants.

You cannot expect your child to perform perfectly the first time. Rather, you will reward small steps toward the goal, a procedure we call (10)_____.

Over time as your child learns the skill, you should be able to (11)_____ out rewards like snacks and activities, but don't forget to continue paying (12)_____ to his successes.

**Answers:** (1) rewards, (2) more, (3) attention, (4) snacks, (5) immediately, (6) activities, (7) more, (8) token, (9) traded, (10) shaping, (11) fade, (12) attention.

## Increasing Independent Play

By now you may be saying to yourself what other parents have said aloud: "These teaching suggestions are fine, but I can't spend my whole day playing with her. How can I get her to play by herself—even for a little while?" This is a good question. Let's talk about two ways to increase independent play: noticing it when it happens, and fading out your attention.

*Noticing Independent Play*   We are inclined to "leave well enough alone." That is, we usually tend not to disturb moments when a child plays alone, for fear that our attention might put an end to what she began herself. Thus, while we can easily see how effective rewards are in teaching, we can just as easily forget that they are also effective when aimed at the child's on-the-spot attempts at play. A word of encouragement or praise for play alone today will make it a bit more likely to happen again tomorrow.

---

###    Noticing

As Mrs. Chu begins to sit down for a quick cup of coffee, she pauses: Janice has picked up a magazine and is looking at the pictures. Before, she might not have interrupted these rare moments when her daughter is occupied, but she's learned the power of just a word of praise.

"Janice, that's good. You're looking at pictures."

Janice looks up, smiles, and quickly goes back to the magazine.

---

## Fading Out Your Attention

Most of the fun of playing for your child has come from the fact that you—your attention and rewards—have always been there. For many children (especially at first), it is not the toy that keeps up their interest but the constant attention of the "teacher." To teach independent play, you will have to begin to remove that attention very gradually.

When she can do the activity by herself, move a little bit away. Perhaps sit near her and "read" a magazine, looking up every so often to offer a word of encouragement. As she pays attention to the task for longer periods, progressively move farther away, for more time. The time will come when you can start her on the task, leave the room, and return a few minutes later to praise her and perhaps give a snack reward.

What do you do if, as you fade out your attention, your child stops playing, wants to follow you, or becomes disruptive? You might scold her or encourage her to go back, but these would only be rewarding and increase the chances that she would follow you again in the future. If one of these things happens, maybe you have not structured the task well enough or have moved away too quickly. Try again. Make the task a bit more simple, and explain again that she should finish the task and then you'll look at it. Do this in a matter-of-fact manner so as not to make a rewarding game of her following you and your explaining the rules. After a few tries, it should be successful.

---

###  Fading Out

Michael and his mom had come a long way! At first it was just matching the two apple pictures, then trees and birds. Pretty soon he could match a whole stack of cards, with Mom's praise.

Not so long ago, Mom stopped handing Michael each card. And then she moved away a little, praising his efforts every so often. Now she just gets him started and leaves the room—Michael's too busy to notice!

---

## Observing and Troubleshooting

You should use the list of steps you wrote on page 118 as a guide to measuring progress. Perhaps jot down the date your child masters each step. Or you can keep a diary, writing notes about your teaching sessions and keeping track of your child's perfomance milestones. Whatever you do, keep some record of his—and your—progress.

At this point, you may want to take another look at Chapter 7 for ideas about what to do when teaching goes well . . . and when it doesn't.

## Sample Teaching Sessions

Parents tell us that case examples help them understand what to do in a teaching session. Therefore, we have included two brief accounts of teaching sessions, using principles that should be familiar to you by now.

First, let's return to Jason and Mary Beth to see how Jason might have set out to teach his young cousin using the teaching strategies outlined in this book.

---

### ◈ Jason and Mary Beth (*continued*)

Jason comes through the gate, smiles a quick hello to Mary Beth, and goes to the corner of the yard. Mary Beth plays with her pail and shovel, watching as Jason clears toys and twigs from his "teaching corner" of the yard.

Mrs. Sullivan watches from the living room window. For the past 5 days her teenage nephew Jason has come over after tennis practice to teach Mary Beth to play ball. And each time has seemed so much like the time before: the same clean corner of the yard, the same medium-size rubber ball, the same 10–15 minutes, even the same variety of snacks.

Jason walks over to the sandbox and says, "Come on Mary Beth, time to play catch."

Jason no longer has to hold Mary Beth's hand for the short walk over to the teaching corner. This was only necessary for the first 2 days of teaching. Today she follows him eagerly.

"Good girl, Mary Beth. You came over here all by yourself." He immediately gives her a piece of cookie.

With the playground ball in his hand, Jason positions himself directly in front of Mary Beth, only a little more than her arm's length away.

"OK, Mary Beth. Catch the ball."

Mary Beth stretches out her arms and cups her hands. (Jason can't help but think how quickly she learned this behavior. She needed physical assistance with it only on the first day.) He flips—almost drops—the ball gently into her hands.

"Good, Mary Beth. You caught the ball."

"Michael Jordan she's not," thinks Jason, "but she's definitely on her way."

---

If we were to return to Jason and Mary Beth a month later, who knows where we might find them? Maybe they'd be bouncing the ball back and forth between them, throwing it into a wastebasket, rolling it at a target, or perhaps they'd be only a little further along than they are now. We cannot say how quickly Mary Beth will learn, but we do know that now she is learning.

## ✍ A Step-by-Step Teaching Session

***Setting Out***  Mrs. Watkins had decided to teach Darryl, her 6-year-old son who has mental retardation, how to play with some simple toys. He had not progressed very far on his own, so she thought that perhaps regular teaching sessions would work better.

***Targeting a Skill***  She'd begin with a puzzle. He could put in a puzzle piece with much help and showed some interest in puzzles. Also, fine motor skills were in his individualized education program at school, so she and his teacher could be working toward similar goals. Too, if he could learn to do a puzzle, she thought, he would have something to do by himself. So this seemed like a good skill to teach.

***Establishing Steps***  She got a four-piece wooden puzzle and jotted down the steps she would follow. (First, take out one piece and guide him to put it back in . . . .)

***Picking a Reward***  Of course she'd need a snack reward—at least at first—and she'd use Cheerios, Darryl's current favorite.

***Setting the Stage***  It's time to start. Mrs. Watkins checks out the kitchen, the place she's chosen as her "classroom." "The dog has to go," she thinks. "So does the stuff on the table: the bills, the napkins, the salt shaker. Everything's all set now. Oops, forgot to move the kitchen timer. Darryl really likes to hear it ring, but having it on the table now will only distract him. He can play with it after he does some work. She puts the puzzle on the empty table and sets a cup of Cheerios on the far corner (so Darryl won't dive for them as soon as he comes into the room).

***Teaching*** Now she's ready, and she announces to the family that she and Darryl will be in the kitchen for the next 15 minutes, and that she doesn't want to be disturbed. In the living room, Darryl is sitting in "his" chair twirling a spoon between his finger. "Darryl, let's go do a puzzle." As she takes his hand, she slips the spoon into her pocket.

When they enter the kitchen and get near the table, Mrs. Watkins lets go of Darryl's hand, goes to his chair, and motions to him to come and sit down.

"Darryl, sit here."

After closing the door, Mrs. Watkins takes Darryl by the hand and guides him to his chair. "Good boy, Darryl, you are sitting down." As she praises him, she gives him a Cheerio.

Putting the puzzle in front of Darryl, she takes one piece almost all the way out. "Darryl, put the piece in." She takes his hand and helps him push the piece into the space. "Good, Darryl." Another Cheerio. They do the same step four times in a row, and each time she helps him a little less. By the fourth time, she doesn't even have to touch his hand to guide him; he reaches up and pushes the piece in by himself.

This time she takes the same piece all the way out, hands it to Darryl, and tells him, "Put it in." He needs a little help the first time, but after that he can put it in himself and earns several Cheerios—and Mom's tickles.

The next step, according to the program, is to take two pieces out and hand them to Darryl one at a time, telling him, "Put it in." Darryl takes the first puzzle piece, aims at the puzzle, and misses the space. His quick exit from the table knocks the chair over.

***Observing and Troubleshooting*** Mrs. Watkins has seen this happen before, and knows that Darryl is upset because he failed. Firmly, but calmly, she returns him to the table. After he sits down, she goes back to the first step of the program (taking one piece almost out and helping him push it in the space).

"Good boy, Darryl; you put the piece in the puzzle." She gives him another Cheerio and a big hug, and as she pushes the puzzle away she reaches for the timer and hands it to Darryl.

> "That's enough work for today." Watching him with the timer, she says proudly, "Know something, Darryl? We're both doing just fine."

Appendix D contains some program suggestions for teaching play skills. There are sections on Skills for Playing Alone and Skills for Playing with Others.

# Chapter 12

# Independent Living: Self-Care Skills

Like most parents of children with special needs, you have real concerns about your child's future. These increase with adolescence. "Where will she be 10 years from now—or 25 years from now?" "Will there be a place for her in the community?" "What will happen to him when we're no longer around? Who will manage for him?"

These are difficult issues, and there is no way to address them simply. However, you cannot ignore them or expect that the future will somehow take care of itself. The responsibility for planning and preparation lies in large part with you.

**One kind of preparation for your child's future that you can do right now is to teach him to be more independent.** If you look closely at your child's typical day, you'll likely find that your help is very much a part of it. Our goal, therefore, is for you to teach your child to perform more capably some basic activities of daily living by himself. We have chosen three areas to consider. This chapter examines one of those areas: self-care skills. Chapters 13 and 14 look at home-care skills and information skills, respectively.

Self-care skills are activities of dressing, grooming, and health care that your child needs to perform to get the day started and to have a good appearance in public. We assume in this chapter that your child can already perform most of the "basics" described in Chapter 9—putting on pants, a shirt, socks, and shoes; buttoning and tying; washing hands and face—but that he needs to learn to perform these skills on his own, at appropriate times, and as part of a smooth routine. In other words, we assume that your child can already perform the *actions* of many basic self-care skills. Our emphasis in this chapter is on teaching your child to make

131

*decisions* related to these skills, such as when the skill should be performed, what materials are needed, and when the skill is completed. For example, even though your child can quite capably put on a pullover sweater (actions), she may still need you to decide if it is cold enough for a sweater, to choose a sweater that matches her slacks, and to check her over to make sure it's put on right (decisions).

# Before You Begin: Three Teaching Points

## Expectations

Perhaps the most important decision you will make as a teacher is to determine how much to expect your child to do. You must walk a fine line. If you expect too much, you risk frustration and failure. If you expect too little, you can slow down your child's progress.

We encourage you, therefore, to take a careful look at your child's day to determine the areas in which you can expect her to do more for herself. To be sure, it's sometimes uncomfortable to take risks (such as sending her to the store alone). However, such risks—when they're reasonable—are necessary. **Expecting more from your child** is the first essential step to her increased independence.

## Assistance

As you examine your child's day, you will also need to look at your role in it. To become truly independent, your child will need to begin skills and carry them through to completion without your reminders, suggestions, or direction. Think about today. Did your child have to remember self-care skills she needed to do on her own? Or were you there, for instance, to remind her to brush her teeth? Or to pick out a blouse that matched? Or to zip up her skirt in the back? Or . . . ? To teach independence, you need to look closely at what you do for your child and then decide when and how to fade out your assistance.

## Motivation

Although you may be ready to expect more and to assist less, your child may want no part of this increased responsibility. Consider *his* point of view. He's always had you there to help with self-care responsibilities; for him it's been a pretty good deal.

So what now? You could simply expect him to do more for himself because he "should do it." But this usually doesn't work. To increase your child's motivation to perform these skills, you will need to use some kind of *rewards*. At the least, you will need to reward his increased efforts with your attention, encouragement, and praise. You may need additional motivators as well, and we consider some options in the pages that follow.

If you can approach each day expecting a bit more from your child, assisting him a bit less, and rewarding his steps to independence, you will be off to a very good start!

# Beyond the Basics

Now that your child readily performs many basic self-care skills, you may be overlooking other ways that you can continue to teach. For example, perhaps you see skills that he *does not do* as skills that he *cannot do*— and so you do these activities for him. To increase your child's independence in self-care, your first task will be to recognize activities that your child can learn to do on his own.

Let's look in on Jim and Allison, two young adults with special needs who are functioning well in the community with minimal supervision. As Jim and Allison get ready to leave for work in the morning, they remind us of the many self-care skills they have learned over the years—and of how these skills contribute to their appearance and independence.

---

### &  A Typical Day

**Jim**  "This place needs another bathroom," Jim complained, although with his usual good humor. "If they can spend billions on Star Wars . . . ."

The morning scramble for the two bathrooms was always something of an annoyance for the eight residents of 187 Arcade Street, a group home for young men with mental retardation. Jim showered quickly, brushed his teeth, rolled on his deodorant, and returned to his room with his brush and comb to free up the bathroom.

As he carefully shaved with the new electric razor he had just bought, Jim's thoughts drifted back to his family's home, to when his dad had taught him to shave with his old razor. Jim, now 22, had been in the group home for about a year.

As he quickly buttoned his shirt Jim glanced at his watch and slowed down a bit. He had plenty of time to get to work. Then he noticed something was wrong. "Damn it," he muttered. The left sleeve button was hanging by one thread. Jim hesitated a few moments, and then decided he might as well sew it on so he wouldn't lose it. Borrowing a needle and thread from the house manager, he sat down on the edge of the bed and concentrated intently on this still-difficult task.

Now he *was* running late. He quickly gathered up his wallet, change, keys, and comb, glancing at the checklist he kept on the dresser as a reminder. "I've got everything."

One last check in the mirror . . . .

**Allison**　As Allison opened the living room window she was hit by a wave of cool air. Pulling her bathrobe closer, she looked for a moment at the cloudless blue sky and the sunlight glancing off the cars going by. It was a beautiful day.

Allison tiptoed quietly back into the bedroom, so as not to wake her roommate, and began to select what she would wear. First, she decided on pantyhose and her denim skirt. She really didn't need to dress up so much for her job assembling telephone equipment, but today, well, she just felt like it. Next she pulled on the beige sweater ("It'll be warm enough and matches real good") and just then noticed the spot on the sleeve ("Oh . . . Jill always knows how to take spots out, but she's still sleeping . . . well, I'll wear the yellow one").

Allison was 20 now and managing quite well in the apartment that she shared with two young women. The counselor came by most evenings to help with dinner and talk with the women about their problems. In the morning, however, Allison was on her own.

Now, a dab of cologne. ("Not too much." She remembered her mother's words. It had been about 2 years since she had left home, first for the work training program and then moving to this apartment. But she saw her family almost every weekend.) Allison noticed the Band-Aid on her finger, where she had gotten a paper cut the night before. With a slight grimace she pulled it off and put on a new one. A quick inspection in the mirror: nails, hair, teeth . . . the yellow sweater looked pretty nice after all. She smiled as she went into the kitchen to fix breakfast—Jim would be on the bus.

In the first few minutes of the day, Jim and Allison routinely performed numerous self-care skills. Your child has not mastered as many skills as Jim and Allison have and perhaps may never become as proficient as they are. We include their example, nonetheless, to show you what independence in self-care can look like.

## Self-Care Assessment

Your first task will be to observe your child's day carefully and to become especially aware of *the part you play* in it. Are there some self-care skills that you typically do for your child? Are there others that you must always prompt or remind him to do?

Self-care skills are really mastered only when a person sees *when to use them*, knows *how to use them*, uses them, and checks *whether he has used them well*.

Pages 137–139 contain a list of many self-care skills. Before you begin to teach, you will need to complete this Self-Care Assessment. For now, simply read through these pages and skim the rest of this section. Then come back to these pages and complete the assessment.

It will take you some time to do the assessment well, but we think you'll find it worth your effort. An accurate understanding of your child's skills is always the first step in effective teaching.

After you have rated each of the self-care skills, use Self-Care Skills to Teach (see next page) to begin targeting skills for teaching. First, from the skills rated Mastery Level 1, choose three (or so) that you would most like to teach your child and list them under TEACH BASIC STEPS. Similarly, from the skills rated Mastery Level 2, choose three (or so) that you would most like to develop further, and list them under TEACH INDEPEN-DENCE. Next, from the skills in Mastery Levels 2 and 3, choose several that would logically fit in a routine that you would like your child to learn. List them under DEVELOP A ROUTINE (these might be skills needed to get ready in the morning, eat a meal, and so forth). Finally, from the skills where motivation is rated as "A Problem," choose three that you would most like your child to do regularly, and list them under MOTIVATE PERFORMANCE.

**Self-Care Skills to Teach**

TEACH BASIC STEPS
(from Mastery Level 1)

TEACH INDEPENDENCE
(from Mastery Level 2)

_____

_____

_____

_____

_____

_____

DEVELOP A ROUTINE
(from Mastery Levels 2 and 3)

MOTIVATE PERFORMANCE
(from "A Problem")

_____

_____

_____

_____

_____

_____

# Toward Self-Care Independence

> *Oh, she can brush her teeth very well, but just try and get her to do it.
> Jeff has learned to dress himself, but if I don't suggest colors that
> match, look out! Reshita puts on her dress and then just sits there; I
> have to remind her what to do next.*

Wouldn't you like to think that once you've taught your child a new self-care skill, that's the end of it? You teach it. She learns it. She does it. Often, though, that's not the way it goes. There's never a guarantee that once you teach the basic steps of a skill your child will perform it at the right time or in the right way.

Instead, most parents find three kinds of challenges that show up only *after* the basics of a self-care skill have been successfully learned.

1. Motivating skill performance
2. Making decisions about skill performance
3. Developing daily routines

The remainder of this chapter addresses each of these challenges separately and presents a variety of strategies designed to ensure independent self-care performance.

# Motivating Skill Performance

You can easily think of activities that are much more enjoyable than washing your hands or putting on your pants. Self-care skills are not invariably

## Self-Care Assessment

For each of the skills in this assessment you will be asked to evaluate your child's *mastery* and his *motivation* as described below:

Mastery

1. *Basic Steps Not Mastered.* These are skills for which your child cannot do all of the basic steps; he needs to learn some (or all) of the actions involved.
2. *Needs Assistance with Decisions.* These are skills for which your child can do the basic steps, but needs help in making decisions about skill performance—he needs to be told when to do the skill, or what materials are needed, or how to begin, or whether the skill has been done well.
3. *Can Do Well and Independently.* These are skills for which your child can do the basic actions and make necessary decisions—so that you do not need to be there at all.

Motivation

1. *A Problem.* These are skills that your child does not perform without urging; he needs to be motivated.
2. *Not a Problem.* These are skills that your child performs regularly without special encouragement.

| | MASTERY | | | MOTIVATION | |
|---|---|---|---|---|---|
| | 1 | 2 | 3 | 1 | 2 |
| SKILLS | Basic Steps Not Mastered | Needs Assistance with Decisions | Can Do Well and Independently | A Problem | Not a Problem |
| Basic Dressing | | | | | |
| Puts on underpants | | | | | |
| Puts on undershirt | | | | | |
| Puts on socks* | | | | | |
| Puts on pants* | | | | | |
| Puts on pullover shirt, sweater* | | | | | |
| Puts on front-button shirt, blouse* | | | | | |
| Takes off pullover shirt, sweater | | | | | |
| Pulls zipper up/down (if started)* | | | | | |
| Threads a belt* | | | | | |
| Starts a zipper* | | | | | |
| Buttons* | | | | | |
| Fastens snaps, hooks | | | | | |
| Ties shoes* | | | | | |
| Puts on a slip | | | | | |

*(continued)*

| SKILLS | MASTERY | | | MOTIVATION | |
|---|---|---|---|---|---|
| | 1 Basic Steps Not Mastered | 2 Needs Assistance with Decisions | 3 Can Do Well and Independently | 1 A Problem | 2 Not a Problem |
| Puts on a bra (if appropriate) | | | | | |
| Puts on nylons/pantyhose (if appropriate) | | | | | |
| Ties a necktie (if appropriate) | | | | | |
| Clothes Selection and Care | | | | | |
| Puts dirty clothes in hamper | | | | | |
| Puts clean clothes away | | | | | |
| Folds and hangs clothes* | | | | | |
| Wears clothes that are clean and pressed | | | | | |
| Selects clothes that fit | | | | | |
| Selects clothes that match | | | | | |
| Selects age-appropriate clothes | | | | | |
| Selects clothes appropriate to weather | | | | | |
| Selects clothes appropriate to social occasion | | | | | |
| Grooming and Personal Hygiene | | | | | |
| Uses toilet and toilet paper | | | | | |
| Washes and dries hands | | | | | |
| Washes and dries face* | | | | | |
| Takes bath or shower, with soap and washcloth* | | | | | |
| Uses deodorant | | | | | |
| Washes and rinses hair* | | | | | |
| Brushes teeth* and uses mouthwash | | | | | |
| Cleans ears | | | | | |
| Shaves (if appropriate) | | | | | |
| Applies make up (if appropriate) | | | | | |
| Combs and brushes hair* | | | | | |
| Uses a mirror to spot-check appearance | | | | | |

(continued)

| SKILLS | MASTERY | | | MOTIVATION | |
|---|---|---|---|---|---|
| | 1<br>Basic Steps Not Mastered | 2<br>Needs Assistance with Decisions | 3<br>Can Do Well and Independently | 1<br>A Problem | 2<br>Not a Problem |
| Trims fingernails/toenails | | | | | |
| Uses aftershave/perfume | | | | | |
| Uses a handkerchief/Kleenex | | | | | |
| Takes care of eyeglasses or contact lenses (if appropriate) | | | | | |
| Gets a haircut | | | | | |
| Wipes food/dirt off clothes | | | | | |
| Uses tampons or sanitary napkins (if appropriate) and disposes of them properly | | | | | |
| Health Care<br>Eats a well-balanced diet | | | | | |
| Gets enough sleep | | | | | |
| Exercises regularly (e.g., rides bike, walks) | | | | | |
| Cares for minor cuts | | | | | |
| Treats minor burns | | | | | |
| Identifies cold symptoms | | | | | |
| Treats a common cold | | | | | |
| Treats a common headache | | | | | |
| Treats a common nosebleed | | | | | |
| Treats common diarrhea/ constipation | | | | | |
| Treats common nausea | | | | | |

*For complete teaching program for these skills, see Appendix C at the end of this book.

fun activities. In order, then, to increase your child's motivation to perform those self-care skills he's already learned, you will need to use rewards.

We discussed rewards at some length in earlier chapters—especially Chapter 4—so we will not repeat ourselves here. We would simply add that as your child becomes older, she will become more concerned about her appearance. She may be more motivated to master self-help skills now. Also, your attention and praise for skills well done will take on greater importance. Nevertheless, you still may need to motivate her with more tangible rewards, especially tokens.

## Tokens

Token rewards are among the most flexible and effective kinds of rewards you can use to motivate your child's independent performance. However, because tokens are neither as spontaneous as praise nor as naturally occurring as activities, their successful use does require careful planning on your part. We have discussed tokens elsewhere in Chapters 4 and 9. We review and add new information here.

Tokens can be almost anything: check marks on a piece of paper, plastic chips, even small amounts of money. They're not terribly valuable in and of themselves. They become valuable only when they are traded in or exchanged for something enjoyable. Ten check marks on a chart might, for example, earn a trip to the movies. Fifty chips could mean that your child can buy that new baseball glove. Twenty nickels are valuable because with them you can purchase . . . well, you know how much a dollar buys these days.

Starting a simple token system involves three steps:

1. Make a list of activities your child can perform to earn tokens, and decide how many tokens you will give for each.
2. Make a list of rewards your child can *buy* with tokens, and decide how many tokens each will cost.
3. Teach your child that the tokens he earns are worth something he wants.

Involve your child as much as possible in choosing skills to perform and rewards to buy. It is a good idea to prepare a chart listing the activities and rewards. Here is a simple example, where each activity earns one token and the child has several reward choices at the end of the day.

|  | *Token Earned* |
| --- | --- |
| Make bed in morning | 1 |
| Put breakfast dishes in sink | 1 |
| Set table for dinner | 1 |
|  | *Price* |
| 30 minutes of TV | 3 |
| Extra dessert | 3 |
| Game of catch with Dad | 3 |

For some children, it may be necessary at first to exchange the token for a reward immediately. Once they understand the idea of earning and trading in tokens, you can begin to delay the exchange until evening.

Token systems can become quite elaborate, with many activities and rewards, each with a different token value. Our advice to you, though, is to *keep it simple*. The main reason token systems fail is that the parents find them a burden to maintain. Record keeping may take too much time, or rewards may become too expensive or inconvenient. When parents lose interest and are not prepared for token exchange ("Oh, I didn't have a chance to buy the rewards"), the system will surely fail. So, keep it simple, keep it fair, and keep it going!

Now think for a moment about your child's skills that you listed earlier in this chapter under "MOTIVATE PERFORMANCE." Can you see ways to use your attention, enjoyable activities, or a simple token system to increase her motivation to do these skills?

# Making Decisions About Skill Performance

Even though your child can already perform most (or even all) of the basic dressing and grooming skills, he may still rely on you to direct his performance. You're the one, for example, who signals when it is time to begin a certain skill . . . or to end it and begin another. Perhaps you're the one who makes what might be called "artistic judgments" about the quality of skill performance: Does the plaid shirt (which he knows how to put on) go with the striped pants (which he also knows how to put on)?

This section talks about what you should do to increase the quality of your child's self-care skill performance. Our goal is to have your child make decisions by learning to ask—and to answer—four basic questions:

1. *When* do I need to do the skill?
2. *What* materials do I need?
3. *Which* step is *first*—and then *next?*
4. When have I *finished* and done a *good job?*

One parent we know recently told us how proud he was that his daughter had learned all the skills involved in putting on a pullover sweater ("She can finally do it"). When we asked him to think more about his daughter's performance, however, he soon learned that "doing the skill" didn't exactly mean putting on the sweater independently:

ॐ "I have to remind her when to put on a sweater." (*When do I need to do the skill?*)
ॐ "I help her pick out a sweater that matches what she is wearing." (*What materials do I need?*)
ॐ "She can do it better if I lay it out for her to start." (*Which step is first— and then next?*)
ॐ "I have to check her when she's done—she forgets to pull it down in back." (*When have I finished and done a good job?*)

Even though his daughter knew more or less how to put on a sweater, she was clearly not yet independent in her performance of that skill. She still required too much coaching from her father. If she is to become fully independent in this and other skills, two things will have to happen: 1) her father will have to pull back a little, keeping his coaching to a bare minimum; and 2) her father will have to replace *answers* to his daughter's problems with *questions* about her performance.

The first point is fairly obvious. If parents are always going to be there to offer assistance, they will never know just how much their children will be able to do on their own. Although difficult at first, it's absolutely necessary that you begin reducing all but your most essential help.

The second point is a little less obvious, but it describes what may be the most powerful way to help increase your child's independence. Think of all the assistance you give your child by providing an answer to a problem. The real problem in most cases may be that your child doesn't know which questions to ask. If he could clearly identify the questions, then the answers wouldn't be too difficult to figure out.

Our goal, then, is to get you to change the way you give your help. If you can learn to become a different kind of coach, chances are that your child will become a more independent performer. And the key to success-

## ✍ Asking Questions

Mom: "Getting ready for the dance? What do you need to do first?"

Katie: "Take a shower, clean my fingernails . . . ."

Mom: "What else?"

Katie: "Oh yeah—brush my hair."

Mom: "OK. Is your hair clean?"

Katie: "Not really. I'll wash it."

Mom: (Stops herself before gathering the materials.) "What will you need for that?"

> Katie: "Shampoo, a towel—and the dryer."
>
> *Later*
>
> Mom: "Are you all ready?"
> Katie: "Yeah."
> Mom: "Let's check in the mirror. How do you look?"
> Katie: "My face is clean, and I combed my hair."
> Mom: "What else? How about your fingernails?"
> Katie: "They're OK."
> Mom: "Great! You look real nice!"

ful skill coaching is for you to give fewer answers and ask more questions. Let's look at one example of what we mean.

Note how Katie's mom asks questions rather than telling Katie the answers or showing her what to do. Soon Katie will learn which questions to ask herself. She'll then be well on her way to independence.

Let's consider in more detail each of the four basic questions related to making decisions about skill performance.

## When Do I Need to Do the Skill?

Your child may not know—or may forget—when a skill is needed. Chances are, though, that you are usually there to remind him. As we've described, it is important that you learn to be there less and less—and that your child learn to answer for himself those questions that will guide his performance.

At first it will be hard for you to stand back, especially when you're used to stepping in to give guidance, a suggestion, or a reminder. But from now on ask yourself whether your directions are absolutely necessary. *Wait* before helping out—and see what happens. Perhaps he will figure out how to do it alone. If after a short while he doesn't remember how to do the activity, offer your help as a guiding question rather than as an answer.

**Note:** Help your child discover what needs to be done by asking questions. Avoid directly telling him what to do.

José, Royce, and June have each learned to act more independently because their parents learned to ask guiding questions. Later on, these

---

### ⌀ Guiding Questions

A downpour! José is about to leave for school. Mrs. Hill pauses before she can give her usual reminder ("José, get your rain-coat"). Instead she asks, "José, it's raining. What do you need to wear?" Later, she'll be able to ask an even more basic question—"José, what's it doing outside?"—and José will be able to provide his own answers to decide what to wear.

Royce is about to sit down for dinner, dirty hands and all. Before Dad can say for the millionth time, "Royce, wash your hands before coming to the table!" he simply looks at his daughter's hands and asks, "Royce, are you ready for dinner yet?"

June has dressed herself for church, and it's almost time to leave. Mom's quick glance reveals a dirty smudge on June's face. Before the words come out—"Go wash your face!"—Mom catches herself and asks instead, "June, did you look at yourself in the mirror?"

---

parents—and you—will fade out such questions. For example, you might eventually ask a general question: "What do you need to ask yourself, Billy?" In this way your child begins *to ask himself* the specific questions and is really beginning to guide his own performance.

## What Materials Do I Need?

Once your child knows what he needs to do and when to do it, he must be able to get the proper materials together. For some skills, the materials will be obvious—face washing requires soap, washcloth, and towel, and these should be easy to locate. But for other skills, he'll need to make more difficult decisions. For instance, your child may realize that he needs to dress warmly on a cold day. But many decisions remain: Which clothes are warm? Which clothes match? Should he wear casual or more "dress-up" clothes?

To get your child thinking about materials, begin to make comments about them whenever he is performing a self-care skill. Get in the habit of making statements like:

⌀ "Do you think this shirt is clean enough?"
⌀ "This sweater matches really nicely."
⌀ "Where do we put the toothpaste when we're done brushing teeth?"

Now we'll look at an activity designed to help your child *plan* his performance and *anticipate* what he'll need.

***Problem-Solving Game***  This game can be played during spare time: while driving together in the car, waiting for supper to get ready, or whenever. The idea is to create situations that may come up from time to time and to practice planning for the materials that would be needed at those times. The following questions will give you an idea of what we mean. You, of course, should think of situations that fit your home and your child best.

- ॐ "If it were raining now, what would you be wearing?"
- ॐ "What would you need in order to sew a button on your shirt?"
- ॐ "What do we take when we go to the beach?"
- ॐ "What would you do if you got a little cut on your finger?"
- ॐ "What should you pack in a toilet kit for an overnight trip?"

Remember, when it becomes necessary to gather the right materials for self-care skill performance, think of yourself no longer as the parent who does the gathering but as the parent who asks the questions. If you ask the right ones, your child will soon get used to preparing his own materials independently.

## Which Step Is First—and Then Next?

Your child may be unsure of how to start a skill or confused about which step comes next. Even if she knows when to do the skill and gets her own materials, you may be preventing her independence by helping her with the beginning steps.

For example, perhaps you

- ॐ Lay out his sweater on the bed
- ॐ Loosen shoelaces so that she can put her shoes on more easily
- ॐ Thread the needle for her
- ॐ Remove the old razor blade and insert a new one
- ॐ Put a vitamin pill by his plate
- ॐ Turn on the water for his shower or bath

While these actions may have been helpful to your child as he learned each skill, they may not be helpful now. Your first step will be to become aware of when you provide this help; you can then learn to fade out such assistance.

Part of doing so will once again involve asking questions. For instance, as your child gets his shoes out of the closet, you can ask, "What will you need to do before you put them on?" Or, in the case of the razor blade, you might ask, "Do you think this blade is sharp enough?"

In many cases you'll have to do more than just ask questions. You'll have to show your child exactly how to do these first steps, so that your help won't be necessary any longer.

Here are some guidelines for making your help less and less necessary:

⌀   At first, have your child watch closely while you perform the first step. Describe the process aloud, slowly and carefully.

⌀   Next, guide her through the process, emphasizing each portion aloud as she goes.

⌀   Later, have her attempt the step on her own, as you give only verbal guidance for each part.

⌀   Eventually, as you fade out your instruction, she'll be able to do it herself.

---

### ⌀   Sneakers: The First Step

Jessie's mom would quickly loosen the laces each time Jessie was ready to put on her sneakers. It was time now to help Jessie become completely independent in this skill. Mom first had Jessie observe the process carefully for a few days. She made sure Jessie was listening attentively to the description of each step. Next, she showed Jessie how to do it herself by helping her as needed with each part of the process. Before long Jessie was picking up her sneakers and loosening the laces herself—she had learned this first step just as she had learned the others.

---

## When Have I Finished and Done a Good Job?

Your child is now on his way to knowing *when* to perform self-care skills, which *materials* to use, and how to get started on the *first step*. But how will he know when he's completed that task—when he's finished all the steps correctly?

For most self-care skills, a mirror provides your child with the answer to how well she's performed. Your job is to teach her how to give herself that last-minute check. As before, your use of guiding questions will make that job both easier and more effective. Did I miss anything? Is it on right? Does it look okay?

> ✍   Mirror, Mirror on the Wall
>
> "Ready, Rosina? Let's see, hands clean? Face clean?"
>    "Yeah, and my hair is all brushed and the ribbon matches my blouse and . . . ."

Begin by standing in front of the mirror with your child and asking her the appropriate questions. Have her check her dressing and grooming with you as you ask. Eventually, have her begin asking these same questions himself so that he can guide her own checking.

At first, a checklist next to the mirror may help your child remember all the points to check. You could also give her a picture of someone who is well groomed—maybe even a picture you've taken of her—and have her compare her appearance with that in the picture.

Now think for a moment about your child's skills that you listed earlier under "TEACH INDEPENDENCE." Can you see ways to fade out some of the assistance you give and to use questions to coach him?

# Developing Daily Routines

The skills you listed previously under "DEVELOP A ROUTINE" are mainly ones that your child can do without your help but still needs to learn to put into a routine without your prompting. What we mean by a **routine** is **the complete performance of more than one skill in the proper order, with no prompts from anyone.** Teaching a routine is like building a chain—your child has many of the separate links and simply needs to learn how to connect them in the proper order.

The critical points in any routine are those when the links come together—when, for example, his toothbrushing is done and bedmaking should begin, when bedmaking is complete and it's time to put on his shoes. It is at these *change of activity* times that you are most often needed: to remind, hint, direct, prod, or help. Often children will finish a skill very well and then just drift off—to leafing through a magazine, a daydream, or whatever—even though they "know" what to do next and can readily do it after your reminder. The main skill you will be teaching your child for performing a routine is how to **use the end of one skill as the cue or signal to begin another.** You will teach her to ask herself "What's next?" Letting her come up with the answer is better than your telling her what to do. "What's next?" is a simple reminder that she can always give to herself.

---

### ◌ What's Next?

Quincy put on her skirt and then sat down on the bed again. Mom looked into the room and almost said her usual, "Quincy, put on your shirt." She caught herself just in time, though, and simply said, "What's next?" This time it was necessary for Mom to point at the shirt, but soon Quincy would be able to ask the question alone.

---

Like Quincy's mom, in the beginning you will need to provide signals or cues for "What's next?" In this way, when your child asks the question, the answer will be obvious. One way to provide signals is to have your child carry out self-help activities in the same order each day, at least until they are very well learned. Ending one activity will soon become a signal for starting the next.

Another useful signal is a chart that shows the activities of the routine in pictures or words. Place the chart on a wall where the skills are performed, and check off tasks with him after each one is done. Gradually fade out your assistance by helping him make the check mark on his own as he completes each task. The picture or word for the next task will be his signal, so that he will not need your prompts. After awhile, he will not have to look at the chart as much. The activities themselves will come to be the only signals he'll need for "What's next?"

## Charts

We've talked several times about charts. Let's take a closer look at how charts can be used to guide and reward your child's performance.

1. **Involve your child in making the chart.** Encourage her to ask and answer questions about how the chart will be used. Have her help make the chart and put it up.
2. **Keep it simple.** The best chart is simple and easy to follow. You may want to use bright colors and perhaps a picture to make it stand out, but don't spend too much time making a fancy chart. You'll want to be able to change the chart easily when you need to and make a new one when it becomes filled with checks.
3. **Keep it in sight.** Place it close to where the skill is performed and within your child's reach. A chart will do little good if you keep it tucked away in a closet or drawer. The refrigerator door is a favorite spot.

4. **Stay interested.** The chart will only be meaningful to your child as long as it is important to you. After an initial burst of enthusiasm some parents lose interest in the chart. Over time, the chart may work well to replace your reminders, but it will never replace your interest.

Here is an example of one child's morning routine and the chart that was used for teaching "What's next?"

1. Wash face and hands.
2. Brush teeth.
3. Comb hair.
4. Put on clothes.
5. Put on shoes.
6. Make bed.

---

### ᛒ Jeff's Chart

Tim and Becky, Jeff's brother and sister, shouted, "Hurray, it's pancakes!" Mrs. Grimes flipped the first batch and thought, "You know, it's nice to have a few extra minutes to make them a breakfast they really like, now that Jeff doesn't need me every minute."

Just then, Jeff came in, check card in hand. Mrs. Grimes had given him a check after he brushed his teeth, and now he needed three more checks for taking his pajamas off, getting dressed, and combing his hair.

Mrs. Grimes told Tim and Becky, "Be back in a minute—Jeff's ready to make his bed." Because Jeff hadn't quite mastered this skill yet, Mrs. Grimes still had to provide a little assistance.

"Pretty soon Jeff will be able to get ready all by himself—just like you two."

---

Over time, Jeff will learn to give himself check marks. Eventually he might use a small pocket-size card with words rather than pictures. As always, the completed check card will lead to a reward, worked out in advance between Jeff and his parents. The time will come, of course, when he will not need the check cards and special rewards for the morning routine.

Now think for a moment about your child's skills that you listed earlier under "DEVELOP A ROUTINE." Can you think of ways to use questions ("What's next?") and to make charts to help your child move more smoothly from one skill to the next?

# Final Comments

We realize that the teaching suggestions in this chapter have not been as specific as those in the previous four chapters. Here you are left needing to adapt general strategies to your specific situation. We realize, too, that this is often more easily said than done. **Expecting** more of your child means taking more risks, and it's always hard to decide just how much is fair to expect. **Motivating** an adolescent with special needs is often quite difficult, and it is tempting to throw out the new system on the first bad day. **Assisting** *less* can take even more time at first—you have to watch your child closely, wait until he finishes, and put up with a less-than-perfect performance.

Yet we think you'll agree that the goal of greater independence for your child is worth a special effort from you. It won't always go smoothly or by the book. But if you remember to use the general strategies we've suggested, it is likely you'll be able to watch with pride as she performs more and more of her daily self-care routine on her own.

| | Jeff | | | | | | |
| --- | --- | --- | --- | --- | --- | --- | --- |
| | Sun. | Mon. | Tue. | Wed. | Thu. | Fri. | Sat. |
| 🧼 | ✓ | ✓ | ✓ | | | | |
| 🪥 | ✓ | | ✓ | | | | |
| comb | ✓ | ✓ | ✓ | | | | |
| tissue | | ✓ | ✓ | | | | |
| 👟 | ✓ | ✓ | ✓ | | | | |
| bed | | | | | | | |

# 13

# Independent Living: Home-Care Skills

This chapter presents teaching strategies designed to promote indepen-dent home-care functioning for your child. These strategies are similar to the ones described in the preceding chapter on self-care skills, with some key differences. We focus on these differences in this section. Before we begin, let's look in again on Jim and Allison, whom you met in Chapter 12, as they remind us of the many home-care challenges to be met, even in the course of 1 hour.

---

### ⟲ A Typical Day (*continued*)

Allison burst into the apartment, carrying a bag of groceries. "Jill, you've got to save me. Jim's coming to dinner . . . remem-ber, it's Friday? . . . and this place is a mess."

"Jim? Who's Jim?"

"Come on. Don't be funny. Really, it's 5:15, and he'll be here at 6:00."

"OK. You start cooking, and I'll clean up in here."

"Thanks, Jill."

Jill put down her magazine and thought for a moment: broom, dustpan, cloth, furniture polish, yeah . . . vacuum, too. All prepared, she emptied the wastebasket and straightened up the room. Then, after quickly sweeping the floor, she plugged in the vacuum cleaner for the rug. The noise drowned out the banging of pans and slamming of cabinet doors in the kitchen as Allison got together items she would need to cook

---

dinner. Soon the vacuum stopped, and the living room filled with the lemon scent of furniture polish.

The sun was setting quickly, casting long shadows across the now quite presentable room, as Allison came in and switched on a light.

"Hey, it looks great. Thanks a lot, Jill. Is it getting cold in here?"

"A little."

Allison turned up the thermostat and was heading back to the kitchen just as the doorbell rang, at 5:50! Jim was early!

Jim was put right to work, making coffee in the electric percolator. Allison had put the haddock in the broiler and was just starting the mixer for the dessert when . . . darkness! Jill called from the living room, a little startled but amused too:

"Hey, what happened?"

"I think it is the circuit breaker."

It had happened before, and Allison rummaged hurriedly in the kitchen drawer for the flashlight as Jim volunteered to go downstairs to reset the circuit breaker. Allison flipped off the switch on the mixer and stood by the door so she could yell to him when the lights were back on. Now dinner might be a mess, and they would probably be late for the movies. Anxiously Allison glanced at her watch, only to realize with a quick laugh that she could see nothing in the darkness . . . .

Jim, Allison, and Jill have previewed many of the home-care areas we consider in this chapter. Think back for a moment to the variety of skills involved in cooking their meal, the organization required for cleaning the living room, the routine adjustments of light and temperature, and the unwelcomed maintenance task presented by the tripped circuit breaker. Had we given them more time, and a few more outlets, they might have even done the week's laundry, completing another area we include as home-care skills. For these young adults, performing home-care routines had not been learned magically, but, rather, had required considerable careful practice and instruction.

Many of the home-care activities we address in this chapter are ones that your child may never have tried or ones that he cannot do. Often we tend to think of home-care and maintenance chores as adult responsibilities anyway, tasks that, for reasons of safety or convenience, we've just naturally done ourselves. Protecting children and adolescents with special needs from challenges at home, however, may not necessarily prove to be in their best interest.

## Home-Care Assessment

MASTERY

1. *Basic Steps Not Mastered.* These are skills for which your child cannot do all of the basic steps; he needs to learn some (or all) of the actions involved.
2. *Needs Assistance with Decisions.* These are skills for which your child can do the basic steps, but needs help in making decisions about skill performance—he needs to be told when to do the skill, or what materials are needed, or how to begin, or whether the skill has been done well.
3. *Can Do Well and Independently.* These are skills for which your child can do the basic actions *and* make necessary decisions—so that you do not need to be there at all.

MOTIVATION

1. *A Problem.* These are skills that your child does not perform without urging; he needs to be motivated.
2. *Not a Problem.* These are skills that your child performs regularly without special encouragement.

| | MASTERY | | | MOTIVATION | |
|---|---|---|---|---|---|
| | 1 | 2 | 3 | | |
| SKILLS | Basic Steps Not Mastered | Needs Assistance with Decisions | Can Do Well and Independently | A Problem | Not a Problem |
| Cleaning Puts things away | | | | | |
| Empties baskets and puts out trash | | | | | |
| Sweeps | | | | | |
| Dusts | | | | | |
| Vacuums | | | | | |
| Washes windows or mirrors | | | | | |
| Mops floor | | | | | |
| Waxes floor | | | | | |
| Cleans sink | | | | | |
| Cleans toilet | | | | | |
| Cleans stove | | | | | |
| Cleans oven | | | | | |
| Defrosts and cleans refrigerator | | | | | |
| Washes and dries dishes, pots, and pans | | | | | |

*(continued)*

| SKILLS | MASTERY | | | MOTIVATION | |
|---|---|---|---|---|---|
| | 1<br>Basic Steps Not Mastered | 2<br>Needs Assistance with Decisions | 3<br>Can Do Well and Independently | A Problem | Not a Problem |
| Loads dishwasher properly (if appropriate) | | | | | |
| Shovels snow | | | | | |
| Laundry<br>Separates machine from hand washables | | | | | |
| Separates dry cleaning from washables | | | | | |
| Separates clean from dirty clothes | | | | | |
| Separates light from dark clothes | | | | | |
| Washes items by hand | | | | | |
| Hangs items on clothesline | | | | | |
| Properly loads washing machine (knows what setting to use) | | | | | |
| Measures soap | | | | | |
| Uses dryer | | | | | |
| Uses coin-op machines | | | | | |
| Hangs up clothes neatly | | | | | |
| Folds clothes neatly | | | | | |
| Puts clothing away appropriately | | | | | |
| Irons clothing as needed | | | | | |
| Food Preparation<br>Puts groceries away | | | | | |
| Sets a table | | | | | |
| Clears a table | | | | | |
| Gets snack | | | | | |
| Prepares cold breakfast | | | | | |
| Makes sandwich (no mixing, no cooking) | | | | | |
| Cooks prepared foods | | | | | |
| Prepares hot breakfasts (e.g., eggs) | | | | | |

(continued)

| SKILLS | MASTERY | | | MOTIVATION | |
| --- | --- | --- | --- | --- | --- |
| | 1 Basic Steps Not Mastered | 2 Needs Assistance with Decisions | 3 Can Do Well and Independently | A Problem | Not a Problem |
| Uses oven (sets for temperature/ times correctly) | | | | | |
| Fixes salads and desserts | | | | | |
| Cooks main dish | | | | | |
| Cooks a complete meal | | | | | |
| Finds/replaces food and utensils in designated areas | | | | | |
| Identifies canned or boxed food by labels | | | | | |
| Stores leftover foods | | | | | |
| Identifies and discards spoiled foods | | | | | |
| Identifies and uses utensils and appliances: toaster | | | | | |
| mixer/blender | | | | | |
| can opener | | | | | |
| coffee maker | | | | | |
| Uses measuring utensils | | | | | |
| Replacing Used Items Replaces burned-out light bulb | | | | | |
| Replaces toilet paper roll or bar of soap in bathroom | | | | | |
| Replaces batteries in toy, radio, or flashlight | | | | | |
| Replaces vacuum cleaner bag | | | | | |
| Replaces trashliners | | | | | |
| Tool Use Appropriately uses: | | | | | |
| stepladder | | | | | |
| hammer | | | | | |
| screwdriver | | | | | |
| wrench | | | | | |

(continued)

| SKILLS | MASTERY | | | MOTIVATION | |
| --- | --- | --- | --- | --- | --- |
| | 1<br>Basic Steps Not Mastered | 2<br>Needs Assistance with Decisions | 3<br>Can Do Well and Independently | A Problem | Not a Problem |
| pliers | | | | | |
| measuring tape/yardstick | | | | | |
| rope (ties knots) | | | | | |
| **Routine Adjustments and Maintenance**<br>Plugs/unplugs electrical appliances appropriately | | | | | |
| Adjusts window, shades, and drapes to light or temperature | | | | | |
| Adjusts thermostat | | | | | |
| Adjusts TV, radio (and selects stations) | | | | | |
| Secures the residence (at bedtime, when going out, etc.) | | | | | |
| Makes a bed | | | | | |
| Changes a bed | | | | | |
| Feeds and waters house plants | | | | | |
| Waters, weeds, trims lawn or garden | | | | | |
| Trims hedges, bushes (if appropriate) | | | | | |
| Puts up and takes down storm windows | | | | | |
| Turns lights, TV, and other appliances off when not in use | | | | | |
| Rakes leaves | | | | | |
| Cares for pets (feeding/watering/cleaning up after) | | | | | |
| Cuts lawn | | | | | |
| Puts gas and oil in lawnmower (if appropriate) | | | | | |
| Knows tool safety (especially lawnmower) | | | | | |

(continued)

| SKILLS | MASTERY | | | MOTIVATION | |
| --- | --- | --- | --- | --- | --- |
| | 1<br>Basic Steps Not Mastered | 2<br>Needs Assistance with Decisions | 3<br>Can Do Well and Independently | A Problem | Not a Problem |
| **Nonroutine Repairs**<br>Fixes broken hinge or handle | | | | | |
| Tacks a screen | | | | | |
| Resets a circuit breaker | | | | | |
| Hangs a picture | | | | | |
| Stops a continuously running toilet | | | | | |
| Uses a plunger for clogged toilet or sink | | | | | |
| Patches a crack in plaster | | | | | |
| Rewinds a window shade | | | | | |
| Removes a stain (carpet, clothing, curtains) | | | | | |
| Glues broken items | | | | | |
| Makes simple repairs on eyeglasses | | | | | |
| Unjams a toaster | | | | | |
| Splices a wire | | | | | |
| Paints large surfaces with brush or roller | | | | | |
| Paints small surfaces or trim with brush | | | | | |
| Cleans brushes and rollers | | | | | |
| Knows when to seek professional help for repairs | | | | | |

# Assessment

To begin, just as you did for the self-care skills in the previous chapter, you need to **assess** your child's current performance—and your role in assisting and guiding that performance. We recommend that you use the same strategy with this chapter that we outlined in Chapter 12: 1) skim the chapter and become familiar with the main points, 2) complete the Home-Care Assessment (pp. 153–157), and 3) read the chapter carefully.

As you do the Home-Care Assessment, you will evaluate both your child's *mastery* of each skill and his *motivation* to perform it. For mastery, there are three levels: 1) the child has not mastered the basic steps, 2) the child has the basic steps but needs assistance with decisions, and 3) the child can complete the entire skill well and on his own. Put a check in the box that best describes your child's mastery of each skill.

For motivation there are two categories: 1) motivation is *a problem*—the child does not perform the skill without urging—and 2) motivation is *not a problem*—the child performs the skill regularly and without urging. For those skills at Mastery Levels 2 and 3, indicate with a check whether motivation is a problem or is not a problem.

After you have rated each of these home-care skills, use Home-Care Skills to Teach (below) to select specific skills for teaching three (or so) skills from Mastery Level 1, and list these under TEACH BASIC STEPS. Next, select three skills from Mastery Level 2 and place these under TEACH INDEPENDENCE. For DEVELOP A ROUTINE, use several related skills from Mastery Level 2 or Level 3. Finally, choose three skills where motivation is labeled as A Problem and list these under MOTIVATE PERFORMANCE.

### Home-Care Skills to Teach

**TEACH BASIC STEPS**
(from Mastery Level 1)

**TEACH INDEPENDENCE**
(from Mastery Level 2)

_____

_____

_____

_____

_____

_____

**DEVELOP A ROUTINE**
(from Mastery Levels 2 and 3)

**MOTIVATE PERFORMANCE**
(from "A Problem")

_____

_____

_____

_____

_____

_____

# Toward Home-Care Independence

Cleaning the house, washing clothes, preparing food, using tools, fixing things—we've covered a wide range of activities in the Home-Care Assessment. But how do you begin teaching such a variety of skills? Where do you start?

You've already made a good beginning by carefully assessing your child's performance in these skill areas. Your job now will be to apply the same general principles we covered in Chapter 12—motivating skill performance, making decisions about skill performance, and developing daily routines—to the specific skills you just targeted. Since we cannot cover the many skill areas of home care in the examples that follow, it will be up to you to decide how our example of cleaning a room, for instance, might apply to the task of doing laundry, or cooking a meal, and so on.

# Motivating Skill Performance

The home-care skills listed under MOTIVATE PERFORMANCE are ones that your child can do independently but won't do without considerable prodding. Let's be realistic—the thought of doing many home-care skills, like household chores, just isn't exciting for most of us. So, as in Chapter 12, we'll be talking about rewards for motivating performance of these skills.

All of the approaches considered in the previous chapter for motivating self-care performance apply as well to the performance of home-care skills. You can effectively use attention, activities, or a token program to reward home-care performance. This chapter uses examples related to *household jobs* to further illustrate motivating performance and to show additional strategies that relate particularly well to home care. Such jobs or chores are important for you and your child. By performing them, your child not only feels like a contributing member of the family but also learns habits and skills that will help with later work placements.

How to choose a regular job or chore? First, select a skill for which your child has mastered the basic steps. Second, choose a job that will be useful to the family, rather than one that is obviously created just to give him something to do. Look over the Home-Care Assessment and identify a daily chore that meets these requirements. In addition, think of one or two other tasks that occur less often—emptying the wastebasket, putting groceries away—that could be additional jobs.

Once you have chosen an appropriate skill, three steps are involved in setting up a successful job program.

1. Involve your child in the planning.
2. Make a chart.
3. Provide pay.

## Involve Your Child in Planning

Discuss job choices with your child as much as possible; you can suggest specific jobs and ask her what she would like to do. During the discussion, make an agreement about each job she will do, how often she will do it, and what her "pay" will be. You can agree, at first, to try it for a week—be sure to talk with her during the week about "how it's going." Be certain, too, that she realizes she is being given real responsibility and that each job is important.

## Make a Job Chart

Make a wall chart or a wallet card for her to carry. You (or preferably your child) can record a check mark each day or each time she does a job. This will be a visual reminder for her to do the job and will be an important record to have on "payday." Even better than the check mark is a daily job rating, such as

    0 = Did not do job
    1 = Did little work or had to be prodded
    2 = Did good work
    3 = Did excellent work

Most children and adolescents for whom this chapter is appropriate will be able to learn a rating system such as this, and it gives you a good way to tell your child about the quality of her work. You should always explain exactly why she earned a particular rating (what she did well; where she could improve). After a while, your child may learn this system well enough to give herself ratings and to tell you why she rated her performance as she did.

 ## Use a Job Wheel

Another option is to alternate jobs. You can do so by making a job wheel. This easily made device can include several jobs, with a spin of the arrow deciding which chore your child will do for a given week.

You and your child can make a job wheel without much effort. Use a paper fastener to attach a cardboard arrow to the center of a paper plate. Then draw or write the various job choices around the edge of the plate. The job wheel provides variety and may keep your child's attention better than one fixed job. It will also give him practice with a number of household chores.

## Provide Pay

Providing pay to reward performance of jobs and chores not only enhances motivation but also creates a natural opportunity for building money skills. You are not doing your child a favor by giving her spending money instead of expecting her to earn it. By providing her with regular opportunities to work around the house, and by rewarding her responsible behavior, you will be preparing her well for the future. Although there is a tendency to expect less of an adolescent with special needs, sometimes you can help most when you expect more.

 Payday

Christina's job was to clear the table after dinner, rinse and stack the dishes, and wipe off the table. Her ratings for 1 week (using the 0–3 scale we presented) were as follows:

| Sun. | Mon. | Tue. | Wed. | Thurs. | Fri. | Sat. |
|------|------|------|------|--------|------|------|
| Day off | 3 | 1 | 3 | 3 | 2 | 3 |

Dad, Mom, and Christina had agreed that Sunday would be Christina's "day off." On Saturday evening, Christina's dad sat down with her to review her chart and pay her. This was a good chance to practice Christina's money skills. They had agreed on a pay scale as follows: 3 = 75 cents, 2 = 50 cents, 1 = 0, and 0 = 0. For about 15 minutes, Christina and her dad sat counting and re-counting the change, and then trading it in  for dollars. They chatted about how Christina would spend her earnings of $3.50, and she decided to spend $1.00 on ice cream and save the rest toward a bracelet she wanted. As they headed for the car, it was clear that Christina felt good about the money she had earned and the decisions she had made.

Of course, you can use other kinds of pay besides money. Remember that your praise is always a welcome reward; it should come regardless of what else you give. Also, after your child finishes the job, you could give her a favorite snack, play a game with her, or give her a token to save toward an enjoyable activity. Your choice of pay should depend mainly on your child's abilities and desires. But whatever you do, make certain she receives some reward. She will certainly have earned it.

If you plan to begin a household job, answer the questions below.

What is the regular job that you and your child have selected? Or, what are the jobs on the job wheel?

_____

_____

_____

How will your child be paid?

_____

When will you discuss ratings and progress and hold "payday"?

_____

 Contracting

What's involved in a contract? Think of any contract you may have signed, and you'll discover that its basic elements are really quite simple. First, you agreed to do something, and the other party entered into an agreement as well. Next, it was made clear what would happen—what the reward would be— if both sides made good on their promises. Finally, the contract stated clearly what would happen if the promises were not kept. Contracts are written agreements that make clear *what behaviors are expected and what rewards follow.*

Take advantage of these key features of contracts with your child. For household jobs, once you've observed how well he can perform with some basic rewards, you can sit down with him and discuss what you expect. For instance, how often do you expect him to complete the jobs (every day? three times a week?). The contract, then, should state your expectations and his expectations, and make clear the rewards for his performance. To be complete, you may wish to add a part that explains what happens if one of you doesn't "make it" on a given day or week. For example, is there a chance to make up for a missed day of work? Or, if the quality of the work isn't great, can he correct himself and still get the reward?

You don't always need to write your contracts down. In fact, the contingencies we've been discussing ("When you finish your job, I'll give you a check") are really simple verbal contracts. For longer jobs (cleaning a room, washing and putting everything away after dinner, even getting dressed in the morning), it helps to put down on paper both sides of the contract. Then you can each sign the contract.

If your child has difficulty with reading, don't let that get in the way. You can use pictures and some simple words to make the contract clear. Sometimes contracts can accompany token charts ("If you get five checks each day, then you'll get the trip to the store"). The chart can serve as a daily reminder of the deal you and he have made.

# Making Decisions About Skill Performance

To help your child learn to make decisions about home-care skills, you need to do two things:

1. Be aware of daily opportunities to involve your child in home-care activities.
2. Have your child do progressively more of each chore. Fade out your assistance and instructions.

To see how these strategies might apply to your child, let's take a look at Liz, who has mastered the basic steps of window washing, and her mom, who is using questions to teach independent performance.

## &#x2672; Questions for Independence

**The first question is too general.**

Mom: "How do the windows look?"
Liz: ???
Mom: "Are the windows clean or dirty?"
Liz: "Dirty."
Mom: "What do we do now?"
Liz: "Wash them."

**Mom asks Liz which question to ask herself.**

Mom: "Right! Now, what's the next question you ask your-
self?"
Liz: "What do we need to use?"
Mom: "Right! So what do we need?"
Liz: "Uh—that stuff."
Mom: "Windex?"
Liz: "Yeah."
Mom: "All right, we need Windex. What else?"
Liz: "Paper towels, right?"
Mom: "Good. Where are the towels?"
Liz: "In the kitchen."

**Mom makes sure Liz gets the materials herself.**

Mom: "OK, you go get the Windex and paper towels."

*Later*

**Again, Mom has Liz ask the question herself.**

Mom: "OK, Liz, what's the question you ask yourself?"
Liz: "Where to start?"

**Mom helps Liz know when her job is done well.**

Mom: "Right. That's good, you're wiping over in the corner
first. How will you know when you're done?"
Liz: "No more spots!"

By taking time to use questions and fade out assistance, Liz's mom is
providing valuable guidance toward independent functioning. As an-

other example, let's look at the four basic questions for independence and see how they apply to sweeping. These suggestions could apply to other home-care skills as well.

 Sweeping: From Basic Steps to Independence

*1. When do I need to do the skill?* As you walk through a room with your child, look for places that are dirty and need sweeping. Model how to look carefully. At first, choose days when the floor is either very clean or obviously in need of sweeping. ("Does the floor need sweeping today? Why?")

*2. What materials do I need?* As you perform tasks around the house, say aloud what tools you'll need. ("Let's see, we need a dustpan and broom.") Remember to ask questions with your child. ("The floor is dirty. What do we need?")

As an exercise, you might make up a game with a stack of pictures cut from magazines showing household items (e.g., a broom, window spray, dust cloth, or spoon). Have him sort out "what you need to wash the car" or, later, "what you need to clean a room."

*3. Which step is first—and then next?* Before he starts to sweep, talk with him about what he will do first, next, and so on until completion. Then walk through this plan with him. At each step ask him what the next step will be. Have him sweep from one end of the room to the other or, in small rooms, from each side to the center.

*4. When have I finished and done a good job?* This question really relates to the first question—deciding whether the floor is clean. Help your child learn to ask, "Is it clean? Did I miss any parts?" about each area of the room. You can do so by stopping him at certain points and prompting him to ask these questions. If necessary, point out spots that he has missed. Make sure that you encourage these questions when he hasn't missed any areas, too.

As soon as possible, fade yourself out of each of these steps. Teach your child to ask himself these questions so he will make decisions and perform the skill on his own.

# Developing Daily Routines

A routine involves the complete performance of more than one skill in the proper order, with no prompts from anyone. When your child has learned to ask the right questions and to make the right decisions for a number of home-care skills—for example, sweeping, dusting, vacuuming—he is ready to put them together into a routine (say, cleaning a room).

Home-care routines are in many ways similar to self-care routines. The critical points come when the separate skills are linked together, as, for instance, when sweeping is completed and dusting begins. The main difference is that the "links" of a home-care chain are more complex. They often involve several materials and require more decisions about starting, checking, and finishing. So you'll have to proceed more systematically in teaching your child to perform a smooth home-care routine.

The first step involves sitting down with your child and making a thorough list of the jobs that need to be done to complete the routine. As you identify each separate skill, make a list of the materials needed to perform it (you may wish to use pictures of the materials instead of words).

Here's a possible sequence of skills for cleaning a room. Use it as a guide for other home-care routines.

### Sequence for Cleaning a Room

| Step | Materials |
|------|-----------|
| Empty wastebasket | |
| Move small breakable items to safe place out of the way | |
| (Wash windows) | (window cleaner, paper towel) |

*If using a broom:*

| | |
|------|-----------|
| Sweep floor and rug, and let dust settle | Broom, dustpan |
| Dust (Do higher places first. For example, dust around windows and pictures before baseboards.) | Dust cloth (chair or ladder if necessary to reach high places) |
| Use dust mop on floor | Mop |

*If using vacuum:*

| | |
|------|-----------|
| (Use vacuum attachment on curtains, drapes) | (Vacuum cleaner) |
| Dust | Dust cloth |
| Move furniture and vacuum rug | Vacuum cleaner |
| Replace furniture | |

The skills in parentheses do not need to be done each time your child cleans the room. In fact, you can begin with just two or three of the skills. As these are mastered, you can add the others. Note that some of the steps of the routine, like vacuuming, may require even more teaching before your child becomes totally independent. For example, you may want to teach him to empty the vacuum cleaner when it gets full.

Once you've made your list, have your child begin with the first skill of the routine. He should be able to perform this independently. Teach him to come tell you when he has completed the task, so that both of you can review his progress, put a check mark on the chart, and identify the next skill (and materials) in the sequence. Eventually, you can begin to fade yourself out of the process. He can evaluate his own performance, mark the chart, and check it to find the next step in the routine. In time, he may be able to clean the room without looking at the chart at all.

Remember, the key to this strategy is that *each step of the routine becomes a signal for the next step.* At first, you will have to help with the signal ("What do you do next?"), but you will be fading yourself out as your child learns the routine.

##  Option

Instead of making a number of charts, you might want to make up a card file with pictures of many home-care activities. Each card would show one activity and the materials needed to complete it. For any routine, you can then select the appropriate cards from the file and give them to him in sequence.

## Remember to Reward

As you review each step of the routine with your child, help him develop careful "checking" skills so that he will learn to evaluate his performance independently. Remember that your praise and encouragement, as well as tokens and other rewards, are essential to his developing independence. Call in other family members to see—and to praise—what a good job he did on his own.

Let's look in on Liz, who has mastered the questions and decisions for window washing and vacuuming.

##  Fading Your Help

One down, two cards to go.

"OK, Mom. They're all done."

Mrs. Fields came in to see the clean windows in Liz's bedroom.

"How do they look?" asked Liz.

"Terrific, Liz. They look very nice. What do you do next?"

Liz turned to the second card. Next to the word *VACUUM* was a picture of a vacuum cleaner.

"Vacuum the rug."

"OK, get what you need—and remember what to put away."

Liz gathered up the window cleaner and the paper towels and headed off to the closet while Mrs. Fields sat down again to continue her letter:

> *Teaching seems to be getting easier all the time. Before long, I'll only have to check her after she's fin-*

*ished the whole routine. Still, it's awfully tempting to get up and help, especially when I hear her struggle with the vacuum cleaner. (Will she remember to get under the bed?) But Liz is 13 now, and this is her job—she can do it. The best help I can give her is to stay right here!*

# Household Repairs

We can review the strategies we've talked about for motivating performance and teaching independence by looking at another area of home-care skills: household repairs.

During a typical day at home the need arises for many simple adjustments (closing the window or turning up the thermostat) or routine maintenance chores (watering the plants). All too often we are also faced with the nonroutine: the burned-out light bulb, the tripped circuit breaker, the cracked plaster. It is likely that you end up doing most of these maintenance and repair skills. However, involving your child not only teaches useful skills but also shows him that identifying and solving problems are inevitable parts of daily living. A child who can handle minor unexpected repair problems can avoid situations like the following:

## Preventing Trouble

Anne was working at her evening job washing dishes and was just about to put the last few dishes in the cupboard. Just as she reached for the cupboard door, however, the handle came off in her hand. As she jumped back, three plates went crashing to the floor. Anne hadn't recognized that a loose handle might soon become a broken handle. A screwdriver might have prevented a flood of tears over broken dishes.

Most of us learn to make simple repairs as we go along. For some children, however, such problem solving does not come so easily. When you don't understand why something doesn't work the way it should, or how to deal with it, a little inconsistency can be an upsetting thing. It's helpful, therefore, to give your child ways of dealing with the unexpected. And skills in this particular area—making simple repairs—must be taught intentionally, just like any other skills.

## What Your Child Needs to Know

Teaching simple repairs is pretty much like teaching independence for other skills—the basic steps, or questions, are the same.

1. What do I need to do—and when do I need to do it?
   a. Recognize the problem.
   b. Recognize what needs to be done.
   c. Recognize when professional help is needed and whom to call.
2. What materials do I need?
   a. Gather the necessary materials.
3. Which step is first—and then next?
   a. Complete the steps of the repair.
4. When have I finished and done a good job?
   a. Test the results (and try again if the repair doesn't work).
   b. Put materials away in the proper place.

As seen in the Home-Care Assessment, there are many maintenance or repair skills that you can teach your child. Try to involve your child in these skills as an observer or a helper while you do them. Eventually you'll want her to be the one to do the repair. For now, we consider a way you can teach your child about household repairs and maintenance in structured practice sessions.

## Something's Wrong

Try the "Something's Wrong" game to teach your child the steps in making a repair. Regular teaching at first is best. Carry out the game at least three times a week for a few weeks until she gets the hang of it. After that, instead of these special teaching sessions, you can simply fit some of the "something wrong" ideas and questions into your regular daily routine.

### 1. What do I need to do—and when do I need to do it?

*Recognizing the problem: "Something is wrong!"* The object of the "Something is wrong" game is to have your child identify a problem that you have purposefully created in a specified room or area of the house. For example,

- ✑ Put a burned-out bulb in a light socket.
- ✑ Open a window on a cold or rainy day.
- ✑ Have the TV or radio too loud.
- ✑ Have a messy bed that needs straightening or a sofa cushion placed incorrectly.
- ✑ Have toilet paper or soap missing from the bathroom.
- ✑ Have a very dry plant that needs water (more difficult).
- ✑ Trip a circuit breaker (more difficult).

Look at your assessment of household repair skills in the Home-Care Assessment (see pp. 153–157). Can you think of other problems you can create in your house? List one here:

_____

Next, take your child to the center of an area and say, "Something's wrong: Can you find it?" As needed, show him the area and objects involved in the search. Show him how to investigate the area. Teach him how to test objects to see if they work, to notice where they are placed, to check under things, and so on.

In the beginning, you may need to prompt him by telling him whether he's on the right track. Offer whatever assistance it takes to get him to notice the problem. Ask obvious questions as clues. For example, ask "What if my hands were dirty right now?" (no soap); "Suppose I wanted to sit on the couch and read?" (no light, no cushion). Praise him for finding what's wrong and give him a check or some other reward. Over a period of days, repeat the game with this problem and other simple problems until your child can readily find *what's wrong*.

*Recognizing what needs to be done*   When your child has found the problem, praise him and ask: "What needs to be fixed?" "How do we fix it?" "Can we do that?" If the answer is yes, ask: "What do we need to do first?"

Ask these and the other questions we present each time you work through the problem. Assist your child to give the correct answer, and then fade your assistance over time.

*Recognizing when a professional repair person is needed*   Although this won't be a part of your structured teaching program, you can teach it incidentally as other problems arise in your home. Discuss with your child the various systems in a house that may need repairs: what they're called, what they do, where they are, why they're there, what might go wrong, and whom to call to fix them. These might include the following:

| System | Whom to Call |
| --- | --- |
| Plumbing and heating | Plumber |
| Shingles on the roof | Roofer or carpenter |
| Building structure | Carpenter |
| Paint | Painter |
| Automobile | Mechanic |
| Radio or television | TV repair person |
| Appliances | Appliance repair person |

A helpful aid for teaching about professional help is a set of cards, each with an illustration of one of the above "systems" or "people to call" and each with a local phone number, if needed. Your child can play a game where he tries to match these up. Finding such pictures in magazines may take a while, but this is the type of task that a brother or sister often tackles eagerly, pleased to have a specific way to become involved in teaching.

**2. What materials do I need?**   Ask: "What do you need to fix the _____?" "Do I need a screwdriver?" (yes/no) "Where can you get the _____?"

After your child answers these kinds of questions, have him get the things he needs. Show him where to get them if necessary, but over time fade out this help. Praise him for remembering where to get the materials. Fading out your help will be easier if you begin to develop a small book (or set of cards) illustrating or describing what is needed for simple chores and repairs.

**3. Which step is first—and then next?**

*Completing the steps of the repair*   Ask him: "What do we do first?" "OK, what next?" Keep asking in this fashion as you both work through the task. By having him name each step, you will be helping him to remember the correct sequence.

For many repairs, you can use the backward chaining approach that we discussed in Chapter 9. Do the first steps with him, letting him complete the last step by himself. Gradually, do fewer of the initial steps with him. Let him do more and more of the steps until he can complete the task from the beginning. It's a good idea to make up a list of the main steps involved in two or three repair skills that you'd like to teach. Here's our list for one simple repair: replacing a light bulb.

1. Make sure the lamp is plugged in.
2. Check to see if the bulb is loose and gently turn clockwise until tight. Press or turn switch to test.
3. If original bulb is burned out, get a new one. Place the bulb where it won't get broken.
4. Unplug from wall socket, or turn off switch for ceiling light.
5. Remove the shade or cover, if necessary.
6. Unscrew the old bulb. (Shake it gently to listen for broken filament; you can also try it in another fixture to see if it is burned out.)
7. Screw in the new bulb until snug (but not too tight).
8. Plug in the lamp and test the bulb.
9. Replace the cover, if necessary.
10. Dispose of the old bulb in a safe place.

Why not take a few minutes now and make up your own list for a repair skill?

### 4. When have I finished and done a good job?

*Testing the results* Ask: "Is it done right?" (or "Is it fixed?") Add: "How do you know?" Have your child test the results if necessary, and try again if it is still not fixed. Encourage him to keep trying and to ask for help as needed.

An important part of any problem-solving skill is knowing when and how to ask for help. A child who has learned to ask for help when a repair attempt proves too difficult is much more independent than one who whines, gives up, or tries over and over again with no result. Let him experience the minor frustrations that may arise on the job, and use these occasions to encourage his appropriate questions. Self-evaluation is one of the most important things to teach. Ask him often to check his work and to say if it's done correctly or not.

*Putting materials away in the proper place* For each object he used to do the job, ask, "Where do you put this?" and have him put it away. This will be easier for your child if you have tools and materials well organized, with a place for each. If a material is used up, make a note of it so you can replace it. Again, give him prompts only as he needs them. Remember, your goal is to have your child do the job totally on his own.

**Comments** Every skill you practice in the "Something's Wrong" game will not require all the above steps. Closing a window in a cold room, for example, will not use materials and will probably not need to be broken down into a sequence of steps. "Doing the lawn," however, will require a number of tools and a systematic approach.

After you have practiced this game with your child for a few weeks, it is likely that he'll know it well. You can now incorporate it more informally into your daily routine. Whenever you notice something in need of adjustment, maintenance, or repair, you can call your child over and launch into the game. In fact, after a while you might reverse roles in the "Something's Wrong" game: Have your child create a simple problem and then take you through the problem-solving steps. Almost every day will provide some opportunity for her to develop skills in this area.

---

### ✍ Going Camping

"Here, Mike, see if this works." Mr. Goldstein handed his son the flashlight and turned back to packing the car for their camping trip.

"No. It doesn't work."

"Oh. Fix it, will you?"

Mike should be able to fix it himself now. During the many variations of the "Something's Wrong" game, they had practiced recognizing what's wrong when a flashlight doesn't work. They had gone through replacing batteries a couple of times. Mike would know what needed to be done, and he should know where to look for batteries.

Later Mr. Goldstein glanced casually over at Mike who was now testing the "fixed" flashlight—which still had no beam. Mike carefully unscrewed the cap again, took out the batteries, and put them in once more, this time headed the right way.

"It's fixed, Dad."

"Good work, Mike. Thanks. Put it in the glove compartment, will you? Then let's fold this tent."

---

# Some Final Tips

✍ Teach at a time when there aren't many distractions. Later, when your child is used to the game, get other members of the family to play, too.

- Make sure that the materials needed for the repair are in the storage places where they belong, so your child will be sure to find them.
- Make sure your child looks at you and listens when you give instructions. In the beginning, it's helpful to have her repeat what you've said, to be sure that she's listening.
- If you are using check cards or tokens, have them ready and give one check or token for successfully finishing each step in the game.
- Give checks for paying attention and following instructions. Withhold them if she doesn't. ("You missed that check because you weren't listening. Let's try again. OK?")
- Have your child's rewards on hand when she's ready to cash in her checks or tokens.

# Chapter 14

# Independent Living: Information Skills

Imagine for a moment that you are in a strange land where clocks, signs, price tags, and symbols on the telephone mean nothing to you—they are just pictures and noises. They convey no information. You would certainly feel more than a little confused, even incompetent. But luckily, in our world, you do know how to tell time, read signs and price tags, and make a telephone call. You have learned to depend on these sources of information for getting around, day to day, in the community. Developing these same skills will be central to increasing your child's independence.

This chapter reviews general strategies for teaching information skills that will help your child to function more independently in the community. We pay particular attention here to the use of token systems to build skills and to maintain performance. Appendix E contains step-by-step programs for teaching four information skills in particular:

- Reading sight words
- Using a telephone
- Telling time
- Using money

There are, of course, many other skills that your child might learn in order to obtain information, such as playing a tape recorder, using a TV and VCR, using a computer (see Chapter 15), or reading a map. Each of these would also be taught in the same step-by-step way that we illustrate with the four information skills in Appendix E.

You might associate information skills with school—after all, shouldn't schools teach children how to read or use money? Sure. But

many children sit through years of school programs and never learn these skills completely. One reason is that for many children these skills are better taught systematically and individually. Group teaching, with a whole class, may not provide the close attention required for this learning to be successful.

At home, however, you can set up special teaching times each day to provide the individual attention needed to teach and practice these skills. Also, the programs we present here aren't limited to practice at home; schools and tutoring programs could make good use of these procedures as well. You may wish to share the programs in Appendix E with your child's teachers so that the teaching program, from your child's point of view, is consistent.

Unlike the self-care and home-care suggestions described in the previous two chapters, information skills are usually learned best in structured daily teaching. We recommend setting aside 10–20 minutes each day for your teaching sessions and sticking to this schedule for at least 3–4 days per week. When your child has mastered most of the skill in your teaching sessions, you should begin to practice the skill in his daily routine.

We've described many teaching strategies earlier in this book. Let's take a moment now to review these briefly.

# Decide What to Teach

Which information skill is best? Is there at least one skill your child seems motivated to try? Observe closely to find a skill that she attempts, or perhaps tells you that she'd like to do.

Choose a skill in which you're likely to see some progress, a skill where your child can already do at least some of the initial steps. As always, the idea here is to ensure success.

# Break the Skill into Small Steps

Merely choosing an appropriate skill does not guarantee that your child will learn it. To help ensure success, you'll have to teach individual steps in logical order—and not demand that the whole skill be learned at once.

In the programs listed in Appendix E, we have broken each skill into a number of smaller steps. Yet some of these steps may not even be small enough. If your child is having difficulty mastering them, you'll have to make the steps even simpler.

# Set the Stage for Success

Pay close attention to the teaching setting, especially to the time of day, the location, and the teaching materials.

## When Will You Teach?

Choose a time that won't conflict with other children, a favorite TV show, or the rush to get to school or work. Plan ahead to find a daily time for teaching that is likely to be free from interruption.

## Where Will You Teach?

You will teach some skills where they are naturally used (e.g., using a telephone). You can teach other skills by setting up teaching sessions in the least distracting, convenient area in the home, and then practice them out in your neighborhood (for example, reading sight words or money skills).

## What Materials Will You Use?

By now, you know that the better prepared you are to teach, the more likely that your child will learn. Each information skills program requires special materials, such as words printed on a card, a teaching clock, or coins. Make a teaching box, and keep all the materials you'll need in one organized place.

## What Will Your Attitude Be?

Teaching the child or adolescent with special needs can be a slow and sometimes demanding task. It can also provide many rewards if you have an optimistic, yet realistic, attitude. Do not expect too much, or you and your child will be destined to fail. Follow the step-by-step approach, and be prepared for inevitable delays and setbacks. Your success in teaching will depend in large part on your ability to maintain consistency even in the face of disappointments. Yet do not expect too little, either. Once your child has mastered a step, expect that he perform it regularly.

# Tell–Show–Prompt

You've chosen a skill, broken it down into small steps, and set the stage for success. Now what? How do you actually begin teaching and let your child in on your grand design?

Your child may not know just what you're demanding of her. So, you'll have to tell her exactly what to do (give verbal directions), show her how to do it (model the steps), and sometimes guide her through the initial lesson (give physical guidance).

## Verbal Directions: Tell

Let your child know, as simply as possible, just what she must do to complete the step. To do so, use words she knows, keeping your directions as simple as possible. Make sure that you have your child's full attention before giving directions. And once you use a particular direction, stick with it. Be consistent with the words you use in teaching.

## Modeling: Show

Just telling your child what to do may not be enough. Show her, slowly, and in exaggerated fashion, how to do the step. As she learns to perform the step more and more independently, you should model less and less. Your verbal directions alone will be sufficient.

## Give Assistance: Prompt

Prompting involves giving your child only as much of a hint (by pointing, touching, or speaking) as you think she'll need to succeed. For example, in teaching counting by fives on a clock, you might point with your finger to show where to start and begin to count with her ("5,10, . . . "). Prompts, like modeling, are faded out gradually.

# Rewards

At the end of this section, we present an extended example of the use of token rewards to motivate learning of information skills. Remember, though, that your enthusiastic praise and encouragement are always necessary additions to token reward programs.

# Making Skills Functional

With all these teaching suggestions in mind, you should be ready to take the final step: BEGIN! It may help to remember that parents almost never feel entirely confident as they begin formal teaching sessions. But to be successful, you must at some point take the plunge.

As you begin, we'd like to offer one final reminder: The information skills you'll be teaching will have little value—and may not be retained— if they do not become functional for your child—if they are not practiced and used in daily life. So be alert for daily opportunities—in addition to the teaching session—for your child to practice his new skills. Have him pay the restaurant bill, and count the change with him. Ask him to answer the telephone. Practice reading road signs with him as you drive in the car. Ask him what time it is.

# Token Reward System

We know that it may be difficult for you to sort through all of the information and strategies we've provided in the earlier chapters and decide how they'll apply to teaching a particular skill. It's often helpful, therefore, to view actual teaching examples. So let's look in on the Harrison family to see how they go about teaching time-telling and use a token reward system.

---

### &#x24B7; Telling Time

The day had finally arrived. For over 2 weeks Brian had been saving tokens to buy that deluxe model plane at Neville's Hobby Shop. Mr. Harrison recalled the time he and Brian had decided to make this addition to their list of possible rewards. It didn't seem so long ago that he first decided to try using token rewards in his home. . . .

*Several weeks earlier*

The dinner dishes had been washed, signaling the start of the evening's teaching session in time-telling. Mr. Harrison picked up his usual teaching materials—a toy clock, two check cards with eight spaces on each card, and a pencil. But tonight there would be new material—two red poker chips that Brian could earn after completing his check cards. After earning his tokens, Brian could then exchange them for either an extra dessert or a glass of juice.

***Begin the session with questions your child knows well, and keep the choice of rewards simple at first.*** "All right, Brian, it looks like you're ready to start. Let's see if you can fill up the check card. Are you ready?"

"Yeah!"

"OK, what time does the clock say?"

"Eight o'clock."

"Way to go, son. Here's your first check."

***At first, use immediate exchange of checks for tokens and tokens for rewards.*** Mr. Harrison placed a check mark in the first space on the card, and then continued with a review of some questions that he knew Brian could answer. Within 10 minutes, Brian's first check card was complete.

"Very good, Brian. You've been working really hard, and now you've filled up your first check card. If you give me your check card, I'll give you a token." Brian hesitated at first, so his Dad prompted him to trade the check card for the token.

***Explain the meaning of tokens simply.*** Mr. Harrison explained, "This is your token, Brian. It's like money and you can buy a special treat with it. Would you like to buy a glass of juice or an extra dessert?"

"Can I have both, Dad?"

"Not yet. See, each one costs one token, so you can only buy one for now. If we keep working, you can earn another token and buy something else later."

"OK, the juice."

"OK, Brian. Give me your token, and I'll give you a glass."

Again they made the exchange. As Brian enjoyed his juice, Mr. Harrison felt relieved that his first attempt at using tokens had gone so well.

***Keep the limits you have set.*** After the juice, Mr. Harrison reminded Brian of the extra dessert and asked him if he wanted to work for another token. They agreed to continue, and after a few more minutes of harder questions, Brian earned a second token, which he traded in for chocolate pudding.

**_Continue to praise for work well done and for tokens earned._** Dad praised him for working hard and earning another token. This ended their teaching session, and both father and son felt good that it had closed with a success.

Encouraged by Brian's early enthusiasm for earning tokens, Mr. Harrison figured that he could use them to motivate many other skills throughout the day. He and Mrs. Harrison and Brian together made a list of daily routines Brian was capable of performing. The main problem with these skills was that Brian needed constant reminders to perform them. So, as they decided on a token value for each skill, they added an extra column to their list. This column included a bonus token for performing the skill without reminders.

| | NUMBER OF TOKENS | |
|---|---|---|
| JOB | With reminder | Without reminder |
| Make bed in morning | 2 | 3 |
| Put breakfast dishes in sink | 1 | 2 |
| Collect materials for the day | 1 | 2 |
| Set table for dinner | 2 | 3 |
| Nightly teaching session | 2 | 2 |
| TOTAL | 8 | 12 |

Mr. and Mrs. Harrison reviewed the chart carefully with Brian. They were sure that he could do the skills—in fact, they'd recently worked on fading out their assistance for his bedmaking and table setting. They made certain that Brian was clear about token values, and that he realized how he could get extra tokens ("You have to do it on your own"). The chart was then tacked onto Brian's wall, in plain sight.

The next step was to develop another list—a list of rewards. As before, the family sat down together and worked on finding the items and activities that Brian thought "would be terrific." After some friendly haggling over prices and one or two disappointments (the trip to the Super Bowl would simply have to wait!), Brian had another wall chart that looked like this:

| REWARD | PRICE |
|---|---|
| ½ hour of TV | 4 |
| Extra dessert | 5 |
| Game of catch with Dad | 8 |
| Bowling—one string | 25 |
| Ride to hamburger stand | 30 |
| Movies | 50 |
| Deluxe model plane | 70 |

Note how the Harrison's token system defined beforehand which skills were included and how many tokens each skill could earn. Moreover, the "prices" of Brian's rewards were clear. The Harrisons were not leaving room for arguments later on. Some of the rewards could be easily earned within a day; others would require saving tokens over several days (weeks).

Successful token systems state clearly all the rules so that the choice to earn or not to earn tokens is up to your child. Of course, the success of your token system will depend also on how appealing the rewards are, so be sure to include your child in all discussions, as the Harrisons did.

Setting up a token system in your home will take some time, and likely won't go as smoothly as the Harrison family example—at least not right away. But the benefits of a successful token program are great if you stick with it.

# Questions and Answers About Tokens

## Once I get it started, can I change my token system?

Yes! In fact, we encourage you to review the system with your child at least once a week. First, go over his progress and determine which skills he has mastered or which skills he now does on his own. These might be phased out of your token system eventually. Next you can see which skills are difficult for him, and perhaps adjust either the "requirement" (accept a small step for the time being) or the "pay" (such a skill might earn more tokens). You can also decide whether any new skills should be added to the chart. As special events arise—the circus, a local sports event, a special TV show—you should feel free to add these to your list of rewards. Your token system should be flexible enough to reflect the ever-changing needs of your child. Remember, though, to be consistent with your rules until everyone meets to decide upon a change.

### What about items that my child used to get "for free"? Can I now make them rewards that he must earn?

Of course you can. One of the important things to know about a token system is that it is completely under your control—you make the rules. Listening to a favorite CD, TV time, an hour with Dad in his workshop, a snack . . . all of these things can be included as rewards in your token economy. In fact, many of these will be the most effective rewards you can offer on a day-to-day basis—so use them!

### How do I decide how much to "charge" for each reward?

There is no rule. Some people view tokens as though they were money (say, one token = 5 cents), but this will not be useful in every case. In general, as in the case of the Harrisons, you will want to have a variety of rewards that cover a wide range of prices. Easy-to-deliver rewards should be made relatively easy to earn, whereas special treats, like a trip to the movies, should take several days or a week to earn.

### What if my child falls just one or two tokens short of earning an item that she really wants?

This is always a difficult situation, but the answer is simple. Once you have determined the price of a reward, do your best to stick with it. Remember, consistency is the key to good teaching. However, if you must "give in" (for example, if you've already purchased tickets to the show), make sure that your child performs one or two last-minute tasks and actually earns the tokens and the privilege of her rewards.

### My child doesn't seem to be catching on to the idea of tokens. What should I do now?

It is natural to increase your expectations on the basis of one or two early successes with tokens. Sometimes this can lead to expanding your token system too quickly. In the beginning, keep it simple. Remember, your child will learn to use tokens most effectively if you present them in a step-by-step fashion. In many cases it takes several weeks of immediate exchanges before you can begin to use a chart with choices of rewards. If your child seems to be confused, and tokens appear to be losing their meaning for him, go back to exchanging tokens immediately for small rewards like snacks.

## Can you give me some ideas about how to encourage my child to save tokens?

A main objective in every token system is to phase out the need for immediate exchange gradually. In its place, establish a particular time (at the end of each day, for example, or on Saturday morning) to exchange the tokens your child has earned during the week. In order for this "payday" to work, she will need to learn to save her tokens. Teach saving gradually. In the beginning, have her buy an immediate reward and then save just one or two tokens. After a couple of days, at most, she can trade her "savings" for rewards. Gradually increase the number saved and the length of time before an exchange. It's helpful to make a special chart with spaces that can be colored in as the number of saved tokens increases. In this way your child can "see" how far she has come and how many more tokens she'll need for that special reward.

## Will my child need to be on a token system forever?

No! The goal of a token system is to provide motivation for skills that your child is learning and for skills that your child has already learned but does not perform regularly. Once your child has acquired the skills and uses them regularly, you'll be able to fade out your token system. But don't expect to fade it out overnight. Just as you built it slowly, you'll have to phase it down carefully and gradually. For instance, as your child masters one of the skills on the chart, you can let him know that you expect him to perform it more and more independently for the same pay. Once his mastery is complete, you can omit the skill entirely from the system and expect him to perform it on his own as part of the daily routine. The goal is for more "natural" rewards (praise, sense of accomplishment) to replace the token reward system.

We should remember, though, that some activities will never be much fun for many children and adolescents. Making the bed, taking out the trash, washing the dishes—fact is, these aren't that much fun for us either. Many children receive an allowance and are expected to do some chores. Perhaps as your child masters some self-care and home-care skills—and learns money skills—you can switch from tokens to a regular allowance.

# Chapter 15

## Plugging into the Personal Computer Revolution

Much of the basic information and advice contained in this book is as relevant today as when the material was first published in the mid-1970s. That's less a comment on our farsightedness than a tribute to the wonders and reliability of common sense. This chapter, though, is different. It centers on the personal computer revolution, a technology whose products and capabilities are changing so rapidly that whatever picture we print of them now may well be transformed by the breakthroughs certain to occur tomorrow. Nevertheless, we would be remiss if we let this edition of *Steps to Independence* go to press without at least urging you to become familiar with what personal computer technology can offer you and your child.

The look of today's technology will surely continue to change. Not only will computer capabilities grow more broadly (and more quickly) than we're able to imagine, but computers will become increasingly more available and affordable, more like common household appliances than highly specialized devices. But even knowing that whatever we say about personal computer technology today will be dramatically different tomorrow, we must still risk giving you at least an overview of the personal computer's capabilities.

Based on what we've witnessed since the mid-1980s, there are two compelling reasons for you to become familiar with personal computers:

1. *A Tool Like No Other.* For your child, the personal computer will become increasingly essential for more effective learning, playing, communicating, and, in many cases, working.

2. *Connectedness.* For you and your child, the personal computer will become a dynamic link to vital information you might otherwise never obtain and to individuals you might otherwise never meet.

There's a third reason, too, a reason that parents invariably report to us once they've been introduced to personal computing. *"It's fun,"* they tell us. "Easier than we ever thought it would be. We're having a ball." Maybe that's reason enough.

## No Nuts and Bolts

Think of this chapter, then, not as a lesson in computers but rather as an invitation to understand why many parents just like you would agree that the personal computer is "the technology of independence." Our job here is to get you intelligently excited about new options and opportunities that may become available to you and your child as a result of using a personal computer. For those of you who are not familiar with computers, we would emphasize that it is not necessary to understand how they work or what the various parts are called. In the same way that you can drive a car—a pretty complicated machine—practically without thinking about it, so it is with today's personal computers. Even if you never understand anything about bits or bytes or megahertz, you'll still be able to operate and take full advantage of a personal computer. And you won't believe where it will take you—and your child.

## Asking Around (the World)

When we began to develop this chapter, we thought it would make sense to ask computer-using parents to tell us how they used computers, both for themselves and with their children. Then we'd take the best of what these parents had to offer, blend it with our own observations and experiences, and pass the information along to you.

We didn't ask the question to just a few parents. Nor to a few hundred. Nor to a few thousand. Actually, we asked somewhere between 2 million and 10 million parents (after awhile it became impossible to estimate how many). And the asking, itself, took us not years or months but about 10 or 11 minutes (most of which were occupied with typing the question).

We had help, of course. One personal computer. Connected to a telephone line by a modem. Which, in turn, is connected to a number of vast electronic communities where individuals like you were also connected to their computers. Not necessarily at the same time, of course. That help, that computer, allowed us to pose our question to millions of individuals around the world in just seconds. With one local telephone call.

Sound amazing? It ought to. But more amazing still is how common-place this kind of activity is becoming every day. Parents are connecting with other parents worldwide—or around the neighborhood—at all hours, exchanging questions, answers, anecdotes, tips, contacts, and . . . .

And when the parents stop connecting, that's when the kids begin. Finding pen pals. Finding games. Finding jobs. Engaging in what one technology company describes as "long distance togetherness."

But before we get too far ahead of ourselves, our point simply is this: What could have taken us forever took us almost no time at all. In less than an hour, we started hearing from parents who'd seen our questions and were eager to share their information with you. By the end of the first day, we were flooded with responses. From every corner of the globe. Parents sitting in their kitchens, their dens, their local school buildings, all had three things in common:

1. *Equipment.* They all had a personal computer connected to an ordinary phone line.
2. *Experience.* They all had used their personal computer—some just a little, some a great deal—with their children.
3. *Enthusiasm.* They all sounded like cheerleaders for technology. Here, for example, is just a sampling of what they told us:

> *"Please let all parents out there know that my husband and I would be happy to share our experiences with them."*
>
> *"My 13-year-old daughter has Down syndrome. At present, she completes many of her school assignments—especially her writing assignments—on the computer. She's shown great improvement in both spelling and syntax. Even her content has become less redundant and more complex."*
>
> *"As you probably already know, many parents of children with disabilities have a very active support system on-line. My wife and I continue to be amazed at the wealth of information 'out there' and so easily available to us."*
>
> *"To say that the personal computer has been a valuable resource is the understatement of the year! Our second son (age 7) has Down syndrome, and as soon as he started using our computer he showed an increased ability to learn across the board (letter recognition, spelling, phonics, early math skills, etc.)."*
>
> *"It was truly astonishing to see her suddenly master something that just the day before had given her so much difficulty. Her computer is a better teacher than I am . . . and I'm her mother."*
>
> *"The computer lets Katy control it. And it'll let her repeat something as many times as she wants."*

*"As a parent, I have learned more in the past year that I've been on-line than I did in the previous 6 years all together."*

*"Now I get advice from people all over the world. Many of them have become dear friends to me."*

*"Cool. That's what the computer is. Just plain cool. And if my daughter could speak, she'd tell you the same thing. It's been nothing but cool for her."*

*"The interactive nature of computers plus their infinite patience makes them a natural for kids with mental retardation."*

*"Since I've gotten on-line, I've had instant access to tons of information that I never knew existed and support that I couldn't have imagined."*

*"When no one else can give me an answer, or a next step, I turn to my computer. It's never failed me yet."*

*"The computer is the greatest thing our family has ever received. Period."*

# All About Access

We make no apology for the fact that these statements sound like commercials for computers. They are, in truth, a small but representative sampling of the hundreds of responses we received to the one small question we asked. No one, in fact, said anything negative.

(Well, that's not quite true. A few people did comment that setting up their computer was a little more difficult than they'd been led to believe. Maybe the advertisements, they said, made everything sound a bit too simple. But even in these instances, with persistence and a telephone call to a computer-using friend, everyone did get their computer out of the box and onto the information highway.)

What became clear to us was the observation that once you have access to a personal computer with a modem and an on-line service, you literally have access to individuals like yourself around the globe. Individuals with children not too unlike your own. Parents to whom you can pose the "Has anyone ever noticed . . . " or "Has anyone ever tried . . . " kinds of questions. You'll also have access to siblings of children with disabilities. To special education teachers. To university researchers. To government policy makers. To the companies developing the software programs that make your computer sing and dance. (And tell stories. And teach numbers. And draw pictures. And so on.)

But not only that. You can also contact people interested in the same hobbies as you. And people who are pursuing that hobby in New Jersey. Or New Delhi. Or New Guinea.

And all, still, with the same local telephone call.

# Questions People Ask

Apple Computer's Worldwide Disability Solutions Group receives between 250 and 300 questions a week related to technology for individuals with disabilities. In a year's time, that's a lot of questions. Yet no question has been asked more often—at least twice as often as any other question—than the one we're always unable to answer. The question comes in a variety of forms. It sometimes sounds like this: "Can you tell me what software I should buy for my child who has mental retardation?" Or "I have three students with mental retardation in my classroom. I want them to start using the computer. Which one should I buy?" Or "Can you tell me, please, what is the very best special education software?"

The reason it is impossible for us to give an intelligent answer to such questions is because they do not provide enough information about the children themselves. For example, it would be helpful to have answers to the following questions: Is your child a boy or girl? How old? What grade? Are computers used in his school? What do you want him to do with the computer? What does he want to do with the computer? Play games? Write? Draw? Make music? Make money? What kind of computer did you buy? What kind of computer experience do you have? What kinds of noncomputer activities or subjects does your child enjoy? Do you have friends or colleagues who know about computers? What kind of problems do you think your child might have using your computer? Can he, for example, operate a standard keyboard? Can he see the screen easily and clearly? With a few answers to these questions, we can begin to make much more helpful recommendations. We touch upon several of these questions in the sections following.

# Software

There is simply no such thing as "the very best special education software." Nor is there terrific software designed specifically for children with mental retardation. Instead, there are truckloads of wonderful software programs for education in general, as well as magical and engaging software for kids. These are the programs you'll need to be exploring. Software that teaches, that engages, that is appropriate for all kids. Software that even excites *you*.

Forget for a moment that your child has mental retardation. Think of her instead as just a child. As someone who likes to play, to sing, to learn, to make mud pies or apple pies. This is not to suggest that you deny reality. It's only to help you understand that the very best children's software is software that's developed for *children*. Period. Not for children with mental retardation.

That's where your exploration, then, must begin—in the ever-expanding and fascinating world of children's software. We could spend several more chapters describing how to be a critical consumer in that world, outlining what, specifically, you should look for and what you should avoid. However, there are at least three easier ways for you to dive right in all by yourself:

1. **Find smart friends.** Go meet the people who run the computer lab at your local school or university. These are people who are likely to know little about disabilities, but who will be keenly aware of the best children's software or of a local kid software expert—not surprisingly, in some communities, that expert is often 14 years old. Learn, also, whether there is a local user group in your area. The school folks will know. So will the people at your local computer dealer.

   The goal of this exploration is for you to identify sources of expert consultation and advice, usually available free. You'll find, too, as we always have, that this community of computer users comprises people who love to help—people who see it as a challenge to get you as excited about technology as they are.

2. **Find smart companies or other sources of information.** Contact a company called KidSoft. This company evaluates hundreds of children's software titles on an ongoing basis to identify what they consider to be the best products on the market. Their judgments, in our view, are accurate. And, while they shouldn't be your only source of software information, we think they represent an ideal starting point. The resource list at the end of the chapter provides contact numbers for KidSoft and other companies.

   In addition to KidSoft, there are other groups of information sources you'll find useful. One is represented by the organizations listed at the end of this chapter under the heading "Resources on Computers." These places are waiting for your call. Another source of information is anyplace that allows you to play with software before you actually buy it, such as a local school, a local computer dealer, or a friend. Take advantage of these sources. Use the software yourself. If it doesn't thrill you, if it doesn't at the least make you giggle or guffaw, then probably you shouldn't buy it. Like the best of children's literature or television, the best of children's software has a cleverness and an artfulness woven throughout it that adults recognize too. It shows a respect for children.

3. **Find the information highway.** Another major source of information is represented by the on-line communities mentioned at the beginning of this chapter, communities easily available to you through services such as America Online, CompuServe, and Prodigy. These

services usually charge a flat fee per month plus an additional charge per minute of use. Users may hook up to the services on line by dialing their modem number on the computer and providing credit card information. In these communities, you can review other people's opinions about software titles you're considering (people who have no stake in the product's success) or ask questions such as "Has anyone found a great program for teaching simple math?" or "Who knows of terrific software that keeps young kids riveted for more than 10 minutes?" You will soon feel comfortable asking any questions you want, and before long you'll probably be answering questions posed by others.

In addition to the kinds of commercial telecommunications services just mentioned, the Internet is another vast information resource available to personal computer users. At some point, you should venture onto the Internet. It offers boundless and constantly changing sources of information about mental retardation, disability, education, software . . . virtually anything in the world you can think of. You can access the Internet directly or through the commercial services mentioned earlier or through direct access. Our advice, though, is to hold off until you've become familiar with the basics. Then get a computer-using friend who's already visited cyberspace to show you around.

So much for software, the invisible part of the computer that turns your piece of dull technology into a machine that dazzles and delights. What about the machine itself, the visible part, the *hardware?*

# Hardware

Hardware refers to the parts of the personal computer you can see and touch—the keyboard, the screen, and the unit that sits under or next to the screen. These are the plastic parts of the computer, the parts that you plug in, either to each other or to an electrical outlet. Hardware also refers to the wires and electronic features inside.

If your child has a tendency to be rough on toys or equipment, keep that in mind while you explore. But don't let it frighten you. For all their sophistication and complexity, today's personal computers are remarkably sturdy.

Keep in mind, too, that the companies listed at the end of this chapter manufacture many items specifically designed for children who are unable to use a standard computer in the standard way. Children who are unable to type on a regular keyboard or who can't manipulate a mouse. Children who can't easily view or who might spill or drool on a keyboard. For these children, there is a wide variety of alternative keyboards (larger ones, smaller ones, ones that you can tailor to meet your specific needs) as well as alternatives to the keyboard (switches, touch screens, voice commands) that make it possible for anyone to use the computer.

# The Power of Power

A final piece of advice, which is perhaps the most important: Go for as much power in the computer as you can possibly afford. Don't break the bank, of course, and don't assume you have to buy all the power at the beginning. But do make sure that whatever you purchase can be upgraded as your needs and your child's needs begin to require more oomph.

Today's personal computers come alive with sounds, colors, videos, and animations, suggesting all kinds of opportunities for exploration and achievement. But to reach their fullest potential, they must have appropriate-size "engines" with the proper amount of computing muscle. We've heard it said on more than one occasion that "underpowered children only really need underpowered technology." We've even seen schools that, when they acquire new technology, pass down to the special education students the older, less powerful models. Such language and behavior, in addition to suggesting prejudices, are inherently wrong and potentially damaging to children with special needs. Your child needs as much computing oomph as you can possibly put in front of him or her. Ironically, the more muscular the computer, the easier it is to operate.

So study a bit before purchasing anything. Learn what computers the local schools are using . . . with their most advanced students. Learn also what the local universities are using; they could turn out to be a valuable source of consultation to you later on. Then, when you begin visiting your neighborhood computer dealer, keep the following hardware considerations in mind:

1. **RAM.** You want as much internal memory (RAM, random access memory) as possible. Anything under 8 megabytes of RAM is going to frustrate you in no time. More than 8 megabytes of RAM (12 or 16) is even more preferable.
2. **Storage space.** You want as large a hard drive as possible. Less than 250 megabytes will quickly prove insufficient. Go for 500 (or more) if you can.
3. **CDs.** You want a built-in CD-ROM (compact disc read only memory) drive, definitely. And it should be at least a quad-speed drive.
4. **Color.** You want a color monitor, with a screen size of no less than 14 inches.

Are you confused? Don't worry—really. All we're trying to do is give you some basic guidelines to follow when you begin shopping around.

Any computer dealer will assist you with these guidelines. And if you're not already familiar with the computer jargon, you soon will be.

## Why CD-ROM?

We have emphasized the importance of purchasing a CD-ROM drive. Increasingly, we believe this is essential, for a number of reasons. Since 1977, when the first mass market personal computers became available, the machines relied on software programs to make them operate. If you wanted to write and edit on your computer, you needed to buy word processing software. If you wanted to "draw" or "paint" with your computer, you needed to buy a drawing or painting program.

In the old days (the early 1980s!) those programs were pretty simple. But in no time, the software designers found ways to add more and more features to them. Soon, the word processor not only typed but also checked your spelling and grammar, allowed you to lay out your writing in a variety of typefaces and styles, and so on. The art programs went even further, allowing you to choose from (literally) millions of colors and an endless variety of brushes, pencils, chalks, and so on.

As the programs became even larger, they began to incorporate sounds, animation, and, soon after that, video. It became increasingly less possible for the program designers to fit their work onto a single computer disk, or even onto 10 or 20 disks. Which is why the CD-ROM has gained such importance. It holds an enormous amount of information of all kinds—words, pictures, sounds, videos. And it is this information that keeps children engaged, occupied, entertained . . . and contributes to their education. Don't buy a computer without a CD-ROM drive.

## Which Computer?

But what kind of computer should you buy? Again (biased though we may be toward a particular brand name), we can't tell you which model to purchase. No matter who you ask, everyone has strong reasons for his or her favorite. We can only tell you to look especially carefully at the following factors: price, reputation, word-of-mouth advice, availability of software, ease of use, and reliability of support and service.

Not too helpful here, are we? That's because buying a computer doesn't differ much from buying any other household appliance. If you're a wise shopper in general, you'll buy wisely when you seek out a computer. If you're not, then bring along a friend who is. It's not much trickier than that.

In the end, just be certain that you understand and appreciate the reasons why you are considering this purchase to begin with. We can give you two final reasons based on many years of experience.

1. **Wanderings.**   One of our favorite definitions of teaching comes from the Roman epic poet Quintus Ennius, who described the role of the teacher as "gently guiding a wanderer on his way." Different wanderers have different ways. All good teachers know that. Such teachers are tuned into individual differences, individual needs, individual styles. Little of what they do, as a result, is prepackaged, and much of what they do is experimental. They're constantly trying things, exploring new ways for their wanderers. When these teachers come upon a personal computer, their creativity explodes. This machine provides them with virtually unlimited opportunities to "Let's try this" and "Now let's try that." Magic happens in their classrooms. Kids learn. They progress further, faster, along whatever their way may be.

2. **Steps to Independence.**   Every special educator or therapist worthy of the title has a single criterion for measuring his or her efforts to enhance the quality of life for children with disabilities. Their goal, they tell us, is to get their students to say "I can do it myself." Today most of these professionals tell us that because of the personal computer, that goal is being reached by more and more kids more and more often.

   And parents are reporting the same. Parents like you. Parents who were anxious about riding on the information highway. Parents who didn't understand how their sons and daughters could ever use something as complex as a computer.

   These parents took a risk. And their sons and daughters are today showing them how that risk has paid off.

# Appendix
# Resources on
# Computers

Behind the personal computer are personal—wonderfully personal—people who, we've always found, go out of their way to help parents of children who need special assistance with technology. Some are people who run informal neighborhood clubs. Others run international organizations. Still others run multimillion-dollar companies dedicated to *personalizing the personal computer* to fit the unique requirements of each user.

These people are part of a community of helpers unlike any other. Friendly, understanding, and understandable, they are eager to share suggestions, tips, and techniques on how to make personal computers increasingly useful for you and your child. Most were helped, themselves, along the way to becoming experts on computers. As a result, they view helping others, just like you, as a critical part of their daily mission.

We've listed in this appendix just some of the places where these individuals work. We encourage you to contact them and to become a member of this growing community of helpers.

If you do nothing else, we urge you to call or send a postcard to the two organizations listed directly below. They will help you begin your entry into the world of technology. Ask them to send you basic information about the resources and services each provides. We've known these two organizations since the 1980s, and we continue to be admirers of the example they set for helpers everywhere:

1. **Trace Research and Development Center**
   University of Wisconsin–Madison
   S-151 Waisman Center
   1500 Highland Avenue
   Madison, WI 53705-2280

Phone: (608) 262-6966
TTY: (608) 263-5408
email: info@trace.wisc.edu
Website: http://trace.wisc.edu

If Silicon Valley is the center of the computer world, then Madison, Wisconsin, is arguably the center of the adaptive technology world. The Trace Research and Development Center, located at the University of Wisconsin, is the foremost authority on using technology to help individuals with any kind of disability. Aside from researching the futuristic tools of tomorrow, Trace maintains a database of every adaptive product available today.

2. **Closing the Gap**
   P.O. Box 68
   Henderson, MN 56044

   Phone: (612) 248-3294
   email: info@closingthegap.com
   Website: http://closingthegap.com

   Closing the Gap is an international organization that provides training and disseminates information about adaptive computer technology. In addition to producing a bimonthly newsletter, Closing the Gap sponsors an annual conference at which developers, consumers, and professionals gather to learn about state-of-the-art computer strategies for individuals with disability.

# Wait Just a Minute. . .

Notice anything strange about the information on these two organizations? If not, look again. What you'll find in addition to the standard address and phone listings are a couple of additional avenues for learning more about (and for communicating directly with) them (and with the organizations listed below). This additional information—labeled "email" (for sending a quick note) and "Website" (for accessing the organization's up-to-date resources on the Internet)—tells you how to contact the organizations using a computer and a modem.

You can, of course, still call the organizations directly or send a quick note asking for additional information. But if you have access to a networked computer, we encourage you to use email whenever possible. It's quicker. And it allows more interaction with the individual(s) receiving your inquiry or comments.

We also urge you to visit the Websites of all the places listed in this section. In many cases, you'll feel like you're actually in the place you're visiting. Trying out new software. Learning more about the organization's offerings. Hearing from other users about their experiences with the organization's products and support. And discovering everything the organization has accomplished since this book went to press. Unlike books, Websites are almost always as current as yesterday.

One more thing. As you scan this section, you'll notice that the graphics are quite a bit different from those in the rest of the book. The change was designed to give you a glimpse into the Internet by showing you what various Websites actually look like (at least at the time we're writing this; since the Internet is such a dynamic and robust medium, Websites are being created and modified every day). Because the Internet has so much useful information to offer, we urge you to identify some way for you to become a cyberspace explorer. Does your school have access to the Internet? How about local colleges and universities? Local computer clubs? A neighbor?

Make an effort to visit the Websites of the organizations we've listed. You'll wonder why you hadn't tried to do so sooner. And you'll soon be developing a new list of organizations and personal contacts of your own. Everyone does.

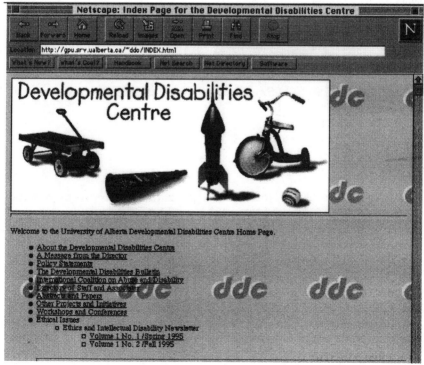

# Other National Organizations

**Alliance for Technology Access**
2173 East Francisco Boulevard, Suite L
San Rafael, CA 94901
Phone: (415) 455-4575
email: atafta@aol.com

The Alliance for Technology Access (ATA) is a nationwide network of resource centers whose members share a common vision of improving the
quality of life for children and adults with disabilities. While each center
is a unique nonprofit organization, all ATA centers provide a range of
services that help parents, teachers, employers, and children and adults
with disabilities to explore computer systems, adaptive devices, and software.

**American Occupational Therapy Association**
1383 Piccard Drive
Rockville, MD 20850
Phone: (301) 948-9626
Website: http://www.infl.com/aota

AOTA is a nationwide organization of professionals concerned with all
aspects of the occupational therapy field. The organization publishes the
*American Journal of Occupational Therapy.*

**American Association of Speech-Language Pathology and Audiology**
10801 Rockville Pike
Rockville, MD 20852
Phone (voice or TTY): (301) 897-5700
email: webmaster@asha.org
Website: http://www.asha.org

ASHA is the largest professional organization for more than 84,000
speech-language pathologists and audiologists. The organization is involved in a number of different applications of computer technology in
the areas of speech and language, including administration, clinical, therapy, school, and research.

**Center for Applied Special Technology (CAST)**
39 Cross Street
Peabody, MA 01960
Phone: (508) 531-8555
TTY: (508) 538-3110
email: cast@cast.org

Founded in 1984, CAST is a nonprofit organization whose mission is to expand opportunities for all people—especially those with disabilities—through the innovative uses of computer technology.

## Mothers From Hell

P.O. Box 21304
Eugene, OR 97402
Website: http://www2.corenet.net/debiski/mfhmemb.htm

Mothers From Hell is a grass-roots organization, specializing in humor, that staunchly advocates for the rights of children with disabilities. "Don't let our name scare you," the group notes. "Contrary to the suspicions of many school district personnel, we do not worship the devil, nor do we tolerate violence as a means of enforcing our children's legal rights. Our common bond is our children, all of whom have disabilities of one form or another . . . autism, cerebral palsy, Down syndrome, Enigma syndrome and DNOS (disorders not otherwise specified)."

## RESNA

1700 North Moore Street
Suite 1540
Arlington, VA 22209-1903
Phone: (703) 524-6686
TTY: (703) 524-6639
email: resnata@resna.org
Website: http://resna.org/resna/reshome.html

RESNA is concerned with transferring science, engineering, and technology to the needs of persons with disabilities. Its members are rehabilitation professionals from all pertinent disciplines, providers, and consumers. Their goal is to promote interaction among these groups to better understand and serve the needs of those who can benefit from rehabilitation technology.

## The Exceptional Parent

1170 Commonwealth Avenue, 3rd Floor
Kenmore Station
Boston, MA 02134
Phone: (617) 536-8961
Website: http://www.families.com

The editorial mission of this acclaimed bimonthly magazine is to reach out to mothers and fathers of children and young adults with disabilities and special health care needs, so they can participate in a network of caring parents and professionals throughout the world. Regular attention is given to technology applications for individuals with disability.

## Selected Companies

There are hundreds of companies supporting the needs of computer users with various special needs, too many in fact to make listing them here anything but frustrating to new users. We've provided you instead with our short list of selected companies in the field. We acknowledge, of course, that anyone else's list may differ and that none of that makes any difference anyway. Because after gaining some experience yourself, you'll quickly develop a list of your very own.

**Apple Computer, Inc.**
Worldwide Disability Solutions Group
One Infinite Loop
Cupertino, CA 95014
Phone: (800) 600-7808 (voice); (800) 755-0601 (TTY)
Website: http://www.apple.com/disability

Through this department, Apple Computer works with key education, rehabilitation, and advocacy organizations nationwide to identify the computer-related needs of individuals with disabilities and to assist in the development of responsive programs. The Worldwide Disability Solutions Group maintains a database of hardware, software, organizations, and publications relevant to special education and rehabilitation. It also maintains an active presence on the World Wide Web.

**Articulate Systems**
600 W. Cummings Park, Suite 4500
Woburn, MA 01801
Phone: (617) 935-5656
email: asisupport@aol.com or support@artsys.com
Website: http://www.artsys.com

Articulate Systems provides technology that enables users to operate a personal computer with voice commands.

**Berkeley Access**
2095 Rose Street
Berkeley, CA 94709
Phone: (510) 883-6280
email: access@berksys.com
Website: http://access.berksys.com

Berkeley Access is a worldwide leader in providing products and information that help individuals who are blind or visually impaired to use technology that relies on graphical user interfaces.

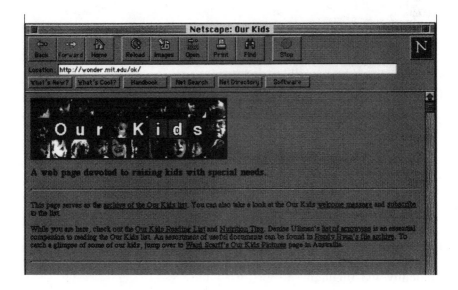

**Don Johnston, Inc.**
P.O. Box 639
1000 N. Rand Road
Wauconda, IL 60084
Phone: (800) 999-4660; (708) 526-2682
Website: http://www.donjohnston.com

Don Johnston was one of the very first companies to focus on the computing needs of children in special education. Today it has expanded to meet the technology needs of all individuals with disability, in whatever setting they may be. Don Johnston is widely acknowledged to be a world-class leader in the field.

**Duxbury Systems, Inc.**
435 King Street
P.O. Box 1504
Littleton, MA 01460
Phone: (508) 486-9766
email: duxbury@world.std.com
Website: http://world.std.com/~duxbury/Duxbury Systems

Duxbury Systems specializes in products that transform computer-based text into braille that can be printed or embossed for individuals who are blind or visually impaired.

**Edmark Corporation**
P.O. Box 97021
Redmond, WA 98073-9721
Phone: (800) 326-2890
email: edmarkteam@edmark.com
Website: http://www.edmark.com/

Edmark is widely known for its innovative educational software products for children with various special needs.

**IBM**
Phone: (800) 426-4832
Website: http://www.austin.ibm.com/pspinfo/snshome.html

IBM Special Needs Solutions Division views technology as a way to enhance the education, employability, and quality of life for all people with disabilities. Under the Independence Series trademark, IBM has developed a number of assistive devices and software tools that make the computer more accessible and friendly to people with vision, hearing, speech, mobility, and attention/memory disabilities.

**IntelliTools**
55 Leveroni Court, Suite 9
Novato, CA 94949
Phone: (800) 899-6687; (415) 382-5959
email: info@intellitools.com

Intellitools is highly regarded as one of the most helpful companies in the community of companies that help. It specializes in products for children who aren't able to operate standard computers in standard ways.

**KidSoft**
10275 N. DiAnza Boulevard
Cupertino, CA 95014-2237
Phone: (800) 354-6150

**Madenta Communications, Inc.**
9411A 20th Avenue
Edmonton, Alberta T6N 1E5
CANADA
Phone: (800) 661-8406
Website: http://madenta.com

Madenta designs adaptive technology to promote independence—at school, work, and home—for all children and adults with disabilities. This company offers a broad variety of hardware and software products that enables special users to use their computers in special—and ordinary—ways.

**Microsoft Corporation**
Website: http://www.microsoft.com

Microsoft develops and distributes software utilities that make it easier for users with disabilities to use a computer (these features are built into Windows 95/NT 4.0). The software can be obtained by calling the Microsoft Sales Information Center at (800) 426-9400. Microsoft Corporation manuals and Microsoft Press books are now available without charge in E-Text format from Recording for the Blind and Dyslexic at (800) 221-4792.

**Prentke Romich Company**
1022 Heyl Road
Wooster, OH 44691
Phone: (800) 262-1984
Website: http://dialup.oar.net/~Pprco/index.html

Prentke Romich Company has been manufacturing communication aids and other assistive technology since the 1960s. Its mission is to help people with disabilities achieve their potential in educational, vocational, and personal pursuits by providing quality language and assistive technology products and services.

**Technical Aids & Systems for the Handicapped, Inc. (TASH)**
Unit 1, 91 Station Street
Ajax, Ontario L1S 3H2
CANADA
Phone: (905) 686-4129 or (800) 463-5685

Affiliated with the Canadian Rehabilitation Council for the Disabled, TASH produces and distributes a wide variety of adaptive technology products for users with special computing needs.

**TeleSensory**
P.O. Box 7455
Mountain View, CA 94039-7455
Phone: (800) 804-8004
Website: http://telesensory.com

TeleSensory specializes in meeting the needs of technology users who are blind or visually impaired.

# Behavior
# Problem
# Management

Chapter 16

# Behavior Problems

Changing a child's problem behaviors is far from simple. Perhaps, like many parents, you tried to make changes before, met with mixed results, and now feel unsure about trying all over again. Nevertheless, a new commitment to reducing your child's problem behaviors can prove as rewarding for you as it has for the many other parents who are now effectively using the approaches described in this and the following chapter. It wasn't easy; this chapter and Chapter 17 require active involvement. But these parents have succeeded in reducing their children's behavior problems—and you can too.

Like the other chapters in this book, this chapter is intended to be adapted and used in ways that you determine make sense for your child. We do not pretend to offer specific solutions for every problem situation; that would be impossible. We do offer our general approach for looking at and eliminating behavior problems so that you have some guidelines for helping your child.

## Identifying the Problem Behavior

Your first task is to decide exactly what is a problem behavior for your child. As you'll see, this may not prove as easy as it sounds. It may be that your child has obvious behavior problems, such as hitting or screaming or running away. Behaviors such as these are generally dramatic and are relatively easily defined as problems. But your child may exhibit more subtle behavior problems—crying when you leave him, wandering aimlessly, or refusing to follow instructions. Let's see how we define a behavior as a problem.

In our experience, it is helpful to organize behavior problems into three categories: behaviors that interfere with learning, behaviors that interfere with skills already learned, and behaviors that are disruptive to the family or harmful to the child.

## Behaviors that Interfere with Learning

*Eileen yells and pushes the materials away whenever her parents try to teach her to identify pictures.* Eileen's problem behavior in teaching sessions is most likely to occur when she is asked to do something new. Her hitting and screaming make it almost impossible for her parents to work with her and, as a result, slow down her learning. "Acting out" of this sort is one way a child's behavior says no to a learning situation, and the result is often that adults quit trying to teach.

Behaviors that limit a child's growth are not always of the dramatic, temper tantrum variety. The child who rocks, wanders aimlessly, or sits absorbed with an object for long periods also misses many opportunities to learn.

## Behaviors that Interfere with Skills Already Learned

*Sarah's mother has to stand over her and constantly urge her to dress herself.* Sarah has learned to dress herself completely, but her stalling forces others to do things for her that she *can* and *should* be doing on her own. Sarah enjoys the attention she gets this way and her mother becomes especially annoyed; she knows Sarah can dress herself.

## Behaviors that Are Disruptive to the Family or Harmful to the Child

*Jackie cries and screams every night at bedtime.* Jackie's crying and screaming at bedtime are very upsetting to the rest of her family. The other children are kept awake, and her parents have to spend much of their evening sitting up with her. It has reached the point where everyone dreads the bedtime struggle.

Behavior problems often lead families to make many compromises in the way they would prefer to live. No doubt you have read the preceding examples with your own child in mind, and it is likely that you see his problems as fitting into one or more of these categories. We'll return to your child's behavior problems shortly. First, however, we want to introduce you to a skill that's essential to managing problem behavior: looking beyond the behavior to the context in which it occurs.

# A-B-C Pattern

Behavior does not occur in a vacuum. Acceptable behaviors and problem behaviors both take place in context. Consider a simple example.

*She dumped out the fingerpaint.* This short phrase clearly defines what took place, right? Well, maybe. To understand what really happened, we must look beyond the simple description of the behavior itself to the conditions that surround it.

The setting, for example, in which the behavior occurs helps us see if the behavior is appropriate. "She dumped out the paint" may be interpreted quite differently depending on whether she did so on the living room rug or on her art desk in the playroom.

What *follows* the behavior helps us predict if it will happen again. *She dumped out the fingerpaint on her art desk* might be followed by: Her mother told her not to let the paint drip on the floor, or her mother helped her spread the paint on the paper. We know much more about "the dumping" when we view it in this more complete context. The setting and what took place before the event (antecedents), as well as what followed it (consequences), are necessary to understand the behavior fully.

Had the antecedents been different, the behavior might not have been inappropriate—and it might have brought better consequences (the A-B-C pattern). Once we can describe both the setting in which a behavior occurs (antecedents), and the actions that follow the behavior in that setting (consequences), we are better able to predict whether the behavior will continue there or not.

A simple rule to remember regarding the consequences of behavior is the following: Behaviors followed by pleasant consequences are more likely to happen again.

A knowledge of antecedents and consequences and their combined effects on behavior helps us to manage behavior in a systematic and successful way. This is the central theme of this and the next chapter, and we return to it often as we examine the variety of ways you can put it into practice for behavior problem management.

Before going into the details of how you can reduce your child's behavior problems, it may be useful for you to see an overview of the approach. Therefore, the next few pages relate the story of one child, Gary, and how his family set out to modify his troublesome mealtime behavior. This simplified account is based on an actual case, as reported by his parents, and is a good illustration of the A-B-C notion. It also introduces several other ideas that are developed in the remainder of this chapter.

## Gary's Story

Gary's mother began: "Gary's really driving us crazy at mealtimes. Every few minutes he jumps up from his seat and ducks under the table or wanders around the kitchen, opening drawers and emptying them out. If we

insist that he stay in his seat, he'll scream and cry. Either way, the meal is hectic."

To form a more exact picture of Gary's problem, we asked the family to keep a record of his behavior. For 1 week—while reacting to him as they always had—they were to note how much time went by after the start of each meal before Gary jumped up. At the end of the week they calculated an average: They added up the daily scores and divided by 7, the number of observations. For lunch (they forgot to time Gary on Monday), they divided by 6.

At the end of a week their record looked like this:

### Number of minutes until Gary jumps up

|  | Sun | Mon | Tues | Wed | Thu | Fri | Sat | Avg |
|---|---|---|---|---|---|---|---|---|
| Breakfast | 18 | 15 | 10 | 13 | 12 | 14 | 16 | 14 |
| Lunch | 19 | — | 11 | 13 | 16 | 16 | 15 | 15 |
| Dinner | 3 | 2 | 5 | 7 | 3 | 4 | 4 | 4 |

Gary's mother talked about the record: "It was a pretty typical week. I was surprised, though, how much sooner Gary gets up during dinner than during breakfast and lunch. I guess I'd never noticed how big the difference is; he almost always stays seated until he's through at breakfast and lunch. When thinking about this, it dawned on me that at dinner my husband is home and we're likely to be talking—or trying to talk—at the table. At breakfast and lunch Gary gets more of my attention. You know, I noticed that Joe and I are usually in the middle of a conversation when Gary jumps up."

Gary's behavior problem occurred when the family's attention was not directed to him. In other words, **the antecedent of the behavior was dinnertime, when Gary did not receive attention**.

She continued: "When he gets up, of course, we have to get up too, run after him, and bring him back to the table. He would miss most of his meal if we didn't, and he would probably destroy the kitchen in the process." **The consequence of Gary's behavior problem was attention from his family.**

"During the week we got the whole family together and talked about what we would do. My daughter suggested that we pay more attention to Gary at dinner, since he usually stayed in his seat when someone was paying attention to him, so we agreed to do this. We also decided to ignore him when he got up. This way, he would get attention only at the table and might decide to stay there. I wasn't too sure I liked the idea, since he might not come back at all. My husband pointed out that he wouldn't go hungry for too long and wouldn't destroy too much. So we decided to try the ignoring approach."

**The family was instructed to continue keeping records**, but just for the dinner meal since the problem more often occurred there. At first

Gary got up very soon and stayed away the entire meal, trying to get the family's attention. After a few days, however, he began to stay at the table longer and to come back on his own after just a few minutes.

"At first I thought we'd never live through it. When he would be emptying drawers or tugging at my sleeve, it was not very easy to ignore him. The whole family was great at helping each other, though. As soon as Gary sat down again, everyone leaped in to talk to him and to give him loads of attention.

"The records showed that the length of time Gary sat at the table before he got up was increasing. During the first week of this program the average time at dinner was 5 minutes. By the next week he was spending most of the meal at the table (13 minutes). By the following week Gary sat 16 minutes, which was the length of the entire meal; he would only get up then if dessert was delayed. We decided to put Gary's progress chart on the wall for everyone to see.

"We all decided we would reward ourselves for helping Gary to make such progress by going to a restaurant for dinner—and now we could even take Gary along."

## Comments

No two children are alike. Each has his own way of doing some things and not doing others. No example we might offer, therefore, could ever make you say, "Yes, that's my child all right!" Yet there are common ways to look at, understand, and change all problem behaviors, no matter how unique your child is.

Let's briefly note some of the things that Gary's family had to do.

### Examine the Behavior

1. **Specify the behavior exactly.** Gary's mother did not talk in general terms. She did not say that Gary was "hyperactive" or had "horrible table manners." Rather, she specifically outlined what Gary did: "He jumps up from his seat and runs around the kitchen."
2. **Take a "before" measure.** Likewise, she did not say that he jumps up from the table "very soon" or "right away." Rather, she timed *how long* Gary sat at the table each meal and wrote down the times. This "before" measure proved helpful in starting a program.
3. **Identify the A-B-C pattern.** The family discovered that Gary's problem occurred at dinner, when their attention was not directed toward him. They also noticed what followed his behavior: their attention! By looking beyond the behavior itself to what came before and what followed, his parents began to get some ideas about how to change that behavior.

### *Initiate a Program*

1.  **Remove positive consequences from the problem behavior.** The family decided that when Gary started to jump up, they would ignore him. Gary soon learned that jumping up provided little attention.
2.  **Provide positive consequences for an alternative behavior.** When Gary was sitting in his seat, or when he returned to the table, he was given considerable attention. Gary learned that the way to get attention was to stay seated.
3.  **Change antecedents.** Gary's family also made some changes in the dinner arrangements so that Gary would be less likely to leave the table. He was brought to the table just as the food was being served, he was seated in a corner (from which it would be harder for him to jump up), and he was given attention during the meal.
4.  **Continue to measure the behavior.** By continuing to keep track of how long Gary sat, his family was able to compare his behavior after the program was initiated with the "before" measure. They were easily able to determine the effectiveness of their approach.

The rest of this chapter considers ways to *examine the behavior*. Chapter 17 talks about how *to initiate—and continue—a behavior management program*.

# Examine the Behavior

Close your eyes for a minutes and picture a child who is hyperactive. Really. Put the book down for just a moment and imagine . . . .

What did you picture the child doing? Was he running around in circles? Climbing up the bookshelves? Bouncing up and down on the sofa? Banging a spoon on the plate? Chasing the cat?

## Specify the Behavior

Perhaps you imagined none of these. Perhaps you pictured them all—and more! In any case, we can be sure you didn't imagine a child sleeping or sitting quietly, so the term *hyperactive* at least narrowed the range of behaviors you might think of. But it did not tell you exactly what the child does.

*To change behavior, you must be able to specify exactly what the child does.* General terms like hyperactive, aggressive, stubborn, or immature may be helpful for general conversation, but they do not pinpoint exactly which behaviors are a problem. A more exact description of behavior is needed.

Note how Gary's mother described his problem as "jumps up from his seat and ducks under the table." This is a more useful description than calling Gary hyperactive, if we actually want to change his behavior. A good description should give something specific *to see* and *measure*.

The following example shows the importance of *specifying the behavior exactly*.

---

### 🍂 Poor Attitude?

Jennifer Yee was a new salesclerk in a big downtown department store. When describing Jennifer, a co-worker said, "She's a good worker, but she has a poor attitude."

Suppose, just for a moment, that you were Jennifer's supervisor. How might you go about improving Jennifer's attitude? You might lecture her; you could praise her on those days when her attitude is better; you could threaten to fire her; you could send her a written warning. But about what? You would have to communicate to her exactly which behaviors you are concerned about and how you want those behaviors to change.

Jennifer's "poor attitude" could be almost anything, such as

⊘ Coming late to work
⊘ Sleeping during staff meetings
⊘ Getting upset when a customer doesn't buy something
⊘ Being impolite when a customer asks for help
⊘ Bringing her St. Bernard to work with her

Therefore, when a co-worker says Jennifer has a "poor attitude," you, as her supervisor, would need to get a more exact description in order to decide whether the behavior should be changed and, if so, how. Each of the behaviors listed might be approached in a different way and some, in fact, might not be viewed as a problem at all by the supervisor.

In order to reduce your child's behavior problems, it is important, just as it was with Jennifer, to know exactly which behaviors you want to change. Here are several behavior problems, first with a general description and then with an exact description. Note that only the exact description enables you to know which behaviors to work on.

| General Description | Exact Description |
|---|---|
| Gary is hyperactive. | Gary jumps up from the table at dinnertime. |
| Eileen has temper tantrums. | Eileen yells and pushes the materials away when she is in a teaching session. |
| Sarah's lazy. | Sarah takes more than 1½ hours to dress in the morning if she does not receive help. |
| Jackie's immature. | Jackie cries each night when she is put to bed. |

Now it's time to identify your own child's behavior problems—in specific terms. Remember that we've said behaviors are a problem if they 1) interfere with learning, 2) interfere with skills already learned, or 3) are disruptive to the family or harmful to the child. What behavior problems does your child have that fit one or more of these categories? Write on the lines that follow exact descriptions for several of the behavior problems you would like to modify.

_____

_____

_____

_____

*Wait a Minute.* Did you actually write down the behavior problems? Are they described as specifically as possible? If so, good. You deserve a break before reading further.

If not, please do. We have found that parents who fill in the blanks are far more successful in reducing behavior problems than those who just read on.

# Measure the Behavior

Once you have defined a problem in terms of specific behaviors, you are ready to measure how often these behaviors occur. We learn little by hearing that Gary jumps up from the table "soon after" dinner begins or that Eileen has tantrums "often." We learn much more by hearing that Gary only stays at the table for an average of 4 minutes or that Eileen has two tantrums each day. Unless we use numbers to describe the occurrence of Gary's and Eileen's behaviors, we cannot know if their behavior is changing over a period of time.

If you rely only on words to describe behaviors, you will never know if what you've modified is more than your vocabulary!

Although the thought of record keeping makes many people nervous, it is essential to reducing behavior problems. And, frankly, as you'll see below, it's no harder than counting or reading the clock.

## Ways to Record Behavior

In many cases, keeping track simply means counting *how many times* the behavior happens—its *frequency* of occurrence. For example,

⊗ Eileen yelled and pushed materials away 2 times today.
⊗ Brendan tears his clothes an average of 7 times a day.
⊗ Bobby hit another child 11 times during recess.

In other cases, keeping track requires timing *how long* the behavior continues each time it occurs—its *duration.* For example,

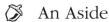

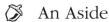 Sarah takes an average of 90 minutes to dress in the morning.

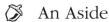 Jill played with the puzzle for 45 seconds before wandering off.

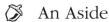 Jackie continued to cry for 25 minutes after being put to bed.

You will record either the *frequency* (how many times it occurs) or the *duration* (how long it lasts) of the behavior problem. In our earlier example, Gary's parents recorded duration—how long he stayed at the table before getting up the first time.

To decide whether you should keep track of the frequency or the duration of a behavior problem, ask the following question: "Which measure will show me if I'm reaching my goal?" Counting "how many times" Sarah gets dressed in the morning certainly will not provide that information because the goal in this case is to reduce the length of time it takes her to dress. However, counting how many times Eileen yells and pushes materials away each day would answer the question because the goal is to decrease the number of such incidents.

 An Aside

There is actually a third way to measure behavior that occassionally applies best: **rating intensity**. Sometimes you are less concerned with how often the behavior occurs or how long it lasts than with how intense it is. For example, if a child talks or sings very loudly, and your goal is to teach him to speak or sing in a "normal" tone of voice, you might want to set up a rating scale for loudness. It could look like this: 4 = much too loud; 3 = too loud; 2 = a little loud; 1 = just right. Then you would use these ratings as your measure of the problem behavior, and monitor whether your teaching resulted in lower ratings. Other examples might be fast talk, quick or slow movements, loud and hysterical laughter, or sloppy writing. In each case an intensity rating would best describe the problem. Can you think of other behaviors where you would rate intensity?

## The "Before" Measure

Your first record keeping will be a "before" measure—recording your child's behavior for 1 week before you begin a specific program to change it. If you continue to measure the behavior in the weeks that follow, you will be able to see if your teaching program is really working.

In our account of Gary's behavior problem, his family kept a "before" record for 1 week. At every meal, they wrote down how long Gary remained seated after everyone sat down. During the week they did not change their usual way of reacting to Gary. This record keeping was easy, it required little extra effort from the family, and it gave them a good record of his behavior problem. You will remember that at the end of the first week their dinner chart looked like this:

**Time in minutes**

|        | Sun | Mon | Tues | Wed | Thu | Fri | Sat | Avg |
|--------|-----|-----|------|-----|-----|-----|-----|-----|
| Dinner | 3   | 2   | 5    | 7   | 3   | 4   | 4   | 4   |

When you begin to take your "before" measure, you might find that sometimes it is difficult to decide whether the problem has occurred. It may be that you still have to define the problem more specifically.

If more than one family member is helping with record keeping, you should talk about what each of you considers to be the problem. Remember, you will be measuring either frequency (how many) or duration (how long). Gary's family measured duration.

The following is an example of specifying a behavior and taking a before measure—in this case, frequency.

---

## ✑ Three and Counting . . .

Here we go again! Ashley was in tears, the castle she had so carefully built was in shambles, and Jonathan was "in trouble," about to get his usual scolding. But first, Mrs. Low put another check on the chart. She was taking a "before" measure of Jonathan's problem behavior, which she had once called "not playing nicely." After thinking about his behavior more exactly, she had renamed the problem "interfering with toys while Ashley is using them." During this "before" week she was responding to Jonathan's "interference" as she always had, with one exception: She was noting on a chart each time this behavior occurred before getting on with the usual scolding. Yesterday the total on the chart was only one, but today it was already three.

In this example, Mrs. Low recorded every time Jonathan interfered with Ashley's play. It was easy to count because it happened infrequently, about three times a day. Therefore, it was possible to record *every time* the problem occurred. With infrequent behaviors, whether you are recording *how many* or *how long*, you should record every time the behavior occurs.

Here are other examples of distinctive and infrequent behavior problems for which you could obtain a complete record over the entire day:

✑ Running away
✑ Violent outbursts of temper
✑ Breaking furniture
✑ Tearing clothes
✑ Fighting
✑ Hitting someone
✑ Screaming

Many behavior problems occur so frequently, however, that you could not get a complete day's record: You would have to follow your child all day to record the problem, and you would have little time to do anything else. For these more frequent problems, you will only record at specific times during the day.

Some problems occur only at a particular time or in a specific situation—for example, at mealtime, bedtime, or during a bath. For these, the observation time is pretty obvious. For other problems that occur at a variety of times during the day, you will need to decide on a specific observation time (or times). Select a time of day (usually 15–30 minutes is long enough) when the behavior is most likely to occur and when you can keep track of it. As much as possible, observe during this same time each day.

You might choose to observe for several 20-minute periods, for the hour immediately following dinner, or whatever. The exact time is up to you, so long as it is a time when the behavior is likely to occur, a time that is convenient for you, and as close as possible to the same time each day. The main point is to be consistent in your measuring; make sure that you measure only for the specified times.

When is a behavior frequent enough to record only at certain times? A rough guideline is as follows: If the behavior occurs more often than once in 15 minutes, record only at specified times. If it occurs less frequently, record every time it occurs throughout the day.

A wrist counter or a supermarket adder is a convenient and accurate way to keep track. A piece of masking tape on your wrist (and a pen in your pocket) makes a convenient substitute for paper, too, and provides a permanent record of the day's activities that you can stick into a notebook. For timing, you can use a wristwatch, wall clock, or even a stopwatch, if you have one.

## &#9998; Hits, Kicks, and Pushes

Bobby would frequently hit, push, or kick his brothers. Now Bobby's teacher has begun to report this same behavior toward other children at school. Clearly, it was time for the family to do something about it. They decided that a good time to observe would be from 6:00 to 6:30 in the evening, just after dinner and when the boys were usually playing. During this 30 minutes, Dad recorded—by putting an X on a chart—every time Bobby hit, kicked, or pushed one of his brothers. At the end of the 30 minutes, Dad totaled the Xs. Below is his chart for a 2-week "before" record.

| Week | Days | | | | | | | Average |
|------|------|---|---|---|---|---|---|---------|
| (Write in Date) | S | M | T | W | T | F | S | for Week |
| **Week 1** 3/21 – 3/27 | X X X X 4 | X X X X X X X X 8 | X X X X X X X X 6 | X X X X X X 4 | X X X X 3 | Not home | X X X X X 5 | 5 |
| **Week 2** 3/28 – 4/3 | X X X X X X X 7 | X X X X X 4 | X X X X X X 6 | X X X X X 5 | X X X X X X X 7 | X X X 3 | X X X X X X X X 8 | 6 |

(Before)

On the first day Bobby hit, kicked, or pushed four times, on the next day eight times, and so forth. His dad figured an average for each week; he rounded up to the nearest whole number, though you may choose to be more exact.

## Record-Keeping Summary

### *What to Observe*

1. Select a behavior problem.
2. Specify the behavior exactly, so that the members of your family can agree upon whether the behavior has occurred or not.

Write the problem behavior here. _____

_____

### How to Observe

1. Decide whether to count *how many* or time *how long* (or both). Ask the question: Will counting "how many" show me if I'm reaching my goal? Write whether you will measure how many or how long here:

_____

### When to Observe

1. If the behavior is infrequent, observe all day.
2. If the behavior if frequent or occurs only in a certain situation, observe for a shorter time period. Write whether you will observe all day or for a shorter time period here:

_____

_____

_____

If a specific time period, when will it be? _____

_____

When you have completed this summary, you are ready to begin taking a 1-week measure of your child's behavior. Fill in the Behavior Chart (p. 227) and begin to record your child's behavior tomorrow. Continue keeping your record until you are ready to begin to modify the problem (first finish reading this chapter). This record keeping should be for at least 1 week.

**Do not go on until you have completed the record-keeping summary.**

# Identify A-B-C Pattern

Earlier we introduced you to the A-B-C notion. Once you have specified a behavior problem and have begun to take a "before" measure of it, you will want to identify the A-B-C pattern in order to initiate a program.

Remember Gary's example:

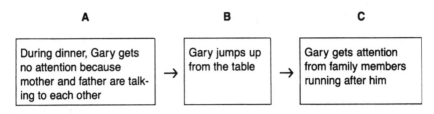

This diagram makes clear how important it is to view Gary's behavior in its context. A behavior problem should not be seen as just the child's problem alone but rather as a give and take between the child and his environment. When viewed in such a context, "problem behaviors" are successful ways the child has of getting what he desires from his environment. And, remember, you and the other members of your family are the most important parts of his environment.

What has Gary learned? He's discovered that a good way to get attention at dinner is to jump up from the table! Furthermore, every time this A-B-C pattern is repeated, Gary learns his "behavior problem" even better. The next time he wants attention at mealtime, he is more likely to use the method that has worked best in the past—jumping up. Gary's behavior problem, it turns out, is not a problem to him at all. It's a solution for getting attention. Remember the rule we mentioned earlier: Behaviors followed by pleasant consequences are more likely to happen again.

Remember to see the A-B-C pattern from your child's point of view. You may not feel that chasing, scolding, and the like are pleasant consequences. Yet, to a child, all of these forms of attention may, in some way, be "pleasant." You'll know if the consequences you provide are rewarding by seeing whether or not the behaviors they follow happen more or less frequently in the future.

Another example shows the importance of discovering the A-B-C pattern. Jackie's family sees *crying* as her behavior problem and begins to look more carefully at its antecedents and consequences. A closer look reveals that it occurs most predictably at two times during the day. First, Jackie cries in the afternoon when her mother tries to hold a short speech-teaching session. Her crying is so disturbing that her mother soon quits teaching. The A-B-C pattern seems to be as follows:

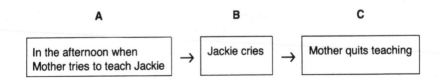

# Behavior Chart

Which exact behavior are you observing? _____

When are you observing it? _____ all day _____ minutes per day

from _____ to _____

Are you charting _____ how often it occurs? or _____ how long it lasts?

| Week (Write in Date) | Days | | | | | | | Average |
|---|---|---|---|---|---|---|---|---|
| | S | M | T | W | T | F | S | |
| Week 1 | | | | | | | | |
| Week 2 | | | | | | | | |
| Week 3 | | | | | | | | |
| Week 4 | | | | | | | | |
| Week 5 | | | | | | | | |

Also, every night it's the same story. Jackie is all smiles until it's bedtime, and then the tears begin. They last, in fact, until Mother gives in and lets Jackie come downstairs again. The A-B-C pattern here is as follows:

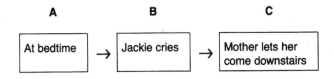

Note that the behavior in each diagram is the same: "Jackie cries." In the teaching session, this behavior makes a difficult task "go away." At bedtime the same behavior now brings attention from the family along with other benefits, such as TV.

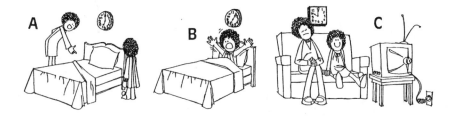

Only by seeing that there are different contexts (A-B-C patterns) to Jackie's behavior are we able to see that different approaches will be necessary. In the teaching instance, Jackie's mother might simplify the speech task so that Jackie can do it easily and then continue to teach right through the crying, having a reward ready for success. At bedtime, Jackie's family might change the consequences by ignoring Jackie's tears. Depending on the context, then, a behavior might be dealt with in many different ways.

Let's think again about your child. Have you identified a problem behavior (or two!) that you want to change? Are you taking a "before" measure? Have you identified the A-B-C pattern? If so, you probably already have some ideas about how to initiate a behavior management program. So—go on to Chapter 17, and let's get started.

# Chapter 17

## Initiating a  Behavior Management Program

This chapter tells you how to carry out a behavior management program. We first look in more detail at one part of the A-B-C pattern (see Chapter 16)—the consequences—to determine how they may be maintaining your child's problem behavior. Then we explore ways to change these consequences. The section following examines the antecedents in the same way.

## Identifying the Consequences

Throughout this book we have talked about rewarding consequences and how they affect what your child does. Indeed, he's already learned two basic things about consequences: He's learned to do what is likely to lead to something rewarding, and he's learned to avoid behaving in ways that would lead to something unpleasant.

In other words, your child already acts according to our familiar rule—as well as according to its opposite:

- ✐ Behaviors followed by pleasant consequences are more likely to happen again.
- ✐ Behaviors that are not followed by pleasant consequences are less likely to happen again.

Remember Gary in Chapter 16? Attention was a pleasant consequence for him. According to the first rule, since his behavior of jumping up from the table was immediately followed by attention from the rest of the family, it is safe to say that Gary's mealtime behavior problem would likely continue.

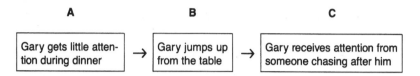

Carefully observe what usually happens to your child immediately after his problem behavior. In what ways do you or other family members respond that might be rewarding to him and therefore encourage his actions to continue? Based on our experiences, we can identify three general kinds of consequences that often encourage problem behavior. We hope that the job of locating the particular ones that motivate your child's behavior problems will be easier after you become familiar with these examples.

## Attention

All children seek attention. The child who works hard in school, helps Mom with the dishes, or shares his toys does so, at least in part, because of the positive attention these behaviors bring from others. It comes as no surprise that hugs, smiles, interest, and praise are rewarding and therefore encourage much "good" behavior. What might come as a surprise, however, is that the consequence that most frequently maintains problem behaviors is also attention.

The attention that follows a behavior problem usually isn't a hug or a smile or a pat on the back. More likely it's a scolding or a frowning or a sharply pitched "Stop it!" Still, from your child's point of view, these kinds of responses are attending to his behavior. Each says to the child, "Because of what you did, I am paying attention to you."

Take Sarah. Although she knows how to dress herself, she stalls and refuses, creating a problem in the morning.

When we examine the A-B-Cs of this situation, it's clear that Sarah has learned a successful strategy for getting her mother to pay attention to her. Isn't it likely, therefore, that so long as her mother continues to coax, Sarah will continue to stall?

## Activities

When an infant cries, we automatically assume he is hungry or in some other way uncomfortable. So we feed him. Or change him. Or sing to him. Or we invent games that capture his attention. And when presented with these activities, his crying usually stops.

As an infant develops, he can either make his needs known without crying or he can satisfy them himself. And he can wait a while, if necessary, for his needs to be satisfied. For some children, however, the ability to say, do, or wait develops more slowly and often to a more limited degree. For these children, needs and desires might be expressed most in the language of behavior. The child might still cry, yell, or hit when she wants something. Parents of these children sometimes encourage behavior problems unknowingly by continuing to reward them with activities.

The parent, for example, who has discovered that three cookies will usually end her daughter's tantrum behavior doesn't realize what the daughter is learning: To get the cookies, all she has to do is scream and kick. Activities, then, like eating, playing games, going for a ride in the car or for a walk outside—these, too, are effective consequences for maintaining problem behaviors.

The following two reactions are typical of ways that behavior problems are unintentionally maintained:

1. *"Oh, let him watch the television. I can't stand to hear him scream about it anymore."*   Once you have said no to something, it's very difficult to "stick to your guns" with your child screaming, kicking, running around the house, or perhaps just looking hurt or unhappy. And surprisingly, as you give in to him and let him have or do what he wished, you find it seems to work—he becomes quiet and happier! For this reason, many families fall into a trap of giving in to—and thereby rewarding—their child's problem behaviors. The immediate result is that the behavior problem seems to stop, and that's certainly rewarding to *you*. But you have to remember what the child learns from this kind of strategy: The next time he wants his way, his problem behavior will probably work.

2. *"If you stop that whining right now, I'll give you a piece of cake."* Often parents will try to "make a deal" with their child *during* a behavior problem. Think again, though, about what this child has learned. To be rewarded for stopping, she must first start. And every time she gets a piece of cake, she's learning how right she was to start whining in the first place.

## Escaping or Avoiding

Sometimes we find ourselves in situations so uncomfortable that all we can think of is "How can I get out?" That situation may be a crowded bus, a boring conversation, or a visit from Uncle Joe's eight children and his German shepherds. Whatever it is, the most rewarding consequence in such situations is to be away from them.

Think now of children who are being asked to learn and who are not experiencing much success. It's not unusual to see a child at school deliberately misbehave, knowing that the teacher will probably send him out of the room for awhile. Without realizing it, that teacher is encouraging his misbehavior. And the next time the child sees the lesson coming, he may not even wait to be in it, but might begin misbehaving early enough to avoid the certain frustration altogether.

Much problem behavior at home is rewarded by this same kind of escape or avoidance payoff. Most often, such consequences will be specific to certain situations such as teaching sessions where the child is being asked to perform new skills or activities that the child just doesn't like, such as bath time or bedtime. Many children soon discover that some well-timed crying and a nicely performed tantrum will get them "off the hook" or even postpone the event altogether.

Remember Eileen in Chapter 16?

| A | | B | | C |
|---|---|---|---|---|
| In the teaching session | → | Eileen screams | → | Mother stops teaching |

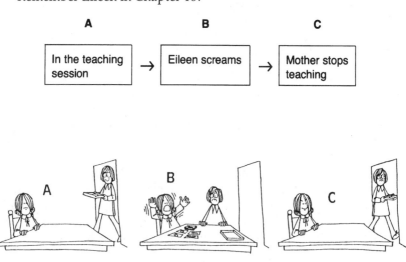

Eileen's escape from the teaching session is obviously rewarding to her. But by ending the teaching session when she did, what behavior has Eileen's mother actually taught her?

Think more about your child's behavior problems. What events usually follow immediately after them? Do you scold, coax, or comfort him in an attempt to quiet him? Do you bargain with him, promising something pleasant if he stops? Do you give in when his problem behavior clearly says, "I want out"?

In the spaces below, write down the consequences you've identified for your child.

| Behavior Problem | Rewarding Consequence(s) |
| --- | --- |
| | |
| | |
| | |
| | |

# Locating a Better Consequence

Once behaviors are understood in terms of the consequences they provide to the child, strategies for reducing problem behaviors become a little more obvious. Indeed, it almost always sounds too simple: To change a problem behavior, you must change the consequences that have been maintaining it. Let's look at several ways you can follow this strategy.

## Ignoring

Ignoring is the surest way of letting your child know that no reward is following his problem behavior. As many parents have discovered, it's one of the most successful strategies you can apply. The problem is, whereas ignoring is the easiest consequence to describe, it is one of the most difficult to practice effectively.

Your child almost always wants your attention. When you ignore him during specific problem behaviors, what you are teaching him is that there are certain ways he will never get it. In other words, if he wants a pleasant consequence to his behavior, then that behavior must be something other than a problem.

In Gary's story, you'll remember that once the family identified their attention as the rewarding consequence, they decided to ignore Gary when he was out of his seat.

Now let's look at another example.

## &#x2684;  Ignoring the Fuss

Almost every morning when her brothers and sisters left for school, Roberta had a temper tantrum: She pounded her fists, pulled at the drapes, and cried. Her mother would try to calm her down by singing a song or playing with her. Sometimes this worked and Roberta would eventually stop; the next morning, however, she would start right in again.

It is not hard to understand why Roberta's tantrums were continuing:

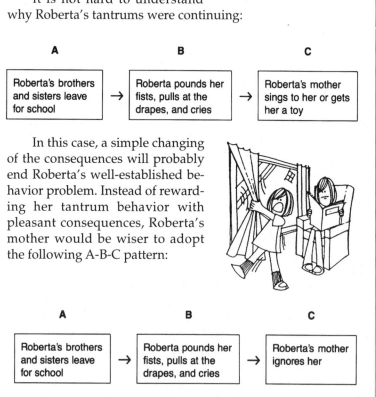

| A | | B | | C |
|---|---|---|---|---|
| Roberta's brothers and sisters leave for school | → | Roberta pounds her fists, pulls at the drapes, and cries | → | Roberta's mother sings to her or gets her a toy |

In this case, a simple changing of the consequences will probably end Roberta's well-established behavior problem. Instead of rewarding her tantrum behavior with pleasant consequences, Roberta's mother would be wiser to adopt the following A-B-C pattern:

| A | | B | | C |
|---|---|---|---|---|
| Roberta's brothers and sisters leave for school | → | Roberta pounds her fists, pulls at the drapes, and cries | → | Roberta's mother ignores her |

Of course, it's important to ignore only those problem behaviors that will not be harmful to your child. Roberta's mother, for example, knew that Roberta wouldn't hurt herself seriously (and the drapes were strong enough!), so she could safely ignore Roberta's tantrums. If, however, Roberta's problem was one of continually running into the street, then another strategy for changing the behavior would obviously have to be chosen. We will consider such alternative strategies in a moment.

First, though, let's briefly consider two questions frequently raised about ignoring.

***Is There a Best Way to Ignore?***    There is really no one best way to ignore; like most parents, you will develop your own most effective style with practice. If, though, you keep in mind *why* you are ignoring, then your ignoring should follow correctly: *You are ignoring so as not to reward problem behavior with your attention.* You are not going to look at it, yell at it, argue with it, or in any way let your child see that you even notice it. Your message to your child must be clear: "Your problem behavior isn't going to succeed any more!"

We understand, however, that when a problem behavior such as screaming or jumping up and down is happening full blast, ignoring seems like the most impossible thing to do. At such times, the best way to ignore is to leave the situation, go to another room, turn on the radio, pick up a magazine, or in some way distract yourself from the problem behavior. You don't want to risk attending to it by accident.

At other times your child may be seeking attention by, for example, interrupting conversations, climbing up on your lap, or pulling on your clothes. If these behaviors happen so often that you consider them a problem, you might try ignoring. It is hard simply to leave these situations, and there's no real reason why you should. Instead, look away, continue doing what you were doing, and, if necessary, remove his hands from you in a firm manner.

***What Will My Child Do When I Ignore?***    As far as your child is concerned, his problem behavior has always worked before. Isn't that, after all, how he learned to get your attention whenever he wanted it? What, now, when his old tricks suddenly fail?

For most children the response to your ignoring is predictable: They will try even harder to get your attention. We might imagine a child, for example, being ignored for the first time saying to himself: "I don't get it. Aren't I yelling loudly enough? Mom always used to try and calm me down by now. Maybe I better add a little crying or kicking—something that'll get her over here."

That's right. In all probability, you can expect your child's problem behavior to *get a little worse* before it gets better. He's probably going to test your new strategy before he begins to learn from it. So in the beginning is where you have to be the strongest. You'll have to continue to ignore even when his behavior is getting worse instead of better. Take heart—it won't be that way for very long.

## Removing the Reward

Just as you moved *yourself* and *your attention* away from the problem behavior, you can also remove activity rewards. Both strategies ensure that the problem behavior will not be followed by anything pleasant.

Some situations practically dictate when you should take a reward away from the child. The following are examples of such situations:

✑ Taking away Kelly's plate for 1 minute when she plays with her food.
✑ Shutting the TV off until Pete stops whining and sits quietly.
✑ Taking the ball away from Fred for 2 minutes when he throws it at the cat.

When you remove a reward, you must always provide an easy way for the child to get it back. So in most cases you will remove the reward for a brief period of time and then return it, as in the following example.

 Penalty: Out of Bounds

Sheila is coloring on the table instead of on her paper. Her mother takes the crayon away for 1 minute. She then gives it back and reminds Sheila to color on the paper.

If the crayon is rewarding to Sheila, then her mother's strategy should discourage further coloring on the table. Perhaps the strategy will have to be repeated several times and with continued reminders. But Sheila will soon learn that she will only be able to keep the crayon if she colors on the paper.

What happens, though, if Sheila starts to cry or rip up the paper after her crayon is taken away? In this case, Sheila's mother would be wise to ignore the outburst as we discussed earlier and return the crayon only when Sheila is quiet.

## Time-Out

When a behavior problem is so disruptive that ignoring proves either too difficult or ineffective, and there is nothing rewarding to take away, a time-out strategy can be used. Time-out means putting the child in a situation where any possibility for reward is completely removed for a fixed period of time, usually not longer than 5–10 minutes. For example,

✑ Sitting on a chair in the corner
✑ Sitting on the floor away from the family
✑ Sitting in the hall alone
✑ Staying in a room alone

Simply and without undue attention, the child should be moved from the place where the behavior problem is occurring to another nonrewarding setting. The length of time is always short and should be specified in advance.

Time-out is not a response made in anger or on the spur of the moment. It is, instead, a strategy planned in advance for dealing with one carefully specified behavior. Going to time-out should never be a surprise for any child. It is common for parents to send a child to his room or make him sit in a corner when he misbehaves. We may resort to such strategies when we are angry, perhaps, or when we just don't know what else to do. We want the problem to go away, literally, and it does. This, however, is not time-out, and there is little reason to expect that the troublesome behaviors removed in this way won't return again soon.

## ⌀ Take 5

The O'Connors had started a program of giving Jimmy a 5-minute time-out (alone in his room) whenever he spit at someone. Being sent to his room was an unpleasant situation for him.

One day, Jimmy and his two older sisters were playing catch. Jimmy missed the ball and spit at one of the girls. His sister immediately whisked him off to his room, being careful to give him as little attention as possible. When the 5 minutes were up, she went to bring him out of his room—but as soon as she opened the door, he spit at her again. If she let him come out to rejoin the game, she would be following his last behavior (spitting) with a reward (ending the time-out). This is exactly what she didn't want to do.

She told him, "No spitting; you stay here for another 5 minutes!" She tried not to give him too much attention, but at the same time made sure he understood why he had to stay. When she came to get him the next time and he didn't spit, she brought him out to play again. Mrs. O'Connor made a special effort soon after that to praise Jimmy for playing nicely with his sisters.

The following list suggests guidelines for how to use time-out in the home. Read the guidelines carefully and discuss them with family members who might be involved. If, after no more than 2 weeks, you find that the problem behavior is pretty much unchanged, you should reexamine what you're doing. Is everyone responding to the behavior in the same way? Is your child discovering ways to make the time-out procedure rewarding? Is he receiving plenty of attention when he's not misbehaving?

### Guidelines for Time-Out

1. Specify in advance the behavior for which your child will be in time-out. This reminder need not be made frequently but rather at those times when it's likely that the problem behavior will occur. Your explanation should be brief and clear, and it should communicate to your child the following:
   a. A precise picture of the problem behavior (in words he can understand).
   b. The location for time-out in your house (a certain chair, a particular place).
   c. How long time-out will last. A common practice is 1 minute of time-out for each year of the child's age. If a child has mental retardation with significant support needs, you might want a shorter time. But it should not be longer.
2. Once you're sure your child knows what not to do, you don't need to say much when he does it. And you shouldn't. This is not the time for apologies or debates. It is the time to act firmly on what you have already said: "When you spit at someone, you go to time-out." Additional discussion at this point will only serve as a reward. So, ignore the crying, the "I'm sorry," the "I won't do it again." These are all predictable responses to being put in time-out; no child, after all, should want to go willingly.
3. "Go to time-out." These words alone will rarely get your child on his way, and they'll probably have to be accompanied by some guiding on your part. Take hold of your child's wrist firmly, not aggressively, and walk him silently to the time-out area. Again, ignore whatever tantrum behavior he may start. Look straight ahead.

   Remember, this time-out strategy is a new one for him, and the fact that you are really following through with it may be the newest and most upsetting part of all. This, however, is what makes it effective.
4. The first few times after you bring your child to the time-out area, it is unlikely that he'll sit there nicely for the 2- to 5-minute period. He might scream, he might kick, he might look for something to throw (of course, if you have left something within arm's reach of the time-out space, then you have simply invited this last behavior). So long as

your child remains seated, however, he should be allowed to do any of these—and to learn that you won't respond with even a glance. If he gets up, however, then you must respond. Gently sit him down again and hold him there until he remains seated without help (or until the time is up).

5.  Have a kitchen timer nearby, and set it when the time-out period begins. Your child will soon learn that his actions during time-out can have no effect on the timer, and by always setting it this way you'll be sure to remember when the time-out period ends. Kitchen timers have helped more than one parent to be consistent with the time-out procedure.

6.  When the time-out period is over, tell her simply, "You can come back now," and look quickly for behaviors to reward when she returns to her previous situation. She may hold a grudge and may even refuse to leave time-out. Fine. Don't make it a struggle. It won't last long. And when she returns, emphasize the kinds of behaviors that will always get your approval and attention.

## Spankings

*"So far you haven't mentioned anything about physical punishment as a way to control behavior problems. I've always found that a well-placed spanking now and then can prove quite effective. Am I wrong?"*

No, you're not wrong. Like yourself, many parents have found that a well-timed spanking—now and then—can put a quick end to certain very annoying or dangerous problem behaviors. We have not included this physical punishment strategy in our discussions, however, because we want you to develop a *systematic* approach to behavior problem management. *Systematic* means planned, not impulsive; it refers to consistency rather than to "now and then"; and it implies long-term rather than temporary solutions. No doubt an occasional slap on the wrist might *appear* effective, but if your concern is to develop a consistent approach instead of a hasty reaction to behavior problems, we would always prefer to use one of the other procedures described, for several reasons.

First, when you hit or spank a child, you are clearly demonstrating a form of behavior he is likely to imitate. And although we can never know exactly where a child first learns this aggressive behavior, it is likely that your reacting to him this way might encourage it further.

Second, the parent who easily or inconsistently uses physical punishment might come to be seen by the child as dangerous or frightening. Effectively teaching your child—or simply enjoying the day with him—will certainly be less possible if he is continually on the lookout for a spanking.

Finally, as we noted earlier, what you may think of as traditional punishments may be seen by your child as a unique form of attention. If so, your punishment will have the effect of maintaining rather than decreasing the problem behavior.

Relative to the other strategies we have discussed, in fact, you teach your child little of value—and much that is negative—through physical punishment. Moreover, there is always a danger that physical punishment will get out of hand and hurt your child. **So for your sake and for your child's, avoid the use of physical punishment and think of an alternative strategy.**

## Cognitive Coping

*"That's easy for you to say. Ignore. Don't spank. But you don't have to be here. Sometimes I get so angry at him."*

If you are thinking something like this, it's understandable. You have lots of company. The most difficult part of managing your child's problem behavior is managing your own anger.

It's a pretty familiar story. Your child does something—throws food, cries at bedtime, throws a tantrum in the market, tells a lie—and you feel yourself getting more and more annoyed and angry. You react—perhaps not in the calm, planned way we've discussed. And maybe later you feel badly that his behavior gets to you so much.

Here's a notion that may sound strange—but hear us out. You are reacting in part to what your child does and in part to what you tell yourself about what he does. Often, what you tell yourself—your "self-talk"—is pretty extreme and leads you to feel frustrated or angry. Make sense? No? Let's suppose he cries at bedtime, and you get angry. If he were a 6-month-old infant you wouldn't get angry. Why not? It's the same crying behavior. Because you would be telling yourself something different about it. Your self-talk about the infant might go something like this: "He's just a baby. He can't understand. He's a happy kid during the day. He'll grow out of this crying."

But your self-talk about your older child might sound like this: "He should act his age. He's ruining my only quiet time. He has so many problems. He'll always do things like this." Some of these self-talk statements blame him for the crying. These can lead you to feel angry. Other such statements, though, use the crying as a takeoff point. They go beyond it to a more general pessimism about his other behaviors and his future. These can lead you to feel depressed.

What you tell yourself about your child's behavior can lead to a host of feelings that might be lessened or avoided altogether if you changed your self-talk. Trouble is, most people really aren't too aware of their self-talk. "He cries, I get angry. I don't stop to think about it." True, but self-talk happens in an instant. Take a few minutes and think about it, especially the next time his problem behavior occurs. Chances are you'll be able to recognize your thoughts—or what we are calling your self-talk.

One mother we know got very angry when her 4-year-old did not do what he was told. She knew she was getting angrier than his behavior justified, but she didn't know why. When she examined her self-talk, however, she realized that her son's misbehavior led to thoughts like, "He's getting to be just like his father." Dad, it seems, had a long history of committing antisocial acts. He had left the family several years earlier and was now in jail. Recognizing this self-talk and then finding more reasonable ways to think about her son's behavior ("Most 4-year-olds don't do what they're told every time. I'll try carrying out a program like they suggest in the book") led to much less anger.

This process of more positive self-talk is sometimes called **cognitive coping**. You are coping with your child's problem behavior in part by changing your thoughts—your cognitions—about that behavior. You are reframing negative cognitions into neutral or even positive ones. Instead of "he's going to be a delinquent," you think "he has some behaviors that he needs to learn to control." The result of successful cognitive coping is a calmer you—a you that is more ready and able to do something constructive about the problem.

One advantage to having a program worked out to deal with a behavior problem is that it gives you some alternative self-talk. Now when the problem occurs, you can say to yourself, "Here's an example of the behavior problem. I need to react to it by [whatever you've planned]. I also need to record it on my chart." Thinking positively about the program you are carrying out, rather than negatively about your child's behavior, may have the additional benefit of leaving you feeling a lot better.

Think—or talk to yourself—about it. It might also be helpful to talk with your mate, another parent, a teacher, or a counselor.

# Encouraging Alternative Behaviors

You can see by now that what we have been calling "problem behaviors" are, from your child's point of view, winning strategies. As far as he's concerned, there's nothing "bad" or "troublesome" about them. He has learned that they pay off.

Now, suddenly, you've decided to remove the payoff. A behavior that might have been scolded before is ignored. When he might have been chased before, he's now put in time-out. You are beginning a strategy to reduce problem behavior. But your child doesn't know that! All he sees is that the behaviors that used to be successful are now met with a different, nonrewarding consequence. And, as a result, he will soon be left to search for new ways to get your attention.

Here is where you can be his most effective guide. This is your chance to teach him appropriate, nonproblem behaviors that will get him what he wants.

You need to make it clear to your child—both in what you say and by what you do—that there is a wide variety of alternative behaviors that will be followed by a pleasant, rewarding consequence.

If we look in once again on Gary's family (see Chapter 16), we see that changing the consequences of his problem behavior (ignoring him when he was out of his seat) was only *part of* their approach. His family also decided to pay special attention to him when he was sitting at the table—to talk to him more often, to comment on his manners, and in general to include him in more of the mealtime activity. They were careful to reward Gary's "sitting" behavior.

If you are to change problem behavior successfully, then you, too, must show your child which desirable behaviors will be rewarded. It sounds simple enough, we know. But keep in mind that we all sometimes tend to "leave well enough alone." And, as in Gary's case, when this happens too often, children quickly look for ways of behaving that are difficult to ignore.

Your search for desirable behaviors to reward will be much more successful if you can think of ones that are incompatible with the problem behavior. For Gary, running around the room and sitting at the table were incompatible. If the "sitting" behavior is strengthened, the "running" behavior will necessarily weaken.

These two A-B-C patterns must exist together if Gary's behavior problem is to be effectively reduced.

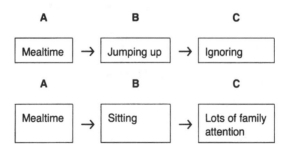

The strategies we have suggested so far, then, are only half-strategies. Take Roberta, for example. When her brothers and sisters leave for school, she pounds her fists, pulls at the drapes, and cries. Although at first Roberta may have been genuinely upset, we saw that her mother reinforced this behavior with attention and a toy. Therefore, it had become a predictable routine.

You'll remember our earlier suggestion that Roberta's mother begin to ignore Roberta during this tantrum. As you can see now, however, that strategy needs to be accompanied by her mother also rewarding incompatible behaviors. She should be ready with attention and a toy immediately when Roberta is not crying and away from the drapes, perhaps playing quietly or talking. An effective plan for reducing behavior problems, therefore, should always include two A-B-C diagrams.

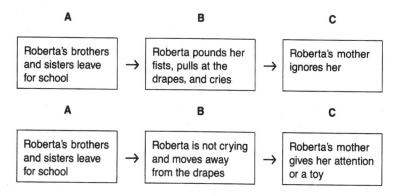

**Every program has these two parts: 1) discouraging the problem behavior and 2) encouraging alternative (incompatible if possible) behaviors.**

For a problem behavior that you wish to reduce, decide on an alternative, incompatible behavior that you can encourage and write it below:

_____

_____

## Contracts

We have talked throughout this book about using rewards to encourage behaviors. We have really been talking about simple agreements or contracts between you and your child. You state what you want your child to do ("Sit down here") and what you will "pay" for the behavior ("and I'll give you a toy"). Contracts can be simple contingencies that you state, or more complex agreements that you write down (as we discussed in Chapter 13 for home-care skills).

You can use simple contracts both to discourage problem behaviors and to encourage alternative behaviors. For example, Jennifer's mother could discourage the problem of Jennifer's crying with this simple contract: "Jennifer, I'm going to count how many times you cry today. If you don't cry more than three times, Dad will play catch with you when he comes home."

This contract assumes that Jennifer's mother knows that playing catch with Dad is rewarding for Jennifer. Mom might make this contract clearer to Jennifer by putting a chart on the refrigerator and drawing a check mark on it each time Jennifer cries. As the contract becomes successful, Mom would reduce the number of crying times allowed to two, then one, and perhaps even zero—though she may decide to leave room for an occasional legitimate cry. She would need to vary the reward some so that Jennifer would not get bored with playing catch.

Sarah's mother could decrease Sarah's stalling while dressing by encouraging the opposite—faster dressing—with this simple contract: "Sarah, I'm going to set the timer for 60 minutes. If you're dressed before the bell, we'll spend 'special time' together tonight."

This simple contract states 1) the desired behavior and 2) the reward. In the days ahead, the timer can be set for shorter periods until Sarah is dressing in a reasonable amount of time. And Sarah can share in deciding the reward. "Special time" might mean 20 minutes when Mom plays with Sarah—and Sarah gets to choose the activity.

José's parents encouraged alternatives to hitting with this simple contract: "José, if you play nicely with your sister until dinner [share toys, don't hit], you can have ice cream for dessert."

You will notice that these contracts reward the child either for reducing problem behavior, for increasing positive behavior, or both. Look for ways to make simple contracts with your child, giving rewards for lower rates of problem behaviors and for alternative positive behaviors. Remember, though, that if your child fulfills her side of the contract, you must always fulfill yours.

## Change the Antecedents

So far, we have talked primarily about changing the consequences of problem behaviors. Essentially, we have only considered the B-C part of the A-B-C pattern. Problem behaviors can also be changed by paying close attention to the antecedents, the A-B part of the pattern.

By antecedents, you'll recall, we mean the situation *just before the problem behavior occurred*. Some antecedents almost seem to guide children to act in troublesome ways. For example, a child might be more apt to cry when he's tired, to get "into things" when he's being ignored, to scream when he cannot do the task, or to fight over a toy with his sister when there's only one toy in the room. The list of situations that can point a child toward problem behaviors is a long one, indeed.

This section considers a variety of ways you can arrange your child's world so that it points him toward appropriate behavior.

***Teach Your Child New Skills***   In addition to encouraging specific alternative behaviors that are incompatible with the problem behavior, you can—and should—teach him a variety of new behaviors as well. A day filled with skills, after all, allows less time for problem behaviors. Gary's parents, for example, while continuing to ignore his "jumping up" behavior, might also have taught him some new mealtime skills, like cutting with a knife, pouring, or serving.

***Reward Your Other Children as Examples***   Show your child what behaviors you would like from him (and show him that these will pay off!) by rewarding your other children when they model these behaviors. This can be a strategy planned with the entire family. Other children can demonstrate the appropriate behavior, and your rewarding can be done in an exaggerated and obvious way. It can also just be done naturally.

For example, when Mark refuses to wash his hands, say, "Come and look, Dad, at how nicely Jimmy is washing his hands." This "rewarding others" strategy is a good one when you want to ignore your child's problem behavior and at the same time encourage an alternative behavior. Simply ignore his behavior, and praise someone else's!

***Set the Stage So Behavior Problems Arise Less in Teaching Sessions***   Even though you attempt to teach your child new skills and show him what is expected, behavior problems will nevertheless still arise while you try to teach. Often ignoring or time-out will not be effective since the child is, in fact, not seeking attention but trying to avoid an unpleasant task. You can help him behave appropriately by making certain that you have given him tasks appropriate to his current skill level and by being alert to cues that the task must be simplified (such as eyes wandering, squirming in the seat, whining, and so forth).

Our earlier chapters on skill teaching have stressed setting the stage for success—essentially arranging the antecedents so that your child will succeed easily. We have discussed aiming demands at your child's skill level and increasing them gradually, by small steps. We have talked also about the importance of choosing easy-to-manage materials, giving understandable directions, eliminating distractions, and so forth. All of these are examples of arranging the antecedents—or *setting the stage.*

***Set the Stage So Behavior Problems Arise Less Throughout the Day*** There are countless times throughout the day when changing the situation just a little reduces the likelihood of problem behaviors—simply giving your child something enjoyable to do, removing breakable objects, providing an extra toy, stepping in to help for a moment . . . .

Think for a moment about your daily routine. No doubt you have already made some adaptations to help your child get through the day more smoothly. Perhaps you eat earlier because that's when he gets hungry. Or you've lowered the toothbrush holder so that he can reach it. Or you cut his meat for him before you sit down to eat. There are countless ways in which you might already have changed antecedents to make problem behaviors less likely.

There are some situations where you can anticipate that your child will be upset—or will upset you! You can readily think of activities where he will be frightened—such as visits to the doctor, dentist, or even barber. You can also think of activities where he may be shy, such as going to a birthday party. You can think of times that he will be demanding (for example, in a toy store), noisy (in a church or temple), or overly active (in a restaurant).

For all of these, and more, use an **early warning system.** Anticipate how your child is likely to feel and behave, and then talk with him or her about the activity in advance. When fear is likely, explain each step of what will happen—and be honest. That is, don't say it won't hurt if it will. Think of some reassuring words that your child can say (*"All kids see the doctor. It's OK. Mom is here."*). Perhaps also plan an enjoyable activity that you can do together after the feared event.

When shyness is likely in social situations, again talk with him in advance—about who will be there, what they will do, and all the fun he's had at previous parties. Arrive early and help him to meet and begin to play with some other children.

When you anticipate noncompliant behavior—such as when it is time to leave that same party!—be sure again to talk in advance about what will happen and what behavior is expected. "We're going to the grocery store. We'll just buy the groceries that are on this list. You can help me put them in the basket. Please don't ask me for other things, because we aren't going to buy any. Do you understand?"

Obviously what you will say will depend on your child's ability to understand and on your own style of communicating. However worded, early warnings can prevent later disasters.

---

### ᐁ  A Caution

Make certain that you do not change antecedents so much that other aspects of your family life are entirely disrupted. Cooking only your child's favorite food may keep him at the table, but what about the rest of the family? Be sure to take them into consideration, too, when changing antecedents. If the change is going to be an uncomfortable one, it should be short-lived as you gradually phase conditions back to normal.

Always remember that you are changing your child's world in order to teach him something. Your own world should not be turned upside down in the process.

---

### Continue to Measure Behavior

Earlier in this chapter we discussed how to keep records of your child's problem behavior for a week or so before initiating a program. It is equally important that you continue record keeping after you begin your program as well. These "after" records will help you decide whether your program is working.

Take your "after" measure beginning with the first day of the program, and in the same way as you took the "before" measure (during the same time every day). Bobby's father (in our example in Chapter 16) kept these "before" records:

| | Week (Write in Date) | Days | | | | | | | Average |
|---|---|---|---|---|---|---|---|---|---|
| | | S | M | T | W | T | F | S | |
| Before | Week 1 3/21 – 3/27 | X X X X _4_ | X X X X X X X X _8_ | X X X X X X _6_ | X X X X X X _4_ | X X X X _3_ | Not home | X X X X X _5_ | _5_ |
| | Week 2 3/28 – 4/3 | X X X X X X X _7_ | X X X X X _4_ | X X X X X X _6_ | X X X X X X _5_ | X X X X X X X _7_ | X X X X _3_ | X X X X X X X X _8_ | _6_ |

His "after" records looked like this:

| | | | | | | | | | |
|---|---|---|---|---|---|---|---|---|---|
| **After** | Week 3 | XXX XXX XX 8 | XXX XXX XXX 9 | XXX XXX XX 8 | XXX XXX 6 | XXX X 4 | XXX 3 | XXX X 4 | 6 |
| | Week 4 | Not home | XXX XX 5 | XX 2 | X 1 | XX 2 | XXX 3 | XXX 3 | 3 |
| | Week 5 | X 1 | 0 | XX 2 | XX 2 | 0 | Not home | X 1 | 1 |

For Bobby, the weekly averages for hitting, kicking, or pushing looked like this.

BEFORE start of program:

1. Week 1: Average = 5 per day
2. Week 2: Average = 6 per day

AFTER start of program:

1. Week 3: Average = 6 per day
2. Week 4: Average = 3 per day
3. Week 5: Average = 1 per day

An average makes week-by-week comparisons easier to understand. As you can see, by the third week of the program, Bobby's problem behavior was greatly reduced.

As you begin your program and are continuing to record your child's behavior, remember that the problem behavior may get worse before it begins to get better. Stay with the program at this early and critical time and expect that very soon you'll see a change for the better. Once you've developed a program that makes sense to you, stay with it for several weeks. Give it a chance to work before you rush to change it.

# Summary

You are now ready to begin a program to reduce your child's behavior problem, using the following six steps:

1. Specify the behavior.
2. Measure the behavior: *Before.*

3. Identify the A-B-C pattern.
4. Change consequences.
   a. Identify a better consequence.
   b. Encourage alternative behaviors.
5. Change antecedents.
6. Continue to measure the behavior: *After.*

A final word: Behavior problem management is the most challenging teaching you will do. You may, therefore, find it helpful in the early stages to reread all or certain parts of this and the previous chapter. By all means, discuss your strategy with other family members and, if desired, your child's teacher or therapist. Once you have come up with an approach that seems sensible, stay with it . . . and good luck!

# David's Story: A Review

"Mom . . . David's up there again."

Having just heard the books falling to the floor, Mrs. McKay really didn't need Judy's signal; she was already on her way to the familiar living room scene. And there was David, playfully toppling over everything that stood in his way as he climbed to the top of the shelves. He loved being up there and hardly seemed to notice the damage his adventures caused.

"Get down from there this minute," ordered Mrs. McKay, and before waiting for David to respond she went over and dragged him off. "I told you not to climb up there anymore, didn't I?" But David simply smiled as he walked out of the room, looking forward, no doubt, to the time of his next adventure.

That evening, after David went to bed, Mr. and Mrs. McKay and Judy discussed ways they might begin to work on the climbing problem. "He's doing it more and more, it seems," said Mrs. McKay; "not listening to me, climbing on the bookshelves, breaking things on his way up . . . . it's terribly frustrating when he does that. Of course, neither of you are home as much as I am, so you don't see it as often. I used to think he did it just to get me upset (and it did!), but I find I keep calmer by telling myself that this doesn't have anything to do with me—he's just a very active kid. Believe me, though, it's got to stop."

"OK. You're talking about his climbing, right?" Mr. McKay asked. "Let's leave it at that for the moment, and forget that he sometimes doesn't listen. Now, how many times would you say he climbs on the shelves?"

"The other night when I was babysitting for him, he went up there six times. I counted," said Judy. "He was really having a ball."

"That's about right," said Mrs. McKay. "Sometimes it seems that whenever you turn your back on him, there he goes . . . all day . . . maybe as many as 10 times."

"All right then. Just so we can be sure, why don't we keep track—like Judy did the other night—of every time David climbs on the shelves. It shouldn't be too hard, since he doesn't seem to worry about giving himself away. We'll just do what we always do when he goes up there, only now, before we do, we'll remember to jot down each time on this chart . . . ." And Mr. McKay prepared the "before" chart.

At the end of 1 week, the McKays' faithfully kept chart looked like this:

| Week | Days | | | | | | | Average |
| (Write in Date) | S | M | T | W | T | F | S | |
| Week 1 | 5 | 9 | 6 | 8 | 7 | 4 | Not home | 6 ½ |

"Well, it looks like you were both right," said Mr. McKay. "The chart shows that David, in fact, climbed a total of 39 times for the week, not counting Saturday when we all went to Grandma's. Divide 39 by 6 days and that comes out to six and a half times a day. He's quite a climber all right."

"So what do we do now?" asked Judy. "Are you going to punish him or something when he does it?"

"I think that David might enjoy climbing just because he looks forward to the way we race in after him," answered Mrs. McKay. "I'm sure he gets a big kick out of all that extra attention."

"Makes sense to me," said Mr. McKay. "It sounds as though if we didn't make such a fuss over his being up there, he'd give up climbing soon enough."

In a few minutes a strategy for ignoring David's climbing behavior was agreed upon. "As you suggested, I'll take most of the things off the shelves—but I'll guarantee you it won't be easy to keep from running in after him. I just hope it works. But I suppose we'll find out soon enough."

Mrs. McKay was right. At times ignoring became almost impossible, especially for Judy who was always excited by her brother's adventures.

But they did it, and at the end of 2 weeks, their "after" records looked like this:

|        | S | M | T | W | T | F | S | Average |
|--------|---|---|---|---|---|---|---|---------|
| Week 1 | No record | 6 | 4 | 4 | 7 | 5 | 4 | 5 |
| Week 2 | 6 | 7 | 7 | 4 | 7 | 3 | 5 | 5½ |

"Now what? For 2 weeks we tried as hard as we could not to give any attention to David's climbing, and now look at him—he's climbing just about as many times now as he was then. And of course he's up there longer because we don't make him get down." Mrs. McKay clearly sounded as though she were giving up. "You know, to tell the truth I never really thought it would work anyway. But I'm glad we at least kept the records to prove it."

"To prove what, Mom?" asked Judy.

"Oh . . . to prove that there are some things that children like David will just always do, I suppose. Or at least that there's nothing we can do to stop him. And we certainly tried as hard as anyone could."

"But we were wrong, that's all," said Mr. McKay. "That's no reason to stop trying. Look at it this way: We took away what we thought was the most rewarding consequence to David's climbing behavior—our attention—and he kept on climbing anyway. That just shows we were wrong . . . and that he must be doing it for some other reason."

"I just think that he does it because he likes doing it," said Judy. "Like I said before, whenever I've seen him climb up there, it looks like he's having a ball."

"So then how do you stop making it fun for him?" asked Mrs. McKay.

They talked for quite awhile until Mrs. McKay finally answered her own question: "Whenever we catch him climbing on the shelves, we march him sternly to his room and make him stay put for 5 minutes, is that it?"

"That sounds right," agreed Mr. McKay. "And let's get him something to climb on outside."

The McKays were now certainly on the right track, but they had neglected the fact that David didn't really mind being in his room at all. Indeed, the first time Mr. McKay went to bring him out of time-out he found David playing happily with his toy soldiers. "He didn't even want to come out. If we're going to make climbing on the shelves have unpleasant consequences for him, then we'd better pick a less happy place for time-out."

It took time for the McKays to work out a successful program for reducing David's climbing behavior, certainly longer than the 2 weeks they originally planned. But were you to look in on them today, you'd find Mrs. McKay's candlesticks back up on the shelves where they had always belonged. The many adjustments they had to make, the way they had to continually rethink their strategy and work together as a team, finally paid off. Their consistent effort was well rewarded.

And as for David, he'll probably develop some new problem behaviors now and then—what child doesn't? But if you were to go and visit him today, you'd most likely find him playing in the backyard on the jungle gym that his father put together.

# Get Ready Skills

## Contents

### Basic Attention Skills

### Basic Gross Motor Skills

### Basic Fine Motor Skills and Activities

This appendix contains programs for teaching get ready skills. The most basic get ready skill is that of paying attention. The first section of this appendix builds upon the suggestions for teaching attention skills that were presented in Chapter 8. We then consider the related but more advanced get ready skills of identifying objects, following directions, and imitating. The child who knows what a ball and basket are (identifying objects), who can "stand on this line" (following directions), and who can "throw it like this" (imitating simple actions) is well on his way toward learning games and other skills.

The second and third sections include suggestions for increasing gross and fine motor skills, respectively, as self-help and play skills naturally build on these. These are simply illustrations—your child's teacher or therapist can suggest many other skills to teach.

Relax. Work patiently with your child on these programs. A teaching session usually will be short, 5 minutes or so. Teaching these get ready skills is especially hard work, but mastery of them will open up all kinds of learning possibilities for your child.

# Basic Attention Skills

## Looking When Called

**Setting the Stage**  Put your child in a chair directly in front of you, close enough so that your knees are nearly touching his. If your child is not likely to stay sitting in the chair, you can back his chair into a corner.

Praise his successful attempts enthusiastically. Use clear, specific language (e.g., "Good! You're sitting!").

Work on each step until your child successfully completes it four to five times. Remember not to push ahead too fast.

**Program**  Hold the reward in front of your face and, guiding your child's head, say, "Danny, look at me." Praise him and give him the reward. "Good! Danny looks at Mommy!" Hold the reward in front of your face and say, "Danny, look at me." This time give less assistance in guiding his head toward your face. Praise him and give him the reward. Hold the reward in front of your face and say, "Danny, look at me." This time just gently touch him under the chin. Praise him and give him the reward. Hold the reward in front of your face and say, "Danny, look at me." Give no physical guidance this time. Hold the reward in front of your face and say, "Danny, look at me." Hold his attention several seconds before rewarding him. Say, "Danny, look at me," and have the reward ready but out of sight. Praise him and give him the reward.

## Coming When Called

In order to begin this program, your child must be able to walk on his own.

*Setting the Stage*   Have your child stand in a corner facing you, and you stand one or two steps away. Each time your child comes to you, praise him enthusiastically and give him his reward. Stay on each of the following steps until your child is successful and comes to you four to five times in a row.

*Program*   With your hand on his shoulder, draw him toward you, saying, "Nick, come here." Touch his shoulder lightly, saying, "Nick, come here." Motion to him with your hands, saying, "Nick, come here." Say, "Nick, come here."

Now that your child will come to you when you call him from two steps away, begin standing farther away. First 3 feet, then 5 feet, 10 feet, then in the doorway of the room (10–15 feet).

Each time you move farther back, call him and also motion to him at first; when he comes successfully five times, then just call him to come.

Progress in teaching this skill may be very slow or fairly quick, depending upon how long it takes your child to learn that he only gets his reward if he comes when you call him.

Don't be discouraged if the program seems to be going just fine and all of a sudden you hit a snag. This

may just mean that you are moving a little too fast or that you need to try a different reward. Back up to a step your child knows well in order to let him experience success. Then begin the next step, spending a little more time on each step from then on. Vary your rewards so that you will always be using something he wants. Remember, it is important that each session end with success.

## Identifying Objects

Identifying (naming) objects like articles of clothing, body parts, or toys will help your child follow directions more easily. Our examples focus on naming toys and body parts, but you can use the same approach with other objects such as clothes and household items.

### Naming a Toy

*Materials* Begin with simple toys that your child will later use in play, such as a ball, doll, book, teddy bear, block, or stacking rings.

*Setting the Stage* Sit facing your child at a table that is completely clear except for the toy you want your child to identify. Alternatively, sit on the floor with your child if she is not likely to wander off. Start with only one toy at a time. For this example, let's start with a teddy bear.

*Program* Hold the teddy bear up so your child can see it; then say very clearly, "Bear. Look at the bear." Next put the bear on the table and say, "Give me the bear." If he doesn't respond, take his hands and clasp them around the bear, helping him to pick it up and hand it to you. Reward him with praise and a bite of his favorite snack.

*Note:* If your child does not respond, have someone else pick up the bear and hand it to you. Repeat this several times. Make sure your child is watching, and make sure he sees you reward the "someone else" for following your directions.

You are clearly showing him what "Give me the bear" means. You have made it easy for him by

- &#x2684; Choosing a useful object to identify
- &#x2684; Having only that one object on the table
- &#x2684; Telling him clearly what to do
- &#x2684; Showing him what to do
- &#x2684; Guiding his hand with yours
- &#x2684; Rewarding his progress

*Next Steps* After your child can give you the bear with your help, gradually phase out your guidance so that eventually he can give you the bear with no physical help at all. Next, teach the name for another toy in the same way. Use a toy that looks very different and whose name sounds very different from the first one. If the first toy was a bear, you might use a top or a stacking ring.

After your child can give you the second toy with no help, put both toys in front of him and ask for one. This will probably be hard for him at first, so you should be prepared to simplify the task by returning to one object if he shows signs of frustration.

Mix up the order in which you present the toys, give help as needed, and don't forget rewards.

### Where Is Your Nose?

*Setting the Stage* In a quiet room or area, sit facing your child on the floor or in chairs that put you both at about the same level.

*Program*   Tell your child, "Clinton, touch your nose," and show him by touching his nose. Tell him again, "Clinton, touch your nose," and take his hand in yours and guide him to touch his nose. Reward him with praise and his favorite snack. Repeat these steps three or four times until he seems comfortable with what you are doing.

*Next Steps*   Say, "Clinton, touch your nose," and show him by touching his nose. Put your hand on his hand and guide him to touch his nose, but take your hand away just before he touches it. Reward him with praise and his favorite snack. Repeat these steps until he can do them successfully three or four times in a row.

*Further Steps*   Say, "Clinton, touch your nose," and just point to his nose. This time just put your hand lightly on his arm to guide him. Reward him after he completes the task on his own. Repeat until he can do this successfully three or four times in a row.

*Final Steps*   Say, "Clinton, touch your nose," and point to his nose. Do not guide him at all. Reward him as soon as he responds correctly. Repeat until he can do this successfully three or four times in a row.

Eventually fade your pointing out so that he touches his nose with only a verbal prompt.

Continue this exercise with different parts of the body, one at a time.

*Note:* If you move to the final steps and your child does not touch his nose without guidance, you'll need to work longer on the previous step. Make sure you practice this step for a while, until your child needs almost no assistance.

## Incidental Teaching

You can further practice these skills incidentally whenever the opportunity arises. Again, keep your demands or prompts simple and give clear, specific feedback. For example, Danny's dad notices when Danny makes eye contact and says, "Good! Danny *looks* at the ice cream cone!" Nick will come to the table with his sister for supper, and Mom says, "Terrific! Nick *comes* to the table!" Clinton's brother takes a tissue and says, "Let's wipe your *nose*." Note that in these interactions you are also encouraging the comprehension and use of language by your child.

## Following Simple Directions

It will certainly be helpful to both you and your child if she learns to follow a wide variety of simple directions: "Look at the airplane," "Put the sweater in the drawer," "Bring the doll to Dad," and so on.

As she learns to identify the names of different toys, articles of clothing, and other objects, she becomes ready to learn to follow directions that apply to them.

You can teach her to understand several simple commands and to know the difference between them. Most of the directions you will expect your child to follow require simple actions: put, give, take, sit, get, stand, pick up, look, throw.

Teaching your child to follow directions involves our same approach, which by now must sound pretty familiar. Here are some guidelines to follow: Pick one simple direction to teach. Use familiar objects that your child can name (bear, block, shirt, etc.). At first, physically guide her to follow the direction. Gradually, give less physical guidance and use gestures to demonstrate the action. In this way, your child sees and also hears what you want her to do. By putting these two kinds of information together, she comes to understand the direction that she hears.

When your child has learned to understand and follow simple directions, she is ready to learn to tell the difference between them. Start by teaching your child the difference between two directions, and when she has mastered these, add more directions, one at a time.

Once your child has learned to discriminate among several directions, make a short list of these and get her to follow them in order. For example,

- ◈ "Look at the ball."
- ◈ "Give me the ball."
- ◈ "Throw me the ball."
- ◈ "Touch the ball."
- ◈ "Give the ball to Daddy."

You may find that your child enjoys continuing this excercise with a variety of different objects. Finally, mix up the objects and the directions. For example,

- ◈ "Look at the book."
- ◈ "Give me the shirt."
- ◈ "Throw me the ball."

## Imitating

Once your child learns to imitate, it will be easier for him to learn new games or play activities by watching other people.

### Clapping Hands

*Setting the Stage*  You and your child should be sitting facing each other, either on the floor or on chairs that put you both at about the same height.

*Program*   Say, "Greg, clap your hands," and show him by clapping your hands. Take his hands and clap them together. Say, "Good clapping!" and give him a piece of his favorite snack. (He hasn't done anything yet except let you clap his hands, but he sees that he gets a snack for doing that.)

Repeat this step until you see he is getting the idea; that is, he is beginning to move his hands to clap by himself. Then go on to the next steps.

*Next Steps*   Say, "Greg, clap your hands," and show him by clapping your hands. Give him less help—just touch his hands to guide him and remind him to clap. Praise him ("Good boy!") and give him his reward.

This time the task was harder. To get the snack, Greg had to do more of the clapping on his own. Eventually, fade out your help altogether. After he can imitate clapping three or four times in a row, teach him to imitate other actions in this same way. Here is a list of other simple actions you can teach.

✷ Stand up
✷ Jump
✷ Touch head
✷ Clap hands (once)
✷ Bang table (once)
✷ Clap hands over head
✷ Put two hands on table
✷ Touch toes

## Something Else to Try

After your child has learned to identify objects and body parts, follow directions, and imitate several different simple actions, he is ready for an imitation game that's similar to, but easier than, "Simon Says." Let's call this game "Dad Says," or "Mom Says," or "Sister Says"(or whoever). Eventually your child may even be able to be leader in this game.

Simply practice going through a list of all the actions your child can imitate. Be sure to make it fun—use rewards, especially lots of laughter and heaps of praise.

"Dad says, 'Clap your hands.'"
"Dad says, 'Touch your head.'"
"Dad says, 'Jump.'"
"Dad says, 'Sit down,'" and so on.

# BASIC GROSS MOTOR SKILLS

## Sitting Down

When your child is physically capable of sitting in a chair and can stand with support, you will want to teach her to sit in a chair by herself and to respond to your request to "sit down."

***Materials***   Use an appropriate-size chair, one in which your child's feet will be on the floor when she is sitting. Have the chair close enough to the table so your child can use the table for support. (It can be a low coffee table, sturdy box, stool, or something else, just so it is at the right level to give support.)

***Program***   Work on this program at times when your child would ordinarily be sitting (e.g., mealtimes, snack times, play times).

Bring your child to the chair; adjust it so the back of your child's legs are hitting the chair (just behind her knees).

Stand behind your child's chair and place her left hand on the tabletop. Place one of your hands on the back of her chair to support it and hold the chair steady. Place your other hand on her shoulder.

Say, "Yoko, sit down," gently pushing down on her shoulder to assist her in sitting.

Enthusiastically praise her ("Good, Yoko, you're sitting down!") and reward her immediately.

Gradually give your child less and less physical assistance. First use just slight pressure on her shoulder, then merely touch her shoulder, saying, "Yoko, sit down." Eventually she will sit down on her own when you bring her to a chair.

## Standing Up from a Chair

When your child is physically capable of standing up on his own, you want him to learn to respond correctly to you by getting out of his seat without your help when you ask him to "Stand up."

*Materials*    Use a chair that allows your child's feet to reach the floor when he is sitting.

*Program*    Standing behind your child's chair, put one hand under your child's arm and one on his back and guide him to a standing position. As soon as he is on his feet, immediately praise him ("Good! You're standing up!") and reward him.

Try this for several sessions until your child begins getting the idea and will cooperate by supporting his own weight once you've guided him part of the way out of his chair.

Gradually give him less and less of your help so that he will be able to do more and more of the standing on his own once you tell him, "Billy, stand up."

Place the chair so that it is against a wall and won't move.

Then stand just in front of him when he is sitting in the chair. Hold out your arms and make an upward motion, but do not lift him. Tell him, "Billy, stand up." Immediately praise and reward him when he stands up.

Eventually you will not have to motion; he will respond simply to the request, "Billy, stand up," and he will have mastered a new task, allowing him more independence.

## Walking

When your child is able to stand by herself, and walk while holding one of your hands, then begin to work on teaching her to walk on her own.

**Materials**     A favorite object or treat. Or maybe just a hug.

**Program**     Have her stand in a corner facing you. You stand just one step away with her favorite toy or treat. Motion to her to come, then give her the toy or treat, enthusiastically praising her for the attempt.

Next, have your child stand with her back to Dad or an older brother and you kneel down a step or so away. Again, motion to her to come to you and reward her with a treat or toy, along with your praise.

Gradually move farther away, requiring your child to walk a few more steps on her own.

## Going Up and Coming Down Stairs

To begin to learn these skills, your child must be able to stand and walk on his own.

**Materials**     The bottom stairstep or, better still, a single step.

**Program**     Begin with only one stairstep for your child to climb. Support his weight and let him hold onto you so that he feels secure as you lift first one of his legs, then the other, onto the single step.

Help him to get his balance so that he is standing steadily on the stairstep.

Keep repeating this each session until your child begins balancing himself without your help.

Gradually lift his feet less of the way up to the step; he will have to lift his feet more and more on his own. When he has learned to lift his own feet onto the step without your physical assistance, it is time to move on to a real flight of stairs.

**Flight of Stairs**     Begin at the bottom of the stairs. Have him hold onto the banister for support. You stand behind him helping him keep his balance.

At first, he needs to climb only one step to get your enthusiastic praise and his reward.

Gradually increase the number of steps he climbs in a session before you reward him. As you are working with him, gradually give less support until he is able to support himself completely by holding onto the banister or wall. Note that children first learn two feet on the same step. Alternating steps comes later.

***Coming Down Stairs***   Your child may be more hesitant, since this is a more difficult task to master. More balance as well as more caution is needed.

When your child is able to climb one or two real stairs by herself, then it is time to have her work on coming down the stairs, starting with the bottom one. Always give whatever support is necessary, then gradually phase it out.

Remember, these tasks may take quite a long time for your child to master. Although you are anxious for her to learn, your patience and small-step expectations are what make your child's success possible!

# Basic Fine Motor Skills and Activities

## Pushing, Pulling, Holding, and Turning

There are numerous basic motor skills that your child will use in self-help and play activities. You can use toys to teach your child these basic motor skills. Toy vehicles such as trucks, cars, or planes, for example, are ideal for demonstrating pushing to your child—simply show her how to push the car across the floor.

There are a number of pull-toys you can buy that are great for teaching your child pulling (all of which are preferred over your cat's or dog's tail!). These toys are usually plastic or wood and can be pulled along the floor by a string. They may be animals that wobble, bop, or hop, or cars that ride along on wheels. You can, of course, make your own pull-toy by simply tying a cord or piece of string to any toy that already has wheels.

Another fun way to teach pulling is to attach a piece of string around one of your child's favorite small stuffed animals. With you and your child seated at a table, lower the stuffed animal down over the edge of the table. Then pull it up, making it suddenly appear. Now place the string within your child's reach and see if she will pull it up; if she doesn't, give her a little help.

Holding is another basic motor skill that your child will need to learn. Begin by showing and guiding her, using a toy or object that she likes and that is easy for her to hold. Some children do not stay interested enough in a toy to actually hold it, so be sure to reward your child's initial touches and grasps.

Turning is a basic motor skill that you can teach using toys as well as objects you might find around the house. Two common store-bought toys that require turning are a jack-in-the-box and a busy-box. Show the child how to turn the handle that winds up the jack-in-the-box. Do most of it for her at first, until the clown is almost ready to pop up. Then help her to turn the handle and watch until the clown pops up. After a while, as you fade out your help, she will be turning the handle again and again! A busy-box can be placed flat on a table or floor or leaned against a wall. Most types have several knobs or handles that can be turned (as well as pushed or pulled, making this toy useful for teaching several basic motor skills). You can also use a kitchen utensil such as a handheld egg beater to teach turning. And don't forget—most doors have knobs that can be turned as well.

The following are suggestions for simple activities that help to develop your child's coordination. They are presented in order of increasing difficulty. For each activity, enthusiastically praise and reward all successful attempts. Guide your child through these activities as needed. When he can do the activity with you successfully four to five times, begin gradually fading out your physical support until he can do the activity on his own.

## Holding and Releasing Objects

*Materials*    Several different objects and an empty shoebox.

*Activity*    Begin with objects that are light, fairly small, and easy to hold (e.g., soft foam or cloth ball, round bath sponge).

Place the object in your child's hand, guide her to the box, remove your hand and hers, and let the object fall into the box.

When she can hold and release these light objects without your physical assistance, introduce objects of different sizes and firmness (e.g., blocks, toy cards, clothespins) one at a time.

Once your child is able to hold and release objects (putting them into the box when you place them in her hands), place an object on the table for her to pick up. Again, start with easy objects to grasp. Physically help her to pick up the object from the table, but then let her place the object in the box as she has learned.

When your child has mastered picking up, holding, and releasing objects, then begin having her take objects out of the box.

## Water Play

*Materials* Plastic containers, measuring cup, a plastic glass, funnel, squeeze bottle, newspapers, and a plastic dishpan.

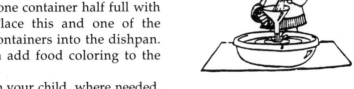

*Activity* Place the empty dishpan on a chair or table, depending upon the height of the child. Put newspapers under it.

Fill one container half full with water. Place this and one of the empty containers into the dishpan. (You can add food coloring to the water.)

Help your child, where needed, to pour the contents of one container into the other. Gradually remove your assistance and add more water to the container. Vary the containers.

This is a fun activity as well as an exercise in attention and coordination. It is a good basis for the future skill of pouring a drink into a glass.

## Putting Objects into Hole in Box

*Materials* Shoebox with a 3-inch square hole cut in top. Several different small objects (e.g., clothespins, large buttons, small blocks, empty thread spools).

*Activity* Have your child drop objects into the hole in the box top. Give her physical assistance as needed. This takes more control than just holding the object over the box and letting it fall in.

## Pinching

*Materials* Peanut butter, honey, jelly, dry cereal, pieces of cookie, and so forth.

*Activity* Place peanut butter, jelly, or honey on your child's thumb and index finger. Pinch them together a couple of times; then have your child lick them off. Do this several times to get him used to having his thumb and index finger work together.

Before meals, when you know your child is hungry, place small bite-size pieces of food between his thumb and index finger. Have him eat them before his actual meal. Help him hold the piece of food, if needed, while he brings it to his mouth. Start with only a couple of bites, then gradually increase the number of bites he eats before his meal.

When your child is able to hold the pieces of food and get them to his mouth after you have handed each one to him, then place one bite of food at a time on the highchair tray, plate, or table and have him pick it up. Help as needed.

This is the motion that is used when picking up small objects such as buttons, keys, poker chips, or money.

# Appendix B

# Self-Help  Skills Inventory

The skills featured in this Self-Help Skills Inventory are the same 30 skills contained in the Self-Help Checklist in Chapter 9. Each skill is broken down into degrees of mastery so that you can determine exactly what your child is currently able to do. This will allow you to plan an appropriate teaching program for your child.

Circle the highest number step your child can do. Circling a step means he can do that step and ALL of the steps before it. For example, if your child can do Steps 1, 2, and 4 of a skill and not Step 3, then you circle 2. Circle a step only if your child can perform the skill completely on his own—this means that he can do it while you are out of the room.

**Note:** Additional skills appear in the Self-Care Assessment (Chapter 12) and the Home-Care Assessment (Chapter 13).

## Drinking from a Cup

0. Cannot hold cup at all.
1. Holds cup and drinks, with your physical guidance throughout.
2. Places cup on table after you assist him to drink and brings cup partway down.
3. Places cup on table after you assist him to drink.
4. Drinks from cup after you help to raise cup partway; replaces cup on table on his own.
5. Drinks from cup after you help him pick it up; replaces cup on table on his own.
6. Drinks from cup completely on his own.
7. Drinks from a variety of cups and glasses, completely on his own.

# Eating with a Spoon

0. Cannot do any part of eating with a spoon.
1. Brings spoon to mouth, with physical guidance from you.
2. Brings spoon to mouth after you fill it and lift it partway.
3. Brings spoon to mouth and replaces it in food, after you fill it and lift it partway.
4. Brings spoon to mouth on own, after you fill it; replaces it in food.
5. Eats on his own with your assistance only in scooping food.
6. Uses spoon independently with soft solids (e.g., mashed potatoes, squash, oatmeal).
7. Uses spoon independently with soup.

# Eating with a Fork

0. Cannot do any part of eating with a fork.
1. Uses fork like a spoon (i.e., scoops with fork).
2. Stabs food with fork, with your guidance.
3. Stabs food with fork, with your directions.
4. Eats soft foods with fork completely on her own.
5. Eats a variety of foods with fork completely on her own.

# Spreading with a Knife

0. Cannot do any part of spreading with a knife.
1. Spreads part of a piece of bread, with your physical help.
2. Spreads a whole piece of bread with your help.
3. Spreads part of a piece of bread with you telling him where to spread.
4. Spreads a whole piece of bread with direction, after you have put jam on it.
5. Puts jam on bread with your help and spreads it on his own.
6. Puts jam on bread and spreads it, with your supervision.
7. Can get jam and bread and spread it completely on his own with no supervision.

# Cutting with a Knife

0. Cannot do any part of cutting with a knife.
1. Finishes cutting through food with your help after you have started the cut.
2. Cuts all the way through food, with your help.

3. Finishes cutting through started food on his own.
4. Cuts all the way through food on his own (you help him hold the food steady with the fork).
5. Holds fork steady on his own (once you have positioned it in the food) while he cuts through the food.
6. Positions fork in the food and cuts entirely on his own, when you tell him to.
7. Uses knife for cutting completely independently with no reminders.

# Removing Pants
# (Does not include unfastening)

0. Cannot remove pants.
1. Pulls pants off one leg after you remove pants from other leg.
2. Pulls both pants legs off from ankle, while sitting.
3. Pulls pants off from below knees, while sitting.
4. Pulls pants down from above knees, then sits and pulls them off.
5. Pulls pants down from mid-thigh, then off.
6. Pulls pants down from hips and off.
7. Removes pants completely, with your supervision.
8. Removes pants completely on her own.

# Putting on Pants
# (does not include fastening)

0. Cannot put on pants.
1. Pulls pants up to waist after you put them on up to hips.
2. Pulls pants up to waist after you put them on to the middle of his thighs.
3. Pulls pants up to waist after you put them over both feet.
4. Stands and pulls pants up to waist after you put them over both feet.
5. Puts pants on one foot and pulls up to waist after you hand them to him.
6. Puts pants on both feet and pulls up to waist after you hand them to him.
7. Puts pants on completely by himself.

# Putting on Socks

0. Cannot put on socks.
1. Pulls socks up from ankles.

2. Pulls socks up from heel.
3. Pulls socks up from toes.
4. Puts socks on completely, with heel in the correct position.

## Putting on a Pullover Shirt

0. Cannot put on a pullover shirt.
1. Pulls shirt down over her head after you place it on her head.
2. Pulls shirt down over her head and you put her arms in; then she pulls shirt down to waist.
3. Pulls shirt over her head and puts one arm in.
4. Pulls shirt over her head and puts both arms in.
5. Puts shirt on after you hand it to her.
6. Picks up pullover and puts it on completely on her own.

## Putting on a Front-Button Blouse, Shirt, or Coat (does not include buttoning)

0. Cannot put on a front-button blouse or shirt.
1. Grasps both sides of shirt front and brings them together after you put both arms through shirt sleeves.
2. Puts one arm in sleeve after you put his other arm in the other sleeve.
3. Puts both arms through sleeves after you hold the shirt for him.
4. Picks up shirt when laid out and puts one arm through.
5. Picks up shirt when laid out and puts both arms through.
6. Puts shirt on completely when laid out.
7. Takes shirt from drawer or hanger and puts on completely.

## Putting on Shoes (does not include tying)

0. Cannot put on shoes.
1. Pushes foot down into shoe after you put the shoe over heel.
2. Pulls shoe over heel after you put the shoe over her toes.
3. Slips her toes into shoe and finishes after you position shoe in her palm.
4. Puts shoe on after you hand it to her.
5. Puts on shoes.
6. Puts shoes on the correct feet completely on her own.
7. Puts shoes on and closes Velcro strips.

# Threading a Belt

0. Cannot thread a belt.
1. Pulls belt through loop after you start it.
2. Inserts belt into one or two loops and pulls it through.
3. Inserts and pulls belt through all loops, with pants off.
4. Inserts and pulls belt through all loops, with pants on.

# Buckling a Belt

0. Cannot buckle a belt.
1. Threads belt and inserts tab end through buckle.
2. Puts tooth of buckle into hole.
3. Buckles belt and inserts tab end through pant loop.

# Zipping Up

0. Cannot zip.
1. Pulls front zipper of jacket up the rest of the way (while you hold the bottom) once you start the zipper and pull it up to chest.
2. Pulls zipper all the way up (while you hold the bottom) once you have started the zipper.
3. Holds the bottom and pulls up with the other hand once you start the zipper. See skills listed under "Starting a Zipper."

# Buttoning

0. Cannot button.
1. Pulls button through buttonhole with one hand after you insert it halfway through.
2. Inserts button into buttonhole while you hold buttonhole open.
3. Inserts button halfway through buttonhole and pulls it through using both hands.
4. Buttons large buttons in view.
5. Buttons small buttons in view.
6. Buttons entire shirt or blouse with verbal direction only.
7. Buttons entire shirt or blouse completely independently.

# Starting a Zipper

0. Cannot start a zipper.
1. Puts insert into slide as you hold the slide of zipper ready.

2. Holds slide steady and places insert in, with direction.
3. Places insert into slide, holds it steady, and pulls up zipper, with direction.
4. Starts zipper completely on her own.

# Tying Shoes

0. Cannot tie shoes.
1. Pulls both laces to tighten.
2. Makes first knot.
3. Makes first loop of bow.
4. Makes second loop of bow.
5. Ties shoes completely.
6. Threads, laces, and ties shoes completely.

# Hanging Up Clothes

0. Cannot do any part of hanging up clothes.
1. Picks up and holds hanger in one hand, holds light coat in other hand.
2. Puts both shoulders of coat over hanger with your guidance.
3. Puts hanger into one shoulder of coat with your guidance, and puts other shoulder of coat over hanger himself.
4. Puts entire coat onto hanger when you tell him what to do.
5. Puts coat onto hanger completely on his own.
6. Hangs up other clothes (shirts, pants, dresses [for girls], etc.).
7. Hangs up all clothes when necessary, with no reminders.

# Drying Hands

0. Cannot do any part of drying hands.
1. Wipes palm of hands while you help hold towel.
2. Wipes back of hands while you help hold towel.
3. Wipes palm of hands holding towel himself.
4. Wipes back of hands holding towel himself.
5. Dries hands completely on his own.

# Washing Hands

0. Cannot do any part of washing hands.
1. Rinses soap off hands.
2. Puts soap on and lathers hands with your help.
3. Puts soap on and lathers hands herself.

4. Turns on water.
5. Turns off water.
6. Washes hands completely on her own.

# Brushing Teeth

0. Cannot do any part of brushing teeth.
1. Brushes teeth with your hands guiding his.
2. Brushes front teeth.
3. Brushes back teeth.
4. Brushes teeth once you have put toothpaste on brush.
5. Brushes teeth entirely on his own (puts toothpaste on brush).

# Washing Face

0. Cannot do any part of washing face.
1. Washes all parts of his face when you guide him with your hand on his.
2. Washes part of his face when you point to or tell him where to wash.
3. Washes all parts of his face.
4. Washes and rinses face completely on his own.

# Bathing—Drying

0. Cannot do any part of drying.
1. Dries upper body with your physical guidance.
2. Dries lower body and back with your physical guidance.
3. Dries upper body with you telling her where to dry.
4. Dries lower body and back with you telling her where to dry.
5. Dries upper body on her own.
6. Dries herself completely on her own.

# Bathing—Washing

0. Cannot do any part of bathing.
1. Rinses soap off with your physical guidance.
2. Rinses soap off on his own.
3. Washes upper body with your physical guidance.
4. Washes lower body and back with your physical guidance.
5. Washes upper body with you telling him where to wash.
6. Washes lower body and back with you telling him where to wash.

7. Washes upper body on his own.
8. Washes lower body on his own.

# Brushing Hair

0. Cannot do any part of hair brushing.
1. Brushes hair with your hands guiding her.
2. Brushes hair with you telling her where to brush.
3. Brushes hair completely on her own.

# Washing Hair

0. Cannot do any part of hair washing.
1. Dries hair with your help.
2. Wets and dries hair with your help.
3. Rinses soap from hair with your help.
4. Lathers hair with your help.
5. Rinses soap from hair on his own.
6. Lathers hair on his own.
7. Puts shampoo in hand and on hair on his own.
8. Dries hair on his own.
9. Completely washes hair on his own.

# Making a Bed

0. Cannot do any part of making a bed.
1. Pulls bedspread over pillow, after you have made the rest of the bed.
2. Folds sheet and blanket down to make a cuff, puts pillow on, and pulls spread over pillow.
3. Pulls up blanket and finishes making bed, after you have pulled up top sheet.
4. Pulls up top sheet and makes bed completely on his own.
5. Makes bed completely on his own and does it daily, without reminders.

# Setting the Table

0. Cannot do any part of setting table.
1. Puts glasses on table with direction once rest of table is set.
2. Puts glasses on table on his own once rest of table is set.
3. Puts spoons on table with direction once rest of table is set, and puts glasses on by himself.

4. Puts spoons and glasses on table by himself.
5. Puts knives and forks on table with direction, and puts spoons and glasses on by himself.
6. Puts knives, forks, spoons, and glasses on table by himself.
7. Puts plates on table with direction; puts knives, forks, spoons, and glasses on table by himself.
8. Puts plates, knives, forks, spoons, and glasses on table by himself.
9. Puts napkins next to plates with directions; puts forks, knives, spoons, and glasses on table by himself.
10. Sets table completely on own.

# Changing a Bed

0. Cannot do any part of changing a bed.
1. Places bedspread on bed after you have done the rest.
2. Tucks top sheet and blanket in at bottom of bed with your physical guidance.
3. Tucks top sheet and blanket in at bottom of bed on her own.
4. Places blanket on bed with your guidance.
5. Places blanket on bed on her own.
6. Places top sheet on bed with your guidance.
7. Places top sheet on bed on her own.
8. Places bottom sheet on bed and tucks it in all around bed with your guidance.
9. Places bottom sheet on bed and tucks in on her own.
10. Changes whole bed completely on her own.
11. Changes whole bed completely on her own, knows when it needs to be done, and does it with no reminders.

# Sweeping

0. Cannot do any part of sweeping.
1. Holds broom and makes sweeping motion with your guidance.
2. Holds broom and makes sweeping motion on his own.
3. Sweeps easy-to-see dirt (large particles of food, paper, etc.) with your guidance.
4. Sweeps easy-to-see dirt on his own.
5. Sweeps floor, getting all dirt into a pile, when you tell and show him where to sweep.
6. Sweeps dirt into dustpan while you hold dustpan.
7. Sweeps floor, getting all dirt into a pile on his own.
8. Sweeps dirt into dustpan, holding it himself.

9. Sweeps floor and picks up dirt in dustpan completely on his own.
10. #9, plus recognizes when floor needs sweeping.
11. #10, plus assesses work and corrects it until job is acceptable.

On the following page is a blank Progress Chart (discussed in detail in Chapter 9) that you may use to list the steps of the skill you intend to teach.

# Progress Chart

Program: _____

| List of Steps | Date | Step | Number of Attempts | | | | | | | | | | | | Notes |
|---|---|---|---|---|---|---|---|---|---|---|---|---|---|---|---|
| | | | 1 | 2 | 3 | 4 | 5 | 6 | 7 | 8 | 9 | 10 | 11 | 12 | |
| | | | | | | | | | | | | | | | |
| | | | | | | | | | | | | | | | |
| | | | | | | | | | | | | | | | |
| | | | | | | | | | | | | | | | |
| | | | | | | | | | | | | | | | |
| | | | | | | | | | | | | | | | |
| | | | | | | | | | | | | | | | |
| | | | | | | | | | | | | | | | |
| | | | | | | | | | | | | | | | |
| | | | | | | | | | | | | | | | |
| | | | | | | | | | | | | | | | |
| | | | | | | | | | | | | | | | |

277

# Appendix C

# Self-Help Skills Programs

## Contents

This appendix contains teaching programs for each of the skills listed in the Self-Help Checklist in Chapter 9. For each teaching program, decide what rewards you will use and have them ready. List several here:

_____

_____

_____

**Note:** It doesn't matter whether your child is right-handed or left-handed for most of these programs. However, if your child is a leftie, you will need to change the directions in a few cases (like starting a zipper).

# Drinking from a Cup

Before you teach this skill, your child should be able to drink from a cup while you hold it.

### Setting the Stage

Use a plastic, tumbler-type cup (no handle) or glass, small enough for your child to grip easily.

Fill the cup one-quarter full with your child's favorite drink.

Begin by planning your teaching times when your child is thirsty and you are not rushed—between meals is suggested. After you both become accustomed to the new program, any time your child has a drink is a time for teaching.

Seat your child at a table in a chair that is high enough for her to drink from comfortably. You can raise the height of a regular chair by using telephone books.

Note that the drink itself should be a sufficient reward for your child—along with your praise, of course.

### Program: Part 1

Standing behind your child, place her hands on the cup and your hands on top of hers throughout the entire session. Do all of the following steps.

1. Bring the cup up to her mouth.
2. Tilt the cup and allow her to take a swallow.
3. Return the cup to the table.
4. Remove your hands and also your child's. Say, "Good! You're drinking from a cup!"

Repeat the above steps until the cup is empty.

Continue with the above program for about four to five sessions or until you feel she is comfortable with your guiding her through Part 1 of the program.

Be sure that your guidance is light enough that your child does some of the work. She must be firmly holding onto the cup before you can begin Part 2 of the program.

When she is aware of the whole skill sequence of drinking from a cup, move on to Part 2 to teach her step by step.

## Program: Part 2

As your child masters one step and is able to perform it successfully for four or five sessions without your physical assistance, it's time to move on to the next step.

1. Continue guiding your child as in Part 1 of the program until just before her cup reaches the table. Then remove your hands from hers and allow her to complete the task by placing the cup on the table. This is her first step toward independent drinking!
2. Remove your hands from hers when the cup is three quarters of the way down to the table.
3. Remove your hands when the cup is one half of the way down to the table.
4. Remove your hands when the cup is one quarter of the way down to the table.
5. Remove your hands when she has swallowed, and let her return the cup all the way to the table. Your child has now mastered the last half of drinking from a cup! It's time to begin fading out your assistance on the way up to her mouth.
6. Assist your child with the cup until it is on her mouth. Remove your hands. Let her tilt the cup and take a swallow. Now she can return the cup to the table unassisted.
7. Assist your child with the cup until it is almost to her mouth. Remove your hands and let her bring it to her lips and take a swallow. Again, she can return it to the table unassisted.
8. Continue to fade out your assistance until your child masters the entire task.

# Eating with a Spoon

## Setting the Stage

Use a plastic bowl. A suction bottom or damp paper towel will keep the bowl from slipping.

For all three meals serve foods that can be eaten easily with a spoon. Examples: mashed potatoes, squash, bite-size pieces of hamburger, hot cereal, thick stews, applesauce.

Seat your child at a table in a chair that is high enough for him to eat from comfortably. You can raise the height of a regular chair by using telephone books.

## Program: Part 1

Standing behind your child, place the spoon in his hand and place his other hand on the side of the bowl. Place your hands on his throughout the meal.

1. Fill the spoon using a scooping action from right to left (if your child is left-handed, go from left to right).
2. Bring the spoon up to his mouth and let him eat the food from the spoon. Say, "Good! You're eating with a spoon!"
3. Return the spoon to the bowl and allow him time to swallow the food.
4. After he has eaten four or five spoonfuls, put the spoon on the table for a short rest.
5. Repeat the above program until mealtime is over, and then for another four or five meals or until you feel he is comfortable with your guiding him through Part 1 of the program. When he is aware of the whole skill sequence of eating with a spoon, move on to Part 2 to teach him step by step.

Notice that the steps in Part 2 teach three skills, using backward chaining for each: 1) getting the spoon to the mouth, 2) getting the spoon back into the bowl, and 3) scooping food.

## Program: Part 2

As your child masters one step and is able to successfully perform this new step for four or five meals in a row, it's time to move on to the next step.

1. With your hand on your child's hand, guide the spoon up to his mouth. Remove your hand from his. Allow him to eat the food from the spoon and remove the spoon from his mouth. Replace your hand on his and guide the spoon back to the bowl. Say, "Good! You're eating with a spoon!"
2. Remove your hand from his when the spoon is almost up to his mouth. Allow him to place the spoon into his mouth, eat the food, then bring the spoon a little farther down from his mouth. Then replace your hand on his and guide the spoon back to the bowl. Say, "Good! You're eating with a spoon!"
3. Remove your hand when the spoon is about halfway up to his mouth. Allow him to bring the spoon up to his mouth, eat the food, and bring the spoon halfway down to the bowl. Then replace your hand and guide the spoon back to the bowl. Say, "Good! You're eating with a spoon!"
4. Remove your hand after you have guided your child to scoop the food onto the spoon. Allow him to bring the spoon up to his mouth, eat the food, and bring the spoon back down to the bowl. Replace your hand on his and guide him in scooping. Say, "Good! You're eating with a spoon!"

Now your child has mastered all but the action of scooping the food onto the spoon. This is the most difficult step to master. When fading out your assistance in scooping, instead of removing your hand, hold your child's hand with a looser and looser grip until you are barely guiding his hand through the scooping action. Then place your hand on his wrist, then elbow, and guide him as necessary. Finally, remove your hand and the task is his!

**Note:** When you are guiding your child with your hand on his wrist, you can give this guidance by sitting next to him during meals.

# Eating with a Fork

Your child should know how to eat with a spoon before you begin to teach him to eat with a fork.

## Setting the Stage

Begin with a plastic bowl rather than a plate. This will make stabbing easier. A suction bottom or damp paper towel will keep the bowl from slipping.

Use foods that can be cut into pieces large enough to stab. Examples: chicken, carrots, waffles. Avoid foods like boiled potatoes or hamburger that will crumble when stabbed.

Seat your child in a chair that is high enough so that he can eat comfortably. You can raise the height of a regular chair by using telephone books.

## Program: Part 1

Stand behind your child and place a fork in his hand. Check the illustration—this is the correct position. If this is too difficult or uncomfortable for your child, he might be able to hold it another way and still learn to eat with a fork. Place your child's other hand on the bowl to keep it in one place.

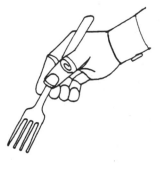

Guide your child through the following steps:

1. Place your hand around his hand and guide him in stabbing a piece of food with the fork.
2. Release your hand as he brings the fork up to his mouth.
3. When he returns the fork to his plate, place your hand on his again and help him to stab another piece of food. Say, "Good! You're eating with a fork!"

Continue in this manner until the meal is over.

When your child has mastered using the fork for stabbing with your physical guidance, it is time to fade out your assistance. Move on to Program: Part 2.

## Program: Part 2

Stay on each of the following steps until he can perform that step easily through four to five meals.

1. Guide your child to stab the food by placing your hand on his wrist.
2. Guide your child by placing your hand on his forearm.

3. Guide your child by placing your hand on his elbow.
4. Remove your hand altogether and be ready to help him as needed until he can use the fork on his own, and the skill is his!

Now that your child is able to stab food when it is in a bowl, begin using a plate and help him as needed.

# Spreading with a Knife

Mealtimes, or whenever your child normally eats a snack, are good times for teaching.

### Setting the Stage

Use easy-to-spread foods that your child likes. Certain foods (butter and jam) are easier to spread on toast; others (ketchup, mayonnaise, and mustard) are easy to spread on plain bread. Decide which foods to begin with on the basis of which the child likes best.

    In this program we use the example of spreading jam on toast. Get the toast ready by spooning enough jam to cover the slice onto the upper corners. (For a right-handed child, put the jam in the upper right-hand corner; for a left-handed child, put the jam in the upper left-hand corner). Use an easy-to-hold, blunt table knife.

### Program

Stay on each step, giving your child less and less assistance, until he can successfully do the step without your physical guidance for four to five teaching sessions. Then move on to the next step.

1. Have the child watch as you pick up and position the knife in one hand and hold the toast steady with the other. Spread the jam diagonally across the bread and cover about one third of the slice with each long, smooth stroke. When you have covered two thirds of the bread (two strokes), help him to position the knife in one hand and to hold the toast with the other. Lightly guide his hand as he completes spreading the jam. Say, "Good! You can spread with a knife!"
2. You spread one third (one long stroke) of the toast, then give him the knife and guide him in spreading the jam. Remove your hand

and let him do the last stroke. Say, "Good! You can spread with a knife!"

3. You place the jam on the bread and help him with the first stroke. He can now finish spreading the jam himself. Remember to praise him.

4. You place the jam on the toast and help him as needed to hold the toast while he spreads the jam. Say, "Good! You can spread with a knife!"

5. Gradually phase out your assistance in holding the toast until the task is his.

When your child can successfully spread with a knife, you can guide him in getting the jam out of the jar by using either a spoon or a knife. Have him spread with different foods (for instance, peanut butter) using toast, and then switch to bread.

# Cutting with a Knife

Your child should already know how to stab and eat meat using a fork, and know how to use a knife for spreading before beginning this program.

### Setting the Stage

Begin with foods that can be easily cut, such as pancakes, hamburgers, zucchini, fish, slices of ham, and bologna.

Use an easy-to-hold table knife.

Place a rubber place mat or wet paper towel under the plate to prevent slipping.

Mealtime is the best time for teaching this task. Have your child cut all her meat at the beginning of the meal.

Seat your child in a chair that is high enough so she can eat comfortably. You can raise the height of a regular chair by using telephone books.

**Note:** Your child can earn checks toward a special dessert or a favorite toy to play with after her meal.

### Program

Stay on each of the following steps, giving your child less and less assistance, until she can successfully do the step without your physical guidance for three or four teaching sessions. Then move on to the next step.

1. Standing behind your child, position the knife and fork in her hands. Be sure the knife is in her favored hand, which is usually the strongest. Place your hands on hers and cut most of the way through the food. Remove your hands and say, "Cut your food," and let her finish cutting through by herself. Remember to praise her. Say, "Good! You cut your food!" **Note:** You may have to help her hold her fork in place longer than you will have to help her hold the knife.
2. Repeat Step 1. However, this time remove your hands sooner and let her complete more of the cutting task by herself. Remember to praise her for cutting the food.
3. Position the knife and fork in your child's hands. Remove your hands and verbally direct your child to "Cut your food." Praise her for finishing the task. Say, "Good! You cut your food!"
4. Verbally direct your child to "Pick up the knife and fork." Help her as needed to position them for cutting. **Note:** Once she has cut one bite, she may need help in positioning the knife and fork for the next cut.

When your child is able to cut her food with your verbal directions, begin to phase these directions out one at a time until the task is hers. Later, with more difficult foods to cut (chops or steak), you may need to go back and help with some of the steps.

# Removing Pants

## Setting the Stage

Begin with short pants and underpants with elastic waistbands. These are easiest to remove.

Begin with his shoes off, as this makes pants easier to remove.

If pants have a button, snap, or zipper, you should undo these for your child.

Begin with him standing. It is easier to pull pants down while standing, then remove them while sitting on the floor, bed, or chair—whichever is easier for your child.

Stay on each step, giving your child less and less assistance, until he can successfully do the step for four to five teaching sessions without your physical guidance. Then move on to the next step. Have your child's rewards ready.

**Program**

1. With your child standing, you pull his pants down to his ankles. Have him sit down, then remove his pants from one foot. Say, "Take your pants off." Place his hands on the pants and guide him with your hands on his to pull the pants off his other foot and have him hand them to you. Then say, "Good! You took your pants off!" and give him his special treat.

    **Note:** Remember to remove the pants from the same foot first each session; following a routine will make his learning easier.
2. With your child standing, you pull his pants down to his ankles and then have him sit down. Say, "Take your pants off." Place his hands on the pants and guide him in pulling the pants off one foot. Let him take his pants off the other foot and hand them to you. Say, "Good! You took your pants off!" and give him his special treat.
3. With your child standing, you pull his pants down to his knees and place his hands on the sides of his pants with his thumbs inside the waistband. Say, "Take your pants off," then place your hands on his and guide him in pulling his pants down to his ankles. Have him sit down. He can now finish taking his pants off and hand them to you. Say, "Good! You took your pants off!" and give him a special treat.
4. When your child is able to take his pants off from his knees without your physical guidance, begin helping him remove them from mid-thigh, then hips, then waist.
5. Gradually give him less and less assistance until he is able to take his pants all the way down and off without any physical assistance from you after you have unfastened them. The skill is now his!

# Putting on Pants

### Setting the Stage

Begin with short pants or underpants with an elastic waistband, since these are easier than long pants.

If pants have a button, snap, or zipper, you should fasten them for your child.

Have him sit to put the pants over his feet, and stand to pull them up.

Stay on each step, giving your child less and less assistance, until he can successfully do the step for four to five teaching sessions without your physical guidance. Then move on to the next step. Have your child's rewards ready.

## Program

1. With your child sitting, you put his pants on both feet, then have him stand up. Pull the pants up to his hips. Then place his hands on the sides of the pants with his thumbs inside the waistband. Say, "Pull your pants up," and guide him with your hands on his to pull the pants up to his waist. Then say, "Good! You pulled your pants up!" and give him his special treat.

2. You put your child's pants on up to mid-thighs. Place his hands on the sides of the pants with his thumbs inside the waistband, saying, "Pull your pants up." Guide him with your hands on his to pull the pants up to his hips. Then allow him to finish pulling the pants up to his waist. Say, "Good! You pulled your pants up!" and give him his special treat.

3. Continue in the above manner, helping your child after you have put his pants on up to his knees, then later his ankles.

4. Sit beside your child and put the pants on one foot for him. Place his hands on the pants and, with your hands on his, say, "Put your pants on." Guide him in putting his pants on the second foot. Have your child stand up and finish putting on his pants without assistance. Praise him and give him the special treat.

5. With your child sitting, place his hands on the pants, saying, "Put your pants on." Guide him in putting his pants on the first foot. Remove your hands and he can now finish putting his pants on. When he has mastered this step, the task is his and he will be able to put on his pants without assistance once you hand them to him.

# Putting on Socks

## Setting the Stage

Use a loose-fitting sock.

Sit next to your child on the bed, floor, or chair, depending upon which is easiest for her.

Do the program for both socks at least once each teaching session.

Stay on each step, giving your child less and less assistance, until she can successfully do the step for four to five teaching sessions without your physical guidance. Then move on to the next step. Have your child's rewards ready.

## Program

1.  With your child sitting, you pull the sock up to her ankle for her. Then help her put her thumbs inside the sock and pull it up the rest of the way, giving her physical guidance as needed. Say, "Good! You put your sock on!" and give her the special treat.
2.  You pull the sock up to the heel. Say, "Put your sock on!" again helping her when needed. Then say, "Good! You put your sock on!" and give her the special treat.
3.  You pull the sock on to just over her toes. Say, "Put your sock on!" helping her when needed. Then say, "Good! You put your sock on!" and give her the special treat.
4.  Hand her the sock and direct her hands to her foot, saying, "Put your sock on!" helping her when needed. When the sock is on her foot, say, "Good! You put your sock on!" and give her the special treat.

Remember, progress comes slowly, and in general you will be giving her less and less assistance as you continue to give her verbal directions and praise.

# Putting on a Pullover Shirt

## Setting the Stage

Begin with a short-sleeve shirt or undershirt, since these will be easier than a long-sleeve shirt.

Begin with a shirt that is loose—maybe a size larger than he usually wears. Avoid turtlenecks for now.

Prepare the shirt for your child by laying it front-side down and then rolling the back half up from the bottom to the armholes.

**Note:** This is not the way most people learn to put their shirts on, so it may be unclear and seem awkward at first. Try it yourself and with other family members to become familiar with the program before you begin teaching your child.

Stay on each step, giving your child less and less assistance, until he can successfully do the step for four to five teaching sessions without your physical guidance. Then move on to the next step. Have your child's rewards ready.

# Program

1. Standing in front of your child, place both of his arms through the shirt and into the sleeves. Then lift his arms up over his head to bring the shirt into position with the neck opening on top of his head. Gently put his arms down to his sides. This will bring the shirt down over his head. Say, "Put your shirt on!" and place his hands on the bottom of the shirt with his thumbs tucked in the rolled-up part and guide him as needed in pulling his shirt down to his waist. Then say, "Good! You put your shirt on!" and give him his special treat.

2. You place both his arms into the shirt sleeves and lift his arms up over his head, saying, "Put your shirt on." Guide him as needed in putting his arms down to his sides. Remind him to finish by telling him to pull his shirt down. When he is done, say, "Good! You put your shirt on!" and give him his special treat.

3. You place both his arms into the shirt sleeves. Then say, "Put your shirt on"; guide him as needed in lifting his arms over his head. When he has brought his arms down and pulled his shirt down to his waist, say, "Good! You put your shirt on!" and give him his special treat.

4. You put the shirt on one arm. Help him in grasping the rolled-up shirt at the bottom with the hand that is already through the shirt sleeve and say, "Put your shirt on." Guide him as needed in putting his other arm in. When he has finished putting his shirt on himself, say, "Good! You put your shirt on!" and give him his special treat.

5. You hand him the rolled-up shirt and help him to grasp it at the bottom, saying, "Put your shirt on." Guide him as needed in putting his other arm in. When he has finished putting his shirt on himself, say, "Good! You put your shirt on!" and give him his special treat.

6. You hand him the rolled-up shirt and help him to grasp it at the bottom, saying, "Put your shirt on." Guide him as needed in putting his arm through. Then help him to release his grasp from the shirt and to grasp it again with the hand that is already through the shirt sleeve. He can now finish putting his shirt on. Say, "Good! You put your shirt on!" and give him his special treat. This is the most difficult step to master, so it will take more sessions than the other steps.

7. With the shirt laid out on the bed, front-side down, say, "Put your shirt on." Place his hands on the bottom of the shirt back and guide him in gathering the shirt up to the armholes. He can now finish putting his shirt on. Say, "Good! You put your shirt on!" and give him his special treat. Once he has mastered this step the task is his, and he will be able to put his shirt on without your assistance after you have laid it out for him.

# Putting on a Front-Button Blouse, Shirt, or Coat

## Setting the Stage

Begin with short-sleeve blouses or shirts, since these are easiest to maneuver. Avoid tight-fitting blouses in the beginning.

Stand behind the child when you are giving her assistance.

Try out this program yourself and with other family members first, since it is different from the way most people put on a blouse or shirt. Put a blouse or shirt on a bed and go through each step. What appears to be a complicated program is really quite simple, if you try it out first.

Lay the blouse on the bed (the neck of the blouse should be closest to you) with the front sides up. Open both sides of the front and lay them flat on the bed.

Have the child's rewards ready.

When first introducing this program to your child, you put her blouse on with her doing all the steps in the order presented below for four to five teaching sessions or until you both feel comfortable with this method. Remember to praise and reward her for her cooperation. Then move on to teach her step by step as outlined in the program.

## Program

1. Have your child stand facing the collar of the blouse, which lies on the bed as pictured. As you guide her to lean over the blouse, say, "Put your arms in." Guide both of her arms through the armholes and all the way through the sleeves. Have her now stand up straight.
2. Your child's arms are on the back side of the blouse. Place her hands so that they grasp the bottom of the blouse (which is now on top!).
3. With your hands on hers, guide her to lift her arms up and over her head, saying, "Put the blouse over your head."

4. Remove both your hands and hers from the blouse and guide her arms down to her side. The blouse will fall into place.

5. Guide your child's hands to reach back, grasp the blouse, and finish pulling it down; say, "Pull the back down."

6. Place her hands on each front edge of the blouse and assist her in pulling the blouse front together. Say, "Good! You put your blouse on!" and give her the special treat. Then button the blouse or shirt for her.

Stay on each step, giving your child less and less assistance, until she can successfully do the step without your physical assistance for four to five teaching sessions. Then move on to the next step.

First you do Steps 1 through 5 with your hands guiding hers. Then remove your hands and help her, as necessary, with Step 6 (pulling the front of her blouse together). Then say, "Good! You put your blouse on!" and give her the special treat.

Remove your hands after Step 4. Say, "Pull the back down," and guide her as necessary with Step 5 (pulling the back down). When she finishes the task by pulling the front together, praise her and give her the special treat.

Continue in this way, removing your hands a step sooner each time she has mastered a step until she can put her blouse on without your assistance—after you have positioned the blouse on the bed for her.

Help her as needed to position the blouse on the bed. Praise and reward her with the special treat.

If your child has already partially learned to put on a blouse a different way, then you might want to continue to teach that way. Think about the steps involved and write them down.

# Putting on Shoes

### Setting the Stage

Use a loafer or low tie shoe (sneakers are too tight fitting and difficult to handle when first learning).

With the lace shoes be sure to loosen the laces really well and pull the tongue way back.

Sit next to your child on the bed, floor, or chair, depending on which is easiest for him.

Do the program for both shoes at least once each teaching session.

Have your child's rewards ready.

## Program: Part 1

With your hands on your child's, guide him through all of the following steps.

1. Place the shoe, with the sole down, in the palm of his opposite hand. Say, "Put your shoe on."
2. Slip the shoe on over his toes.
3. Place the index finger of his other hand (his left hand if you are putting on his left shoe) in the heel and help him to pull the shoe the rest of the way over his heel.
4. Place this foot on the floor and help him push to be sure his foot is all the way in the shoe. Having your child stand up may help. Say, "Good! You put your shoe on!" and give him his special treat for his cooperation. Now you tie the shoe for him.

When your child is able to successfully put his shoes on with your physical guidance, then it is time to begin teaching him step by step. Move on to Part 2.

## Program: Part 2

First do Steps 1, 2, and 3 of Part 1 with your hands guiding his.

Remove your hands and have him do Step 4 (pushing foot down in shoe); say, "Put your shoe on." Guide him if needed.

When the shoe is on, say, "Good! You put your shoe on!" and give him a special treat for his success.

When your child is successful with Step 4 (for four to five sessions), then remove your hands after Step 2.

Help him by guiding him when necessary with Step 3 (pulling shoe over heel with index finger). This is the most difficult step, so it may take many sessions before he is ready to go on to the next step.

Continue in this way, removing your hands a step sooner each time he has mastered a step, until he can successfully put his shoes on without your physical assistance.

At this point you may still need to encourage every step, telling him, "Put your shoes on." Gradually fade out your directions so that he can do all the steps with no assistance.

# Threading a Belt

## Setting the Stage

Use a belt your child can handle comfortably: not too wide if he has small hands, and not too narrow if he is awkward with small things.

Choose a pair of pants that has large, easy-to-handle loops. Plan teaching sessions when he would normally be putting on pants.

Make this skill easier for your child by teaching him with his pants off. This way he can see everything he is doing and will not have to reach behind his back to thread the belt.

Have his rewards ready.

Threading a belt is different from most dressing skills, since the child is not putting an article of clothing on his body. Therefore, it might not seem as unnatural to undo what he has just done and practice the skill several times in one session. (With a young child this can be made into a game: "the train through the tunnel" or "snake in the hole," etc.) When he has threaded his belt for the last time in a given practice session, have him put on his pants and guide him through the steps of buckling his belt, since this will be one of the skills you will want to teach in the future.

## Program

Stay on each step, giving your child less and less assistance, until he can successfully do the step without your physical guidance for four to five teaching sessions. Then move on to the next step.

1. Thread the entire belt for your child. Tell him what you are doing. "I'm pulling the belt through the loops," and demonstrate how you "push it in" the loop and "pull it through."
2. Thread the entire belt except for the last loop. You start the belt tab in the last loop and then say, "Pull it through." Have him pull it through and then say, "Good! You put the belt on!" Give him his special treat.
3. Continue as in Step 2, having him pull the tab through one more belt loop each time until he can pull it through them all after you have inserted the belt tab in each loop.
4. For all but the last loop, insert the belt for him and have him pull it through. On the last loop say, "You put it in," and have him insert it and pull it through. If necessary, guide his hand in inserting the belt for the first few times.
5. When your child has mastered inserting and pulling the belt through the last loop, have him do the same for the last two loops, and then three loops, and so on, until he can thread the entire belt on his own.

When your child can thread his belt with just your verbal directions, begin phasing these directions out one at a time until he can thread his belt independently with just one direction—"Put the belt on your pants." When he has mastered this skill you can, if desired, have him thread his belt with his pants on. He will require your physical guidance for the loops in the back. Gradually phase this assistance out until he can perform the entire task on his own.

# Buckling a Belt

## Setting the Stage

Your child should already know how to thread his belt through the loops (see threading program) before you begin this program.

Use a belt for teaching that has as large a buckle as your child can handle comfortably. Use a belt that is long enough so that the tab will reach through the first pant loop, since it is easier to buckle with a long tab end.

Begin with the belt threaded and the pants on your child. Wear a belt yourself, so that you can model the steps for him. Place yourself beside him in such a position that you can both model and guide him. Have the child's rewards ready.

Begin by buckling your child's belt with him. Do all the steps below in the order presented, physically guiding his hands and giving verbal directions for four to five teaching sessions. Remember to praise him and reward him for his cooperation. Then begin to phase out your guidance as outlined in the program.

## Program

1. Hold the buckle in one hand. Say, "Hold the buckle."
2. Insert the tab end of the belt into the buckle with the other hand. Say, "Put the belt through the buckle."
3. Pull the tab end back with one hand until comfortable, then push the belt buckle flat against the body with the other hand. Say, "Pull."
4. Maintain pressure on the tab end with one hand while pushing the tooth into the nearest hole with the other hand. Say, "Put it in the hole."
5. With one hand lift up the other end of the buckle (if it has one), and with the other hand push the tab end under it. (For some belts, this step is unnecessary.) Say, "Push it through."

6. Insert the end of the tab into the belt loop with one hand. Say, "Put it through the loop."
7. Pull the tab through the belt loop with the other hand. Say, "Pull it through."

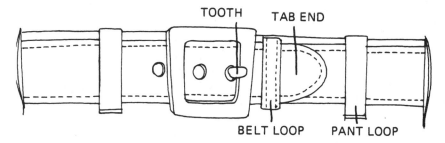

Stay on each step, giving your child less and less assistance, until he can successfully do the step without your physical guidance for four to five teaching sessions. Then move on to the next step.

You do Steps 1 through 6 with your child. With him watching you, show him on yourself how you pull the belt tab through the loop. Give him verbal directions—"Pull the tab through the loop"—then guide him as necessary to do this on his belt. Praise him by saying, "Good! You buckled your belt!" and give him his special treat.

You do Steps 1 through 5 with your child. Demonstrate Step 6 (inserting the belt tab into the pant loop). Then say, "Put it through the pant loop," and guide him as needed. He can now finish by doing Step 7 himself. Remember to praise him and give him his special treat.

Continue in this way, first demonstrating the step, then verbally directing him and guiding him as needed with each new step. He will be finishing more and more of the task as he learns each step, until the task is his. Remember to praise him with each step mastered.

When your child can buckle his belt with just your verbal directions, begin to phase out these directions one at a time until he can buckle his belt independently with just the one direction: "Buckle your belt."

# Zipping Up

## Setting the Stage

Begin with front zippers (jackets, sweaters), since these are easier than those that zip on the sides (skirts) or that are in positions harder to reach (pants, dresses).

Attach a small object (e.g., charm) onto the zipper tab with string or a key chain if your child has trouble holding on to the zipper tab.

Stay on each step, giving your child less and less assistance, until he can successfully do the step for four to five teaching sessions without your physical guidance. Then move on to the next step. Have your child's rewards ready.

## Program

1. You start the zipper and zip it up to the middle of your child's chest. Place his left hand on the bottom of the zipper to hold it down. Place his right hand on the zipper tab; say, "Pull up your zipper." Place your hands on his and guide him in zipping up the rest of the way, saying, "Look! You pulled up your zipper!" and give him his special treat.
2. You zip the zipper up to the middle of your child's chest. Then saying, "Pull up your zipper," help him to hold the bottom of the zipper with his left hand. Remove your right hand from his and guide his hand, if needed, in pulling up the zipper. Say, "Good! You zipped it up!" and give him his special treat.
3. Have him start pulling up the zipper from a couple of inches lower each time he masters a distance. Continue to help him to hold down the bottom of the zipper. Praise him each time he finishes the zipper. When he is able to finish zipping all the way from the bottom of the started zipper, begin phasing out your assistance in holding the bottom of the zipper (Step 4).
4. Have him pull the zipper all the way up with his right hand, but when he is a few inches from the top, remove your left hand from his and say, "Hold on." Have him finish the zipping without your guidance. Praise him and give him the special treat.
5. Remove your left hand from his hand (which holds the bottom of the zipper) a couple of inches sooner each time until he can do the whole task of zipping, once you have started the zipper, without your assistance. The new task is his!

When your child can zip up front-top zippers without difficulty, begin to work on trouser or skirt zippers. Holding and pulling up smaller zippers is more difficult, so it may be necessary to start at Step 1 again. In any case, give your child clear verbal directions, lots of praise, and special treats for each step he masters.

# Buttoning

## Setting the Stage

The larger the button and the easier it fits through the buttonhole, the easier the task.

Button all of the buttons for the child except the middle one. This button is the easiest for her to see, so it is the one she should begin with.

The illustration and directions are for a girl's blouse. If your child is a boy, the buttons will be on the opposite side, so reverse all right and left directions in the program (and, of course, use the term *shirt* instead of *blouse*).

If a mother is teaching a daughter, Mother should wear one of Dad's shirts. If she is teaching a son, her own blouse should be worn. By standing in front of the child she then provides a mirror image and the child can imitate her actions. A father teaching a son should demonstrate standing beside him.

Stand behind or beside your child when giving physical guidance. Wear a blouse or shirt yourself so you can demonstrate each step for her during teaching sessions. Have the child's rewards ready.

There are four main steps in buttoning:

1. Holding the buttonhole open
2. Inserting the button
3. Pinching the button to pull it through
4. Pulling the buttonhole edge of the shirt over the button

The following program teaches these steps through backward chaining.

## Program

Stay on each step, giving your child less and less assistance, until she can successfully do the step without your physical guidance for four to five teaching sessions. Then move on to the next step.

1. You insert the button halfway through the hole and hold the button. Say, "Button your blouse," and guide her to pinch the buttonhole edge of the material between her thumb and index finger of her left hand and pull the material over the button. Say, "Good! You buttoned your blouse!" and give her the special treat.
2. After you have inserted the button halfway through the hole, have the child pinch the button with the thumb and index finger of her right hand. Then let her finish by pulling the buttonhole edge of the material over the button. Say, "Good! You buttoned your blouse!" and give her the special treat.
3. Help the child pinch the edge of the button with the thumb and index finger of her left hand while you are holding the buttonhole open for her. Say, "Push it in," and guide her to insert the button into the hole.

Remind her to pinch the other end of the button with her right hand. She can now finish buttoning by pulling the buttonhole edge of the material over the button. Praise her and give her the special treat.

4. Help her to grasp the buttonhole with the thumb and index finger of her right hand, making sure that the tip of her thumb is in the buttonhole. Guide her, as she inserts the button into the hole with her left hand, to move her right index finger so she can grasp the button with her right thumb and index finger as the button comes through the hole. She can now finish buttoning the button herself. Praise her and give her the special treat.

   **Note:** Step 4 contains two different tasks—holding the buttonhole open and moving the index finger down to grasp the button. Since we perform them almost as one step, they are taught together.

5. When she can button the middle button without your help, then you button one less button and guide her when necessary until she buttons all the buttons.

Begin now to work on buttoning smaller front buttons and side buttons. Since these are more difficult, it may be necessary to back up and begin with earlier steps. Remember to give clear verbal directions, lots of praise, and special treats along the way.

# Starting a Zipper

Your child should already have mastered pulling up a zipper, unassisted, before you begin teaching this skill.

### Setting the Stage

Use large zippers—they are easier for a child to handle. Begin with a coat or heavy sweater where the end of the zipper is within easy reach. Save light jackets for later.

Put a zipper-front coat or sweater on yourself so you can demonstrate (model) each step as she is learning. Stand behind or beside the child while you are guiding her. Have the child's rewards ready.

### Program

Stay on each step, giving the child less and less assistance, until she can successfully do the step without your physical assistance for four to five teaching sessions. Then move on to the next step.

1. Make sure your child is looking at the zipper, then position the fingers of her left hand around the insert part of the zipper. Place her right

hand on the slide. With your hands on hers, say, "Start your zipper," and guide her in raising the insert and placing it all the way down into the slide. Say, "Good! You started the zipper!" Now guide her left hand to hold on to the slide bottom. Remove your right hand from hers. Direct her to take the zipper tab with her right hand and pull it up.

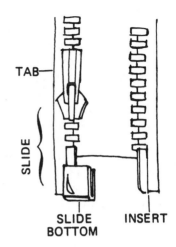

2. With your hands on hers, guide her in placing the insert partway into the slide; say, "Start your zipper." Remove your left hand from hers and let her push the insert all the way into the slide. Assist her in holding the slide bottom with her left hand while she starts zipping up with her right hand.

3. Help her hold the slide in her right hand as you have in previous steps. Then say, "Start your zipper," and have her place the insert all the way into the slide by herself. Say, "Good, you started the zipper." Remind her to hold the bottom of the slide with her left hand while she starts to zip. Remember to reward her. Now that she can put the insert all the way into the slide with her left hand, it's time to start phasing out your assistance in holding the slide steady with her right hand.

4. Remove your right hand from hers a little sooner each time that she places the insert into the slide, until your assistance is no longer needed and the task is hers. This is a difficult step and may take more time than the others for your child to learn.

Once she has mastered starting a large zipper, begin to teach her on a smaller one (light jacket). Help her as needed. This may mean starting with Step 1 again.

# Tying Shoes

### Setting the Stage

Use two pairs of shoelaces—one black and one white. Cut one quarter of each lace off and discard it.

Tie the cut ends of a black lace and a white lace together to make one lace. Then tie the cut ends of the other two laces together for the other shoe.

Lace up each shoe so that the excess black lace is on your child's left (when shoe is on her), the excess white on her right.

Choose a position (sitting in a chair, standing with foot on stool or chair, or bending over from a chair) that is comfortable for your child.

Do the program when your child normally puts on her shoes. Also, hold practice sessions with a shoe on the table in the same position as if it were on your child's foot (i.e., heel close to her, toe away). Be sure to lace the practice shoe with a black and white lace first.

This is a difficult program, so practice it yourself and with other family members until you are comfortable with it before teaching. Have your child's rewards ready.

**Note:** You may want to offer your child an extra special reward (say, a toy she's been wanting) for learning this difficult task. Reward her as usual for each teaching session also.

## Program

### *Tying the First Knot*

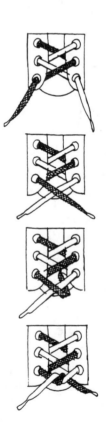

1. Take a lace in each hand, between thumb and index finger (black in left, white in right) and pull the laces tight by pulling up. Then drop them.
2. Cross the white lace down toward the heel of the shoe and drop it. Cross the black lace down over the white lace and drop it.
3. Pick up the tip of the black lace with the right hand. Put the tip of the black lace under the white, pushing it through toward the toe of the shoe, then drop it.
4. Pick up the tip of the white lace with the left hand and the black with the right. Pull both to tighten, then drop both laces.

Stay on each step, giving your child less and less assistance, until she can successfully do the step without your physical assistance for three to four teaching sessions. Then move on to the next step.

Do Steps 1 through 3 for your child. Then guide her to pick up the tip of the white lace with her left hand and the black lace with her right, saying, "Pull them tight"; guide her as needed. Then say, "Good! You made the knot!" and give her the reward.

You do Steps 1 and 2 for her. Guide her to pick up the tip of the black lace with her right hand and put it under and through the white lace toward the toe of the shoe. Verbally direct her to "Pull them both tight." Praise her and give her the reward when she finishes making the knot.

Continue in the same fashion, doing one less step for her each time she masters a step until she can make the first knot without your physical assistance. Then move on to teach her to make the bow.

### Making the Bow

1. Use the thumb and index finger of the left hand to pick up the black lace one third of the way from the knot.

   Use the thumb and index finger of the right hand to hold the same lace two thirds of the way from the knot.

   Make the loop by bringing the right hand to join at the bottom of the black lace at the knot.

   Have your child hold the bottom of the looped black lace firmly with the thumb and index finger of the right hand, and let the left hand go.

   Place the newly joined black loop down on top of the white lace so that it lies on the shoe with the black loop facing sideways and pointing to the left side of the shoe.
2. Pick up the white lace in the right hand and place the white lace over the black loop with the end of the white lace pointing toward the toe of the shoe. Then drop the lace.
3. Hold the black loop in the thumb and index finger of the left hand fairly close to the knot.
4. Place the index finger of the right hand on top of the white lace one third of the way up from the knot (the end of the white lace is still facing the toe of the shoe).

   Push the white lace through the opening from behind the black loop, pushing the lace toward the heel of the shoe. Remove the right index finger.

   Pick up the newly made white loop between the thumb and index finger of the right hand and pull both loops tight.

Stay on each step, giving your child less and less assistance until she can successfully do the step without your physical guidance for three or four teaching sessions. Then move on to the next step.

Teach your child to make the bow in the same way as you taught her to make the first knot.

Begin by doing all the steps for your child except the last one. Give her directions and physical guidance as needed with each step she is learning. Give her clear verbal directions along the way: "Pull the lace," "Hold the loop," "Hold it here," "Pull both loops tight."

Remember to praise and reward her as she learns each step, until she has mastered this new and difficult task.

When your child has mastered tying shoes with the black and white laces, then lace her shoes with regular laces and help her as needed.

# Hanging Up Clothes

Your child should be able to button and zip clothes before beginning this program.

### Setting the Stage

Use a large wooden hanger, and place it on the bed.

Begin with an article of clothing that is easy for your child to handle, like a shirt, blouse, or light coat.

Place the article on the bed with the front facing up and the collar away from you.

Have a stool ready if your child cannot reach the clothes rod in the closet. Have your child's rewards ready.

### Program

1.  Pick up the hanger and hold it in your right hand. Say, "Pick the hanger up in this hand."
2.  While leaving the coat flat on the bed, pick up the shoulder on your left with your left hand. Say, "Hold the coat up here."
3.  Slide the hanger into the left sleeve with your right hand, then set it down and remove both hands. Say, "Push the hanger in here."
4.  Hold the hanger steady by pressing on it lightly with your left hand. Say, "Press the hanger here."
5.  Hold up the shoulder on the right side with your right hand. Say, "Hold the coat up here."

6. Place the right shoulder over the exposed part of the hanger. Say, "Put the coat over the hanger."
7. Fasten the coat near the top so it will stay on the hanger. Say, "Button the coat."
8. Grasp the hanger near the hook part, lifting it off the bed, and then hang the coat up. Say, "Hang up your coat."

**Note:** Do not pick the coat up by the hook, since you will have to shift hands before the coat can be hung on the closet rod.

Stay on each step, giving your child less and less assistance, until she can do the step without your physical guidance for three or four teaching sessions. Then teach her the next step.

With your hands on your child's, guide her through Steps 1 through 7. Tell her what you are doing as you guide her. Remove your hands and say, "Hang up your coat"; help her as needed. Praise her with, "Good! You hung up your coat!" and give her the reward.

With your hands on your child's, guide her through Steps 1 through 6. Remove your hands and say "Button (or zip) up your coat." Help her as needed with this, then say, "Hang up your coat." She can now do this step herself.

Continue in this way, removing your hands a step sooner each time she has mastered a step until she can successfully do all the steps involved in putting clothes onto a hanger without your physical guidance.

When your child is able to use the hanger with just your verbal directions, begin to phase out these directions one at a time starting with the last direction, "Hang up your coat," until she can do all the steps involved with no directions from you.

# Drying Hands

## Setting the Stage

Use a large towel. Fold it over the rack and fasten the two sides together just below the rack with a safety pin so that it won't slip off the rack.

Make sure the rack is low enough for your child to reach easily. If not, get a wide stool for her to stand on.

Have your child's rewards ready.

## Program: Part 1

With your hands on your child's hands, guide her through the following steps.

1. Place one of her hands behind the towel.
2. Wipe the palm of her other hand.
3. Turn her hand over and wipe the back.
4. Place her dry hand behind the towel.
5. Wipe the palm of her other hand.
6. Turn her hand over and wipe the back. Say, "Good! You dried your hands!" and give her a special treat for her cooperation.

When your child is able to successfully dry her hands with your physical guidance, then begin to phase out your assistance. Move on to Part 2.

## Program: Part 2

First do Steps 1 through 5 with your hands guiding hers. Then remove your hands and, guiding her, if necessary, with your hand on her elbow, have her do Step 6. Say, "Good girl! You dried your hands!" Give her a special treat for her success.

When your child is successful with Step 6 for four to five sessions, then remove your hands after Step 4 and have her do Steps 5 and 6, guiding her when needed.

Continue in this way, removing your hands a step sooner each time she has mastered a step until she can successfully do the task on her own.

# Washing Hands

Your child should be able to dry his hands before beginning this program.

## Water Play

Water play is a good way to get your child accustomed to water flowing over his hands before beginning the actual hand-washing program. Place several small plastic containers into a plastic dishpan with a small amount of water in it. Help your child in filling the containers and pouring the water out over his hands. Use cold water for this, since he will be learning to wash his hands with cold water.

Add a bar of soap cut to fit the size of his hands. Help him pick the soap up out of the water and place it into a container. This will give him practice in grasping, holding, and releasing the wet, slippery soap. These play skills will make the task of learning to wash hands easier for both you and your child.

Also, in the weeks or months before beginning to teach hand washing when you are washing your child's hands for him, follow the sequence of steps listed in this program. Later, teaching will come more easily.

## Setting the Stage

Every time his hands are washed is a good teaching time.

Use a low stool with a wide base if your child needs it to be able to reach the sink.

Cut a bar of soap so it fits into the palm of his hand, since this will be easier for your child to handle. Also, new soap is easier to hold.

Use a soap dish, wet washcloth, or wet paper towel to help prevent the soap from slipping off the sink.

Mark the cold water faucet with bright colored tape or nail polish. (If there is one faucet for both hot and cold water, then you adjust the water temperature for your child before teaching.)

Have your child's rewards ready.

## Program: Part 1

Stand behind your child and, with your hands on his, guide him through the following steps.

1. Turn on the cold water.
2. Place both his hands under the water; say, "Wash your hands."
3. Help him pick up the soap using one or both of his hands—whichever is easier for him.
4. Rub the soap between the palms of his hands. This might best be done by first having him hold the soap with one hand, and rubbing the other hand on the soap, then switching hands.
5. Place the soap back down on the sink.
6. Rub the back of one hand with the soapy palm of the other.
7. Do the same for the back of his other hand.
8. Place both hands under the water and rinse his hands, rubbing them together until the suds are gone.

Say, "Good! You washed your hands! Now let's turn the water off." Help him turn off the water.

**Note:** Always use the same hand order when doing Steps 4, 6, and 7, as this routine will make his learning easier.

For some children, turning off the water may be rewarding in itself. If this is enjoyable for your child, fine, but if he could be reinforced more by a special treat, give it to him for his cooperation.

When your child is able to wash his hands with your physical assistance, begin teaching him step by step. Move on to Part 2.

**Program: Part 2**

As your child masters one step and is able to successfully perform this step without your physical assistance for four or five teaching sessions, then it's time to move back to the next step (backward chaining).

Guide your child through Steps 1 through 7 in Part 1. Then remove your hands and help him as needed in rinsing his hands (Step 8). (Guide him by placing your hands on his elbows to direct them under the running water.) Then say, "Good! You washed your hands!" Help him as needed in turning off the water, then give him his special treat.

When he has mastered Step 8, remove your hands after Step 6 and guide him as needed (your hand on his elbow) to rub the back of one hand with the soapy palm of the other hand, saying, "Wash your hands." He can now finish the task by rinsing his hands. Help him if needed in turning off the water. Then say, "Good! You washed your hands!" and give him his special treat. Continue to teach each step in the sequence using backward chaining.

# Brushing Teeth

### Setting the Stage

Use a soft, child-size toothbrush. If the toothbrush is hard, run it under hot water to soften it. Use tasty (not strong or stinging) toothpaste—there are brands especially for children. Prepare the toothbrush by putting the toothpaste on the brush for your child.

After meals and before bed are good times for teaching. Stand behind or beside your child while guiding her. Use a wide-base stool or carton, if needed, so that she can see in the mirror.

Remember one rule: Brush the way the teeth grow—down on the top teeth and up on the button. Have the child's rewards ready.

Place the toothbrush in your child's hand and physically guide her through the steps below for four to five teaching sessions. Remember to praise and reward her for her cooperation. Then move on to teach her step by step as outlined in the program.

### Program

1. Say, "Show your teeth." You show your teeth for her while she is looking in the mirror. (Open lips and smile with your teeth together.) Say, "Good! I see your teeth."
2. Place the toothbrush on the front teeth. Brush in an up-and-down motion, saying, "Brush up and down." Continue brushing up and

down for the fronts of teeth on the left side of her mouth and back to the front teeth again.

3. Take the toothbrush out of her mouth and turn her wrist so the toothbrush is now pointing toward the right side of her mouth. Place the brush on her teeth and brush in an up-and-down motion on the right side of her mouth. Remove the toothbrush, offer her a sip of water to rinse her mouth, and say, "Spit it out." Show her this if she does not know how.

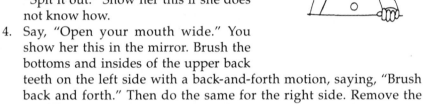

4. Say, "Open your mouth wide." You show her this in the mirror. Brush the bottoms and insides of the upper back teeth on the left side with a back-and-forth motion, saying, "Brush back and forth." Then do the same for the right side. Remove the toothbrush and offer her a sip of water to rinse her mouth.

5. Say, "Open your mouth wide again." Brush her lower back teeth, first on the left, then on the right, saying, "Brush back and forth." Remove the toothbrush and offer her water to rinse her mouth. Praise her by saying, "Good! You brushed your teeth!" and give her something special to play with for her cooperation.

With your hand on your child's, do Steps 1 through 4 with her, then guide her in the following way with Step 5:

1. With your hand on her wrist for four to five teaching sessions
2. With your hand on her forearm for four to five teaching sessions
3. With your hand on her elbow for four to five teaching sessions
4. Remove your hand, point to show her the area, and give verbal directions throughout the step

With your hands on hers, do Steps 1 through 3 with her, then guide her as above with Step 4; she can now finish with just your directions. Continue in this way, step by step, until she can brush without any physical guidance, but with verbal directions for each step.

When your child can brush her teeth with your verbal directions, begin to phase out these directions one at a time until she can brush her teeth independently, with just the one direction, "Brush your teeth." You can then teach her to prepare the toothbrush and to clean it after brushing.

# Washing Face

## Setting the Stage

Stand your child in front of a mirror to let her see her actions, to keep her attention, and to make the task more enjoyable. Use a wide-base stool, if needed, for your child to reach the sink.

Begin teaching after meals. It is easier for your child to know her face is clean if she can see it's dirty before she washes. When both you and she become familiar with the program, any time you would wash her face becomes a teaching session.

Wait to use soap until your child is able to wash her face well with just a wet washcloth. Wet the washcloth and fold and tuck it around your child's hand like a mitten. Have the child's rewards ready.

## Program: Part 1

Stand behind your child. Place your hand on hers and guide her through all of the following steps, giving verbal directions with each step.

1. Rub one of her cheeks with the washcloth. Say, "Wash your cheek."
2. Rub her chin. Say, "Wash your chin."
3. Rub her other cheek. Say, "Wash your cheek."
4. Rub her upper lip and mouth. Say, "Wash your mouth."
5. Rub her nose. Say, "Wash your nose."
6. Rub her forehead. Say, "Wash your forehead."

Say, "Good, you washed your face," and give her a special treat for her cooperation.

When your child is able to wash her face with your physical assistance, then it is time to teach her step by step. Move on to Part 2.

## Program: Part 2

When your child is able to successfully do a step without your physical assistance for four or five teaching sessions, then it is time to move on to the next step.

1. With your hand on your child's, guide her through Steps 1–5 of Part 1. Then remove your hand and say, "Wash your forehead." Point to her forehead with your finger. Guide her as needed. You may have to remove your hand gradually; that is, guide her from the wrist and then from the elbow. When she has finished, say, "Good! You washed your face!" and give her the special treat.
2. Remove your hand after Step 4 and say, "Wash your nose." Point to her nose with your finger. Guide her as needed. When she has

washed her nose, point to her forehead and say, "Wash your forehead." When she has finished, say, "Good! You washed your face!" and give her the special treat.

3.  Continue in this way, removing your hand a step sooner each time she has mastered a step, until she can wash her face without your physical assistance. At this point you are still giving her help by pointing to each part of her face and giving verbal directions.

4.  Phase out your help by gradually pointing less but still giving verbal directions. When she is able to wash her face with just your verbal reminders, begin to phase out your verbal directions one at a time until she can do all the steps in face washing with no assistance from you.

# Bathing

### Setting the Stage

Put a rubber mat or a large bath towel in the tub to prevent slipping.

Have a small-size bar of soap and a washcloth easily reachable. Have a towel ready that is small enough for your child to manage easily.

Fill the tub with about 4 or 5 inches of lukewarm water.

Make bathing enjoyable; have bathtub toys handy and let him have a short play period when finished washing.

### Steps Involved in Bathing

1.  Step in, sit down, wash face.
2.  Wash ears.
3.  Wash neck.
4.  Rinse off soap.
5.  Wash chest.
6.  Wash arms and shoulders.
7.  Wash lower back.
8.  Rinse off soap.
9.  Wash legs.
10.  Wash feet.
11.  Move to kneeling position.
12.  Wash genital area and buttocks.
13.  Sit down.
14.  Rinse off any soap.
15.  Get out of tub.

**Alternative:** Showering. It is more difficult to teach your child to take a shower. You'll likely be most successful if Dad gets in the shower with him or Mom showers along with her. Demonstrate the steps, and gradually fade out your guidance. This will be a long process, but one that you can eventually monitor from outside the shower. Once your child is pretty good at showering, you can begin to teach washing hair (see p. 314).

## Steps Involved in Drying

1. Dry face.
2. Dry ears.
3. Dry neck.
4. Dry chest.
5. Dry arms and shoulders.
6. Dry back.
7. Dry legs.
8. Dry feet.
9. Dry genital area and buttocks.

We have presented the steps involved in both bathing and drying. You should teach these two skills at the same time.

While you are bathing and drying your child, follow the steps as outlined above, referring to the various parts of his body as you go.

## Program

Use backward chaining and stay on each step until your child can do it without your physical assistance for three to four teaching sessions. Then move on to teach him the next step up.

Begin by doing all the steps for your child in both bathing and drying except for the last step of each.

Give him directions and physical guidance as needed with each step he is learning.

Remember to give him clear verbal directions: "Wash your feet," "Wash your arms," "Dry your feet," "Dry your arms."

Always praise and reward him with his special treat each time he has finished a task.

**Note:** For most children, a playtime in the tub after washing is rewarding in itself. However, be sure to reward your child after drying also.

When your child can bathe and dry himself with just your verbal reminders, begin to phase these out one at a time until he can take his bath and dry himself on his own.

Gradually remove yourself from the bathroom, allowing your child to finish more of the tasks without you there until he can go in and take his bath independently once you have filled the tub for him.

# Brushing Hair

## Setting the Stage

Part your child's hair before beginning. Position the brush in your child's hand so she is comfortable holding it.

Teach brushing hair in front of a mirror; this provides motivation as well as something to model while you are guiding her. Stand behind your child with both of you looking in the mirror.

Practice brushing hair when it is relatively free of tangles (e.g., after washing hair is not an ideal time).

Have the child's rewards ready.

Begin by brushing your child's hair with her. Do all the steps below in the order presented for four to five teaching sessions. Remember to praise and reward her for her cooperation (watching in the mirror, standing quietly, etc.). Then begin to phase out your assistance as outlined in the program.

## Program

1. If your child holds the brush in her right hand, brush the left side of her hair first. Begin at the part and stroke down the left side of her head. Say, "Brush down." Make sure in early sessions that your guidance is slow and easy. Avoid pulling hard on snarls, since this discomfort could discourage her from wanting to brush her hair.
2. Follow the brush with a downward stroke using her free hand; say, "Smooth your hair."
3. Bring the hand with the brush over her head. Tell her to "Brush down." Brush the back of her hair using three long strokes. Follow each brush stroke with a smoothing down stroke using her free hand, saying, "Smooth your hair."
4. Brush the *right* side, smoothing down her hair with her free hand after each stroke. Tell her each time, "Brush down," then, "Smooth your hair." When finished, praise her. Say, "Very nice! You brushed your hair!" Tell her how pretty she looks. For a girl, a pretty ribbon or barrette may be a special treat.

There are five steps in phasing out your assistance. Stay on each step until she comfortably does it and seems ready to do more without your help. Make sure you let her do as much of the skill as possible. Guide her in the following way through all of the steps involved.

1. With your hand on her wrist.
2. With your hand on her forearm.
3. With your hand on her elbow.
4. Without your hands guiding her, but giving her verbal directions. You might have to point at first to the areas needing brushing.
5. With no directions other than giving her the brush and saying, "Brush your hair."

Remember, progress comes slowly. You are giving her less and less assistance (as you continue to give her praise and rewards) throughout the teaching program.

When your child can brush her hair completely by herself, continue to praise her, as this will help to make hair brushing part of her daily routine. When your child has mastered the use of the brush, then guide her in the same manner using a comb.

What about tangles? Help her to hold her hair above tangles to prevent pulling. A brush is easier and pulls hair less, so loosen tangles with a brush before combing.

# Washing Hair

Your child should be used to the shower before you teach her to wash her hair in the shower.

### Setting the Stage

Use one of the "no tears" shampoos, but have a towel handy just in case.

You may want to teach hair washing in the shower or at the sink, depending upon which is the more convenient in your home.

If you choose to teach hair washing in the shower, it should be taught at the end of the shower. You probably will be assisting your child from outside the shower, but wear something you won't mind getting wet.

When teaching hair washing at the sink, a container is helpful for wetting and rinsing, especially if the hot and cold water come out of different faucets.

In this program, it is assumed that teaching will take place in the shower. However, the steps are essentially the same when using the sink.

**Note:** A hand mirror is a good reward for some children. Show her how she looks with lather on her head. Also, let her see that the soap is gone after rinsing.

## Program

1. Wet hair thoroughly.
2. Put shampoo on hand, then onto hair.
3. Rub the shampoo into scalp until it lathers.
4. Rinse by putting head under the shower several times, working hands through hair until it squeaks.
5. Dry hair with a towel.

Stay on each step until your child can successfully complete that step three or four times without your physical assistance; then move up to the next step.

Help your child to wet her hair. Do Steps 2 through 4 for her and then say, "Dry your hair," giving her assistance as needed. Praise her for completing the task.

Help your child to wet her hair. Do Steps 2 and 3 for her and then say, "Rinse your hair." Give her physical assistance and be sure to point out the squeaky sound hair makes when all of the soap is really out. Let your child finish drying her hair and then give her the reward.

Help your child wet her hair. Complete Step 2 for her and then begin lathering. Say, "Rub the soap all over your hair." Gradually fade out your assistance so that your child is eventually doing all of the lathering herself. Then let her finish the task. Remember to praise her and give her the reward.

Help your child wet her hair. Direct her to put the shampoo into her hand and then onto her hair. Give her assistance as needed. Let her finish washing and drying her hair and remember to praise her.

When your child is able to wash her hair with just your verbal directions, begin to phase these out, one at a time, starting with "Dry your hair," until she can wash her hair without any directions.

# Making a Bed

## Setting the Stage

Tuck in the sheets, blankets, and bedspread securely at the foot of the bed.

Move the bed away from the wall if it is difficult to reach all sides of the bed. Remove the pillow from the bed. Have your child's rewards ready.

Physically guide your child through the steps below for four to five teaching sessions. Praise and reward her for her cooperation. Then move on to teach her step by step as outlined in the program.

## Program

1.  Pull the top sheet up as far as it will go and smooth out the wrinkles. Say, "Pull up the sheet."
2.  Tuck the sheet in on both sides. Say, "Tuck in the sheet."
3.  Pull the blanket up and smooth out the wrinkles. Say, "Pull up the blanket."
4.  Tuck the blanket in on both sides. Say, "Tuck in the blanket."
5.  Put the pillow on the bed. Say, "Put the pillow on."
6.  Pull the spread up and over the pillow. Say, "Pull up the spread."

**Note:** If the spread is long enough, make a crease by tucking about an inch of the spread under the bottom of the pillow.

Stay on each step, giving your child less and less assistance, until she can successfully do the step without your physical guidance for three to four teaching sessions. Then move on to the next step.

Physically guide your child with Steps 1 through 5, then say, "Pull the spread over the pillow." Help her as needed, then direct her to "Pull the spread over the pillow." Praise and reward her.

Continue to remove your physical guidance a step sooner each time she has mastered a step, until she is able to complete the entire task with just your verbal directions throughout each step. Remember to praise and reward her.

When your child can make the bed with only verbal directions for all steps, you will want to gradually fade out these directions. Begin by giving directions for all steps except the last one ("Pull the spread over the pillow"). Next leave out the directions for the last two steps. Continue in this way until your child can complete the whole task from the single direction, "Make the bed."

To help your child become more independent in bedmaking, you can teach her to separate the sheet from the blanket, after a night's sleep, and tuck them in at the bottom. Have her remove the pillow before proceeding to make her bed.

# Setting the Table

Make sure your child understands all the concepts you will be using when giving directions for setting the table (e.g., "next to," "beside"), as well as the names of the pieces of tableware he will be using.

### Setting the Stage

Arrange place mats on the table before you begin the teaching program; these will help your child space the table settings and know how many places are needed. "Homemade" place mats consist of a large piece of paper or paper towel. These are ideal for teaching, since you can draw outlines of the tableware on them before you begin.

Pull the chairs out from the table so your child can get around the table easily.

Place the correct number of plates, glasses, folded napkins, and silverware out on the table. (You should teach your child to fold napkins at another time.)

Teach your child before meals. Then use the table your child has set for the meal. If you are teaching at other times, however, a snack or a "mock" meal can be a fun reward after the table is set. Have your child's rewards ready.

Have your child watch as you set the table according to the steps below for two to three teaching sessions. Reward him for paying attention. Then move on to teach him step by step as outlined in the program.

### Program

1. Place all the plates on the place mats. Say, "Put out the plates."
2. Place all the napkins on the place mats. Say, "Put out the napkins."
3. Place all the forks on the napkins. Say, "Put the forks on the napkins."
4. Place the knives on the place mats. Say, "Put out the knives."
5. Place the spoons next to the knives on the place mats. Say, "Put out the spoons."
6. Place the glasses on the place mats. Say, "Put out the glasses."

When your child masters one step and is able to perform this new step for three to four teaching sessions with just your verbal reminders, it is time to move on to the next step.

You do Steps 1 through 5 with your child watching. Then say, "You put the glasses out." Show him where they go on the outlined place mat. Hand the glasses to him one at a time. Praise him with, "Good! You helped set the table!"

This time you set the stage by drawing the outline on the place mat of everything except the glasses. Do Steps 1 through 5 with your child watching. Then say, "You put the glasses out." Put one out, then hand him the rest, one at a time for him to put out. Praise him with, "Good! You helped set the table!"

You do Steps 1 through 4 with your child watching. Then say, "You put out the spoons." Show him where they go on the outlined place mats. Hand them to him one at a time and guide him as needed in putting out the rest of the spoons. Then say, "Good! Now put the glasses out!" and he can finish setting the table.

This time set the stage by drawing the outline on the place mats for everything except the glasses and the spoons. You do Steps 1 through 4 with him watching, and then say, "You put out the spoons." Put one spoon out for him, then hand the rest to him one at a time. Guide him as needed in putting the rest of the spoons out. Then say, "Good! Now put the glasses out!"

Continue as above to do one step less each time your child masters a step without any outline drawn on the place mats, until he can perform the entire task of setting the table with blank place mats and verbal directions.

Now that your child can set the table with your verbal directions, you will want to begin fading out your directions for each item except the last one—glasses. Tell him, "Finish setting the table"; remember to praise him when he has completed the task. Next leave out the verbal directions for spoons and glasses. Continue in this manner until your child can complete the whole task from the single direction, "Set the table."

Have your child help in getting the tableware out and putting it on the table. Help him pull the chairs out from the table and put them back in place.

# Changing a Bed

Your child should already be able to make a bed before beginning this program.

### Setting the Stage

Begin with everything off the bed. Check to see if the sheets, blankets, and spread have labels, hems, or something to clearly indicate the lengthwise ends. If they don't, use a laundry marker or sew labels on to mark the ends.

Have sheets, blankets, and spread in order and easily accessible on a chair, bureau, or table. Put the pillowcase on the pillow and have it ready for her also.

Move the bed away from the wall, if necessary, to make it easy for your child to reach all sides. Have your child's rewards ready.

### Steps in Changing a Bed

1. Spread the bottom sheet out on the bed.
2. Tuck it in on all four sides.
3. Spread the top sheet out on the bed.
4. Spread the blanket out on the bed.
5. Tuck the blanket and top sheet under together at the foot of the bed.
6. Put the pillow on the bed.
7. Lay the bedspread out on the bed and straighten out the wrinkles.
8. Pull the bedspread over the pillow.

**Optional:** If the spread is long enough, make a crease by tucking about an inch of the spread under the bottom of the pillow.

**Note:** You may change a bed differently from the way we have outlined. Go through the process yourself and make your own list of steps. It may look different from ours (you may use a fitted bottom sheet or you might tuck the blanket in all the way around the bed, etc.).

## Program

In this program your child can already do some of the steps involved. Expect her to do these as you are teaching her the steps she needs to learn. She can already do Step 6. She will need help with Step 7; then she can do Step 8.

Stay on each new step, giving your child less and less assistance, until she can successfully do the step without your physical guidance for three to four teaching sessions. Then move on to the next step.

Start by telling your child, "It's my turn. You watch." With your child watching, do Steps 1 through 5. Tell her as you go, "I'm putting the bottom sheet on the bed. See, I'm tucking it in all the way around the bed. Now I'm putting the top sheet on. I'm putting the blanket on. I'm tucking the blanket and sheet in at the bottom."

Then say, "OK, it's your turn!" and direct your child to do Step 6 and praise her.

Say, "Let's put the spread on the bed." Physically guide her by helping as needed to put the spread on and smooth out the wrinkles. Say, "Good! You put the spread on!" Now let her finish by pulling the spread over the pillow; give her a reward.

With your child watching, you do Steps 1 through 4, again telling her what you are doing as you go along. Then physically guide her as needed to do Step 5, tucking the sheet and blanket in at the bottom of the bed. When she has finished tucking them in with your help, praise her with, "Good! You tucked them in!" Direct her to finish making the bed and give her a reward.

Continue in the same fashion, doing one less step for your child as she masters each previous one until she can change her bed with just your verbal directions. Remember to explain to her what you are doing while you model.

Then physically help her as needed with the step she is learning, and direct her to finish. Praise and reward her throughout.

When your child can change the bed with only verbal directions, you will want to gradually fade out these directions.

Begin by giving directions for all new steps, except the last one (placing the bedspread on the bed). Next, leave out the directions for the last two new steps. Continue in this way until your child can complete the whole task from the single direction "Change the bed."

# Sweeping

This program contains many skills (holding the broom, sweeping large pieces of paper, moving furniture, etc.). Your child may already know how to do some of these skills, whereas he may need to learn others. Read this program and decide which sections are relevant for your child.

## Materials

Old newspapers, masking tape, a dustpan, a dust brush, a trash basket, and a broom small enough for your child to handle comfortably.

## Setting the Stage

Teach in a small room with no carpet and not too much furniture. Most kitchens fit this description.

Make a large square in the middle of the floor with masking tape about 4 or 5 feet by 4 or 5 feet. Have your child's rewards ready.

## Program: Part 1

Stay on each of the following steps, giving your child less and less assistance, until he can successfully do the step without your assistance for three to four sessions.

1. Teach your child how to hold the broom. You should model this for him. Say, "Hold the broom," and if necessary, physically assist him in positioning his hands. You may find it helpful to him to put some tape markers where his hands should be on the broom handle. Praise him: "Good! You're holding the broom!"

2. Crumple up one page of a newspaper and put it on the floor outside but near the square. (Note: A torn-up Styrofoam cup is especially good for this.) Show him how to sweep inside the square with a slow, exaggerated sweeping motion. Take the paper back outside the square, and say, "Sweep the floor."

   He may need your physical assistance for the first few trials in learning the sweeping motion. Praise him, saying, "Good! You're sweeping!" Give him his reward.

3. One piece at a time, start adding more pieces of crumpled paper for him to sweep inside the square until he can sweep 6–12 pieces of paper into the square.

4. Gradually increase the distance of the papers from the square until you are placing them near the sides and corners of the room. In this way, your child is learning to sweep from all parts of the room into a central pile. Remember to praise and reward him.

5. Gradually decrease the size of the masking tape square until it is about 2 feet by 2 feet. In this step, your child is learning to make a pile of dirt (papers) in the middle of the floor.

When your child can sweep crumpled newspapers from all sides of the room into the small square in the middle, it is time to start teaching him to do this with dirt. Move on to Part 2.

## Program: Part 2

It is a big jump from crumpled newspaper to little bits of dirt, so start making the pieces of paper smaller and smaller by tearing up and crumpling the newspaper.

Continue to make them smaller, at your child's own pace, until he is able to sweep fairly small bits of paper into a pile in the square.

Switch from having him sweep crumpled paper to sweeping floor dirt. This may be a big step for him, so first model it for him. (It could also be helpful if there were enough dirt so that he could easily see what he was sweeping. After meals may be a good time.)

Say, "Sweep the floor," and have him sweep the dirt into a pile in the square.

Check to make sure he is getting most of the dirt. If necessary, help him sweep some of the dirt, and then let him finish. Gradually increase the amount of dirt he sweeps. Praise and reward a good job!

When your child is able to sweep the floor dirt into a pile inside the square, begin teaching him to use a dustpan. After your child has swept the dirt into the pile, hold the dustpan for him and have him sweep the dirt into the pan with the dust brush. Help him as needed and remember to praise him. Say, "Put the dirt into the basket," and give him his reward.

Demonstrate for him how to hold the dustpan and sweep the dirt in with the dust brush. Then give them both to him and help him as needed. Direct him to "Put the dirt into the basket," and help him as needed. Say, "Good job!" and give him his reward.

Your child is now ready to learn to move chairs and sweep under furniture. Show him how to move kitchen chairs, sweep under the table, and put the chairs back. Let him do it, giving him help as needed. If necessary, small pieces of tape can be used to mark the proper position of each chair.

# Appendix D

# Play Skill Programs

## Contents

### Skills for Playing Alone

### Skills for Playing with Others

This appendix contains programs for teaching play skills—those for playing alone and those for playing with others.

## Skills for Playing Alone

This section presents brief programs for teaching four individual play skills. The goal of individual play skills is for your child to play alone, to enjoy herself without your having to be there with her.

"Stacking rings" is one of the easiest games for you to teach and for your child to learn. "Stringing beads" is included as an example of activities that do not require toys bought from stores. "Working puzzles" is a bit more difficult; you must decide which of the many available puzzles is right for your child. "Matching pictures" (lotto) is a more advanced, school-type activity. These are toys that virtually all young children play with. If your child is older, you might want to look for other materials that are more age-appropriate and yet offer the same type of play and learning opportunities.

What does your child learn from these activities? For one thing, each activity involves sitting and paying attention. For another, each involves using eyes and hands together. This builds a child's coordination, which in turn helps in other activities, such as holding a spoon or writing. Also, your child can learn to play each of these games by herself and, therefore, can feel some mastery and control over a part of her world. Last, but certainly not least, play is fun.

# Stacking Rings

## Materials

Use a stacking rings toy, with a post and six rings.

## Setting the Stage

Begin with the two largest rings—put the others out of sight. Keep teaching sessions short (under 10 minutes). Have your child's rewards ready.

## Program: Taking Rings Off

1. Put the two largest rings on the post.
2. Hold the base of the post steady with one hand. Place your other hand over your child's hand, and guide her to the top ring.
3. Tilt the post toward her and tell her, "Lisa, take the ring off." Guide her as needed.

Over time, fade out your physical assistance until you can prompt her with just instructions and by pointing to the next ring.

## Program: Putting Rings On

1. Use the two largest rings. Begin with the larger of the two.
2. Hold the base of the post steady with one hand. Place your other hand over your child's hand, and guide the ring onto the top of the post. Tell her, "Lisa, put the ring on."

3. Remove your hand and hers to let the ring fall to the base.
4. Gradually fade your physical assistance until she can put these two rings on with just instructions and a prompt (pointing).

## Next Steps

Gradually add the other rings, one at a time. Each time, put the new ring within easy reach. Teach her to hold the base of the post with one hand (using physical assistance at first).

## Further Steps

Now that she can put all the rings on, begin to teach her to choose the correct ring.

Start with the biggest and the smallest rings. Place them in front of her, point to the larger ring, and say, "Get the big one." Next, use the second largest and the smallest, and so on. When she learns to select the bigger ring from each pair presented, you can gradually introduce more rings, one at a time, until she can pick the correct one when you put them all in front of her.

## Final Steps

Get her started and sit with her while she puts the rings on, but give her as few prompts as possible. Over time, move farther away. Remember to check back regularly to praise her.

# Stringing Beads

## Materials

Use a short shoelace and wooden or plastic beads with large holes or other beadlike materials. Most children like materials that are brightly colored. If you're feeling ambitious, you might want to involve other family members—brother, sister, Dad, Grandma—in painting empty wooden spools or macaroni to use in teaching stringing.

## Setting the Stage

Make sure that the table or floor area that you are working on is clear except for the materials you will be using. Tie a large knot at one end of the shoelace to prevent the beads from slipping off. Have your child's rewards ready.

## Program: Taking Beads Off

Start with five or six beads or spools already strung on the shoelace.

1. Place your hand over your child's and guide him to the last bead that you put on. Tell him, "Pete, take the bead off."
2. Help him pull it off if necessary.
3. Gradually fade out your physical assistance until he can slide each bead off by himself.

## Program: Putting Beads On

1. Begin with no beads on the shoelace. Put one bead on while your child is watching.
2. Begin another bead. Say, "Pete, put the bead on." Hold the end of the lace and place your free hand over your child's hand to help him slide the bead down to the knotted end of the shoelace. Repeat this until he can slide them down by himself.
3. Start the bead and give him the shoelace, so that he is holding the end in his hand. Guide him as much as necessary.

## Next Steps

1. Now teach him to start the bead. You hold the end of the shoelace and hand him a bead saying, "Pete, put the bead on." With your other hand, help him line up the hole in the bead with the tip of the shoelace.

2. Gradually fade your physical guidance so that he gets the bead onto the tip of the shoelace by himself.
3. Then show him how to hold the shoelace in his other hand and put the lace into the hole himself. You may need to guide him at first.

## Further Steps

Once he can put the beads on by himself, you can use this game to practice colors. Place several different-colored beads (or spools or macaroni) in front of him and ask him for one color. Say, "Put the red one on" or "Put the blue one on," each time pointing to the correct one. After a while, fade out your pointing. You can also have him

⊘ Alternate colors. Begin with two colors (red, blue, red, blue), then use three (red, blue, yellow, red, blue, yellow), then more.

⊘ Do the same steps but with different sizes (big, little) instead of different colors.

### Something Else to Try

A variation on stringing beads is lacing cards. This activity involves the same eye–hand coordination skills as stringing beads, but it's a little harder. Try this activity when your child has mastered beads or spools.

Have her pick a picture from a favorite coloring book and color it. Next, cut it out and paste it onto a piece of cardboard. Then punch holes all around the edge of the picture. Tie a knot in one end of the shoelace. At first you may have to put the lace into a hole and help your child pull it through. Show her how to go from one hole to the next. After a while, as you gradually fade out your physical assistance, she should be able to lace the whole picture by herself.

**Note:** Many different kinds of attractive and inexpensive lacing cards are available in toy stores. Keep on the lookout for those that are sturdy and have large holes.

# Working Puzzles

### Materials

Wooden puzzles, although they are more expensive than cardboard ones, are best. Choose a simple puzzle that has only a few large pieces. The shape puzzle shown here is very good for beginners because each piece is designed for its own hole and because the pieces fit in easily. If you want to use more difficult puzzles as your child gets better at doing puzzles, you will find wooden ones available with more than 20 pieces.

## Program

Begin with one piece. (Leave all the others in.)

1. Take the piece only a little way out. Say, "Charles, put it in." Use some physical assistance to guide him if necessary.
2. Take the same piece halfway out. Say, "Charles, put it in." (Guide as necessary.)
3. Hand him the piece. Point to the correct space, and say, "Charles, put it in." (Guide as necessary, but don't help too soon. Let him try it by himself for a bit first.)

Repeat this with each of the other pieces. Never take more than one puzzle piece out at a time. Gradually remove your physical assistance, until he can put a piece in by himself once you've put it on the table.

## Next Steps

Now take out two pieces.

1. Hand him one and tell him, "Charles, put it in." After he has put the piece in, hand him the other.
2. Put the two pieces on the table and tell him, "Charles, put them in" or "Do the puzzle."

If he is struggling with a piece and getting frustrated, back up a bit—give a little physical guidance.

## Further Steps

Eventually you will spill out the whole puzzle and he'll be able to put it together. Remember, though, that this is your last step; plan to reach it gradually.

## Final Steps

Get him started, and then move away, gradually. After he's learned to do several puzzles, you can create a new game by mixing up all the puzzle pieces. Naturally, it will take him a bit longer to sort them out and complete each puzzle. Remember that this kind of challenge will only be welcomed after he has mastered each puzzle.

### Something Else to Try

Puzzles range in difficulty from very easy to very difficult. (We've been working on some for years without success!) Play with blocks can also vary in difficulty. Blocks are very popular with young children, partly because children can do so many different things with them. Your child can stack blocks, knock them down, line them up, count them, match colors, or point to letters. He can make a castle, a tunnel, a garage, or a space station. When you teach your child to play with blocks, remember—as with puzzles—to begin with a task at his own level.

# Matching Pictures

### Materials

Use a lotto matching game (available in most toy stores). This matching game has a large card with pictures on it and a stack of small cards, each with one picture. Begin with a lotto game in which the pictures are very simple and easy to tell apart.

### Program

Begin by having your child match one picture.

1. On the large card, cover all the pictures but one with blank paper.
2. Give your child the picture that matches the one you've left uncovered.
3. Tell her, "Nina, find this one."
4. Show her how to put the matching card on top of the same picture on the lotto card.
5. Repeat this with a different picture, covering the others on the large card.

**Note:** If this seems a bit too hard for your child, make up your own set of matching cards with colors or shapes, and work on these until she has learned what *matching* means.

## Next Steps

1. Uncover two pictures. First give her one card. Say, "Nina, find this one." When she is successful, give her the other.
2. Gradually uncover the whole large card, giving her one card to match at a time.

## Further Steps

Once she understands the basic idea of matching, you can get other lotto games, with more choices and different objects. Or you can make your own with numbers or letters.

## Final Steps

When she has learned to match all the cards when you hand them to her one at a time, do the following.

1. Give her two cards to match. Tell her you'll look at what she has done after she matches the two cards. (Prompt a bit if necessary.)
2. Gradually increase the pile of cards. When she can do a whole pile without your prompting, leave the room briefly while she is working. When you return to the room make sure to praise her for playing by herself.

## Something Else to Try

When your child has mastered stringing beads and matching lotto cards, you can teach matching beads. String a number of different-colored beads, and leave your string in front of your child. Her task is to make a string that matches yours. As with all of the individual play skills we've talked about, you will

1. Begin with an easy task (for example, three beads).
2. Gradually make it more difficult.
3. Fade out your help until she's doing it by herself.

# Skills for Playing with Others

This section presents brief programs for teaching four activities involving other people. "Bean bag toss" and "Playing ball" are both active games that can involve other children and can be played in countless variations.

In "art gallery" we suggest a number of quieter arts-and-crafts projects that your child can do along with other children, even if he does not do exactly what the others do. "Dramatic play" is more advanced and makes greater use of imagination. All of the games in this section are fun to do with other family members or children in the neighborhood, and none involves expensive materials.

What does your child learn from play with others? He improves in those same areas we mentioned earlier: paying attention, eye–hand coordination, and self-confidence. Also, he learns something about waiting his turn, following rules, and sharing—in short, he learns a bit more about getting along with other people.

# Bean Bag Toss

## Materials

Use bean bags, either store-bought or homemade. To make your own, fill socks with a combination of uncooked rice and puffed rice or some kind of hard, dry beans. Any cardboard carton with holes cut out can be used as the "target," or you can toss the bean bags into a basket. You might want to involve several children or other family members in painting a clown face on a large carton and cutting out the eyes, nose, and mouth as targets.

## Setting the Stage

Find a level surface area outdoors or a space indoors that is free from clutter and all breakable objects. If the game is to be played indoors, you might want to set some rules for the group, such as "The bean bags should be tossed at the target, not at the goldfish bowl." Have rewards ready.

## Program

1. Have your child stand 2 or 3 feet away from the bean bag target. Toss a bean bag. Say, "Throw the bean bag," then hand a bean bag to him and help him throw it.
2. As he becomes more skilled, gradually give him less help and move farther away from the target.

## Next Steps

1. Mark several distances from the target. If you're playing outside, use chalk to draw lines at 2, 4, 6, 8, and 10 feet. If you are inside, use masking tape on the floor or carpet. Have your child begin on the first line and with each successful toss, move back a line.
2. Play a group game, with other children and/or family members. Assign points to be earned from each distance when the bean bag hits the target or lands in the basket. Divide players into teams and keep score.

## Something Else to Try

You can make this game as difficult as you want. Try having children toss bean bags from different positions (kneeling, lying down, standing up on a small footstool). If at least four children are playing, form teams and play each round from one of the different positions.

    A variation of this game is to knock over cups. For this game, stack three to six Styrofoam or paper cups on a low table or chair. Using the bean bag (or a small rubber ball), take turns trying to knock the pile of cups over. Another variation is bowling. You can teach this using plastic bowling pins or empty, rinsed-out soft drink cans.

# Playing Ball

## Materials

Use a large, light ball (a basketball is a good size, but too heavy) or a small rubber ball, depending on your child's size. A Nerf ball is good for many children, especially if they shy away from a ball that is thrown to them.

## Program

Begin by teaching your child the basics of throwing and catching a ball, and then work toward having a game of catch.

1. Stand in front of your child. Put her hands into a "catching" position (hands extended and cupped). Put the ball firmly in her hands, saying, "Catch the ball."
2. Next put your hands a few inches under hers. Motion to her to drop the ball into your hands (and guide if necessary). Say, "Throw the ball." Remember to reward with praise: "Good! You caught the ball!" or "You threw the ball!" Repeat this simple step until she is dropping the ball into your hands with no help.
3. Now move about a foot away. Put her hands in the catching position. Say, "Catch the ball." Toss the ball gently so that it lands right in her hands. Say, "Good! You caught the ball!"
4. Gradually increase the distance between the two of you, each time prompting her to "get ready" as needed, and then tossing the ball into her hands.

## Next Steps

Many children will learn to catch the ball before they will be able to throw it to you. Use one of these steps to teach your child to throw the ball.

1. Involve another person, who can stand behind your child and guide her arms, so that she will feel the correct motion as she throws it to you. Stand a few feet away. *Or*
2. Guide your child to throw the ball at, or into, a target. For example, stand her on a chair, and have her at first drop and then throw the ball into a basket.

## Next Steps

Involve your child in a game of catch with three or four other people. Your child will now be ready to participate in many simple group ball games.

# Art Gallery

There are many arts-and-crafts activities that your child can do with other children or family members. Although each of these could be done alone, we include them here because this type of group play—where everyone is "doing her own thing"—requires some cooperating and sharing, but not strict following of rules or taking turns. Also, each child can work at her own ability level and speed.

We give suggestions for teaching your child several basic art skills. You can build on these—depending upon your child's ability—to make craft projects. Make sure to display the products so that everyone can see and praise them.

## Materials

There are many objects and materials in your house that you can use to interest your child, as well as your other children or the neighborhood gang, in craft activities. Pictured below are some things that you could use:

# Coloring

### Basic

To help your child learn to color within boundaries, use a stencil. (You can buy one or make one by cutting a simple shape in the middle of a piece of cardboard and taping the cardboard to a piece of paper.)

Show your child how to color inside the stencil—point out how it automatically makes a picture. This can be very exciting and rewarding. Let other children help make some stencils and color using them.

### More Advanced

Draw or select simple pictures with heavy boundary lines from coloring books. Encourage your child to color within the lines, rewarding her with praise as you go along. Other, more advanced children can work alongside your child on slightly more complex pictures, or they can draw their own pictures.

### Still More Advanced

Have children create or copy figures, scenes, or objects. Have them work together on a mural. A long piece of brown wrapping paper will give each child a place to work. The better artists can outline pictures and others can color them in.

# Painting

### Basic

Start with fairly large paintbrushes and a large surface to paint. If three or four children are involved, they could each paint a side of a large cardboard carton. (When the paint is dry, the carton could be used for a play table or cut up for a bean bag toss game, puppet theater, play house, and so on.)

### More Advanced

Have children paint smaller objects, such as macaroni or wooden spools.

### Still More Advanced

Encourage children to paint original designs, figures, or scenes. The children themselves can decide on themes for painting: sports, animals, food, favorite games, and so on.

# Playing with Clay

### Basic

Introduce the clay, showing how it can be squeezed, pounded, poked, or rolled.

## More Advanced

Help children roll the clay into hot dog shapes and cut it into pieces with a dull knife. Also try rolling clay with a rolling pin and cutting it with a cookie cutter.

## Still More Advanced

Work as a group making animals (a snake, cat, or duck, for example) or simple toys (truck, house, car) out of the clay.

## Other Projects

There are many craft projects your child and others can do together once your child has mastered the basics of skills such as coloring, cutting, pasting, and painting. An easy activity is to have them cut up scraps of colored paper and paste these into an attractive pattern on a large piece of paper. A more difficult activity is to examine magazines for pictures that all relate to the same theme—boats, animals, sports—and to make an art gallery from the ones that are selected.

# Dramatic Play

This final set of activities, dramatic play, is more advanced than the other activites in this manual.

## Materials

All you need for dramatic play is a quiet area and a few free minutes. You can even do some of these activities in the car (so long as someone else is driving!). It's nice to play these games in a group with several children, but you and your child can still have a good time doing them without others.

## Mirrors

Stand facing your child. One of you is a "mirror," the other looks into the "mirror." The mirror imitates exactly what the other person does. At first, you be the mirror, then let your child be the mirror. Keep the motions slow and repetitive so the other person can follow them.

## Pantomime

Pantomime a very simple action with which your child is familiar: peel a banana, wash your face, brush your teeth, open a window. Do it slowly as the child watches. Then ask your child to guess what you did. When she pantomimes an action, teach her to move slowly and remember details ("How do you peel a banana?" "What does your mouth do when you eat a lemon?" and so on).

## Emotion Land

Choose a few basic emotions such as happy, sad, angry, scared, and surprised. At first, have your child imitate you as you act out an emotion. Next, call out the name of an emotion and instruct him to act it out. Then pick out three spots in a room (couch, corner, chair) and name each one a different "emotion land" (couch is "happy land," corner is "angry land," chair is

"sad land"). Call out "happy land" and when your child remembers where it is, he runs to it and you encourage him to act happy there until you call out a new emotion land.

# Statues

Hang limp with your head and arms dangling. Your child is the "sculptor." He can move your arms, head, hands, eyes, mouth, and so forth any way he wants until he has made a "statue." When he is satisfied with his creation, you freeze.

# Imaginary Play

Imaginary, or pretend, play may be the most advanced of the dramatic play skills. One type of imaginary play is pretending to be someone else: Mommy, Superman, the captain of a ship. Another type of imaginary play is using one object to represent another—pretending, for example, that small stones are coins or a doll is a baby. Even though imaginary play is an entertaining activity that your child might do alone, it can easily be done as part of play with others. Here are some examples.

✥ Tell your child he is Superman, or Daddy, or some other well-known person or storybook character. If your child can do this type of pretend play successfully, have him then "be someone" and you try to guess who he is. Children often enjoy playing this guess-who game with each other.

✥ Ask your child to pretend he is riding on a bus, flying on a plane, sailing in a boat, and so on. Encourage him to use household objects as props.

✥ Finally, if you feel your child is ready for it, try acting out a short, simple play or skit with a few children ("Little Red Riding Hood," "The Three Bears," a TV show, or any other favorite story).

# A Last Word

Congratulations! You've finished a long section, thought about many play ideas, and quite likely tried out a few along the way. We hope you'll try teaching these play skills and adding your own ideas to what we've suggested.

E

# Information Skills Programs

## Contents

This appendix comprises programs for teaching information skills.

## Reading Sight Words

This reading program teaches your child to read survival sight words, a skill that greatly increases his ability to get around in the community without help. The program teaches him to read things such as signs, simple directions, and menu items. These are mostly single words (like "Stop," "Men," "Enter"), although some are phrases of several words (like "Do Not Enter"). This program does not teach a child to read "connected text" (as you are doing right now), and it is not the best approach for children who can already read reasonably well. Rather, the program teaches your child to identify whole words, which simply means that he does not need to recognize or identify individual letters to use this program.

    Read and become familiar with the entire program before you begin teaching.

## Entering Skills

Many of the skills a child needs to enter this sight word program can actually be taught as you go along. However, one necessary entering skill involves being able to see the differences among pictures. Specifically,

1. Your child should be able to match a given picture of a shape or design to the same one in an array of three or more.
2. Your child should be able to match a given word to the same one in an

   array of three or more.
3. Your child should have a sense of the meaning of some words. He

   should be able to tell you or show you the meaning of certain words that you say ("Go," "Stop," or "Out").

    If your child does not have these entering skills mastered, work on them before beginning the sight word program. For the first two entering skills, begin with just two pictures or cards that are the same. Teach your child to place one card on top of the other, as you say, "Find the same." Gradually introduce more cards on the table, so that your child is actually identifying the correct symbol. Remember to scramble the order of this array from time to time.

## Assessment

Your first task is to choose which words you will begin to teach. If your child cannot read his first and last names, these should be the first words you work on. The Sight Word Assessment (p. 344) of common sight words will help you choose others. You should add to this list other words that you know your child will often encounter, such as familiar bus route names. Also, cross out any words that he doesn't yet understand. For example, if he doesn't really understand the idea of *danger*, save the word *danger* for later. In sum, you will want to teach those words that represent objects, actions, and attributes that your child clearly recognizes and that he will most often see in printed form. It might be helpful to ask his teacher to add words he encounters in school.

Numerals—important for time telling, money skills, telephone use, address finding, and other day-to-day activities—are included in the vocabulary list. Most children do better with these after they have already learned several other words.

## Materials

Print the first words to be taught on 3-by-5-inch index cards. Make the letters heavy and dark, ½–1 inch high. Make the letters as much alike in darkness and height as possible.

You should print the words in uppercase, or capital, letters (e.g., "STOP") rather than lowercase letters (e.g., "stop"), even though lowercase letters are often easier to recognize. The reason for using uppercase letters is that signs are usually printed this way.

 Exception

If there are words that your child most frequently sees in lowercase, then you can write these in lowercase letters. Also, teach your child to read his first and last names in both upper- and lowercase. If your child does not make progress with uppercase words, you can try teaching the first few words all in lowercase until he's responding well to the task; then switch back to uppercase.

## Sight Word Assessment

| WORD | Recognizes | Understands | WORD | Recognizes | Understands |
|---|---|---|---|---|---|
| WALK | | | FRONT | | |
| DON'T WALK | | | OFF | | |
| STOP | | | ON | | |
| FIRE EXIT | | | GO | | |
| R. R. CROSSING | | | UNDER | | |
| DANGER | | | TURN | | |
| FLAMMABLE | | | IN | | |
| BEWARE OF DOG | | | OUT | | |
| POISON | | | Favorite Foods: | | |
| CAUTION | | | | | |
| KEEP OUT | | | | | |
| TELEPHONE | | | | | |
| MEN | | | | | |
| GENTLEMEN | | | | | |
| WOMEN | | | DO NOT ENTER | | |
| LADIES | | | NO ADMITTANCE | | |
| NO TRESPASSING | | | BUS | | |
| WET PAINT | | | TAXI | | |
| ENTRANCE/ENTER | | | Names of Family | | |
| EXIT | | | Members: | | |
| REST ROOMS | | | | | |
| NO EATING | | | | | |
| NO SMOKING | | | Numerals: | | |
| FIRE DEPT. | | | 0 | | |
| POLICE DEPT. | | | 1 | | |
| HOSPITAL | | | 2 | | |
| POST OFFICE | | | 3 | | |
| OPEN | | | 4 | | |
| CLOSE | | | 5 | | |
| CLOSED | | | 6 | | |
| LAUNDROMAT | | | 7 | | |
| UP | | | 8 | | |
| DOWN | | | 9 | | |
| PUSH | | | Name: | | |
| PULL | | | Other Words: | | |
| LEFT | | | | | |
| RIGHT | | | | | |

## Errorless Teaching

This program is meant to be errorless; if you are teaching correctly, your child should rarely make a mistake. Do not allow guessing. Encourage your child to take his time and to say, "I don't know," rather than to guess. Encourage him to ask for help when necessary. As he learns, gradually decrease your assistance until he can do the task correctly, by himself, at least five times in a row. Always reward correct answers, and, if occasional errors do occur, simply withhold your reward and go on to the next practice trial. We give some suggestions later for ways to discourage guessing.

## Pretest

Ask your child to play a game with you. Put the word cards in a stack, and show him one at a time, asking him to "Read the word." Put any that he reads correctly on the bottom of the stack, and put those that he misses in a separate pile. Go through the entire stack until you have identified all the words he can consistently read correctly. Don't skip this pretest—you may be surprised at what your child can already do! You'll be using the group of cards he could not read to begin teaching.

## Procedure I. Recognition of Words

This first procedure teaches your child to identify and recognize the words you display. You will also ask him to name the words, but this is only to help him learn recognition better.

At first you will lay out three cards at a time for your child to learn. You can increase this to four and five cards as your child learns the procedure. However, if more cards cause errors, drop back to fewer cards for a while. If your child has a great deal of difficulty starting with three cards, drop back to two, but work up to three as quickly as you can. It will make the program run much more smoothly.

Select three cards. Choose two words that your child already recognizes and one that he does not recognize. (If your child does not recognize any words on the word list, begin with one word and two blank cards.) Try to pick words that don't look alike. For example,

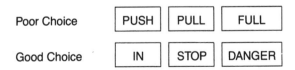

| | | | |
|---|---|---|---|
| Poor Choice | PUSH | PULL | FULL |
| Good Choice | IN | STOP | DANGER |

1. Lay out the first three cards in an even row from left to right in front of your child. Always lay them out from left to right (that's the way we read, so we want your child to learn to look from left to right).
2. Name each card as you put it down. Make sure that your child looks at each of the cards in a left-to-right sequence.
3. Name each word again and have him repeat the word as you point to the correct card. Do not have him "sound out" the word slowly; rather, have him repeat it quickly, so that he recognizes the whole word as a unit. You can gradually discontinue pointing to and naming the words once your child catches on to the task and is not guessing (this may take several days or, perhaps, weeks).
4. Select one card as the first word your child will learn to read. Say, "Find [word]!" Have him either point to the correct card or pick it up and hand it to you. Remember to prevent guessing and to provide help when necessary.
5. When he chooses the correct card, with or without your help, say, "Good! You found [word]. What does this say?" Prompt, if necessary, and confirm the response: "That's right, [word]!"
6. Mix up the cards and repeat. As soon as your child is consistently finding and saying the first word, you should no longer name the cards as you lay them out. (You can make this easier for your child by naming the cards a bit more softly each time, removing your cues gradually rather than all at once.) Simply put them in front of him from left to right, ask him to "Find [word]," and have him repeat the word when he finds it.
7. When he is again consistently finding and saying the first word, teach him the second and then the third words in the same way, using the same three cards. Now practice, mixing up the order of the cards and varying which word you ask for. Remember, it may take several sessions before he is consistently identifying the first three words. Be patient and keep the teaching and learning errorless. Repeat this task until your child is consistently choosing the correct word without assistance every time.

We can now summarize the basic procedure that you will use to teach each new word. Select one new card together with several that he already knows. Then

1. Begin with a series of practice trials in which you name the cards as you lay them out. Work on the new word until your child can find it and repeat it consistently when you ask for it.
2. Next, practice a series in which you don't name the words before you ask for the new word. Practice until he is again performing correctly without help.

3. Finally, practice a series in which you sometimes ask for the new word and sometimes for one of the old ones until he performs smoothly on this task, too.

Remember: Add only one new word to the array until he masters it.

Be sure to mix up the cards each time, and have your child repeat the word when he finds it. After you have taught a number of words, keep the mastered ("old") ones you are not using in a stack. Shuffle this stack from time to time, so that you are using different "old" words along with the new words. This will ensure that your child does not forget any old words while he is learning new ones.

## Procedure II.  Naming the Words

After your child has learned to recognize words with the basic teaching procedure (Procedure I), he should learn to name them by himself, a related skill that is slightly more difficult. The basic steps are the same, with one key difference: When you lay out the cards, point to the new card and ask, "What's this?" Your child's task is to name the word—that is, read it aloud, without your having said the word first. To introduce new words, use the steps in Procedure I (one new word at a time).

Again, do not allow guessing. Encourage your child to take his time and to say "I don't know" rather than to guess. Encourage him to ask for help when necessary. One useful strategy is to have him wait for several seconds before responding (whether he knows the right answer or not). For example, point to the new word in the array, ask, "What's this?" and wait 3–4 seconds for the answer. This will discourage quick guesses, and your child can either give the right answer or say "I don't know" after the short delay.

---

 **Exception**

If your child cannot articulate or sign words clearly enough to be understood, you may want to point to a word and have him select a picture from an assortment to match that word. In this way he can indicate that he knows the word.

---

## Procedure III.  Flash Card Naming

Once your child can smoothly name words pointed out to him in a three- to five-card array, you can help him learn still better with a flash card drill. Put the word cards in a stack and show him only one word at a time. Say, "Read the words." When he reads the top card, put it on the bottom of the stack and show the next card. You should show the cards as fast as your child reads them. Put cards that he misses in a separate pile for review. Remember that he should read each word as a unit and not try to "sound it out."

If you have been rewarding your child for every correct answer, begin to reward him only after he has read several words in a row. Gradually reward larger numbers of words or longer periods of time on the task. Keep doing this as long as your child is accurately learning new words. Don't correct errors on the spot, but go over the missed word pile slowly and carefully, with rewards for each correct response. If he seems to have forgotten a few of these, go back to Procedures I and II and reteach them. Then put them back in the flash card stack.

 **Comment**

You can possibly teach your child a large number of sight words with this program, and you can maintain continued performance with an occasional flash card drill. If your child learns over 100 words and seems eager to learn more, it would be good to seek formal instruction to help him learn to read connected text.

## Procedure IV. Practicing Sight Words in the Community

Once your child has learned to name a word correctly in the flash card drills, you can begin to call his attention to that word as it appears in community settings. As you are driving or walking along, point out words on signs and ask your child to identify them. He may have difficulty at first, since words in the community look different from those on his flash cards.

Cues such as the color, shape, or location of the sign reduce the number of possible names it might have and make choosing the right name easier. For example, a red octagonal sign on the corner must be "STOP," a sign on the traffic light post has to be either "WALK" or "DON'T WALK," and a rest room door will say either "MEN" or "WOMEN" (or their equivalents).

You might want to try another activity for practicing sight words: Make a community words notebook, with photographs or magazine pictures of different signs in the community. Just as with actual community practice, introduce each word only after your child has mastered it in the flash card drill.

# Using a Telephone

This telephone program is designed to help you teach your child to use regular telephones and pay telephones—to answer the phone, take messages, call home, and many other related skills. Some parts of the program (Procedures I and IV) can be taught as opportunities present themselves in your daily routine. Others (Procedures II and III) will probably be easier to teach in structured teaching sessions.

## Entering Skills

Your child should have the following skills before starting this program:

1. She must be able to recognize numerals 0–9.
2. She must be able to speak at least in short phrases, and be able to make herself understood to others without a great deal of difficulty.
3. She must understand short, simple, direct conversation.
4. She must have the motor coordination to hold the receiver and to enter numbers (or she must have a prosthetic device that enables her to do this).

## Assessment

Complete the Telephone Skills Assessment (p. 351) for your child. Each assessment section corresponds to a section of the telephone skills program, so the assessment will indicate the portions of the program you will need to teach. The program is designed to be taught in sequence, from I through IV. In general, though, the order is less critical here than in the other programs, and you may want to work on more than one skill at a time with your child. Of course, if she becomes confused or has difficulty learning this way, go back to teaching the program in order, one step at a time. An exception is the entering sequence: You'll need to teach this in order from the beginning.

## Errorless Teaching

This program, like the others for information skills, is meant to be errorless. In other words, if you are teaching correctly, your child should rarely

make a mistake. On each new step, you should tell her what to do, show her how, and prompt her if necessary. Decrease your assistance little by little as she learns. Do not allow guessing, and encourage your child to ask for help if she needs it, instead of just taking a stab at it. Reward her for successes, whether or not you assist her.

## Procedure I. Answering the Phone

You can probably teach most of this section in your daily routine as opportunities present themselves. With each of these skills, gradually decrease your assistance as your child learns the skill.

**A. *Holding the Phone*** Call your child's attention to the cord. Show her that it comes out at the end of the receiver where you put your

## Telephone Skills Assessment

| | No | Yes With Help | Yes On Own |
|---|---|---|---|
| ENTERING SKILLS<br>1. Recognizes numerals 0–9 | | | |
| 2. Speaks in short, understandable phrases | | | |
| 3. Understands simple conversation | | | |
| 4. Has motor skills to hold receiver and dial | | | |
| TELEPHONE SKILLS<br>I. Answering the Phone<br>   A. Holds the receiver correctly | | | |
|    B. Recognizes the telephone ring | | | |
|    C. Answers and says "hello" | | | |
|    D. Hangs up correctly when call is over | | | |
|    E. Writes or codes simple messages | | | |
| II. Making a Telephone Call<br>   A. Dials (or pushbuttons) a single numeral you show or say | | | |
|    B. Dials a full 7-digit phone number you write down | | | |
|    C. Knows what to do when signal is:.<br>     1. dial tone<br>     2. "dead" phone<br>     3. ringing<br>     4. "busy"<br>     5. operator or recording | | | |
| III. Calling from a Standard Phone<br>   A. Knows own phone number from memory | | | |
|    B. Has notebook or other system for remembering other numbers | | | |
|    C. Knows how to dial 0 and what to say in case of an emergency | | | |
| IV. Calling from a Pay Phone<br>   A. Uses a pay phone correctly | | | |

mouth. Then guide her in picking up the receiver all the way from the cradle and putting it to her ear and mouth. Practice whenever it is convenient (an incoming call is not necessary for this).

**B. Recognizing the Ring** Your child needs to recognize the ring of the telephone, and must learn to distinguish it from other common household sounds such as the doorbell or an alarm clock. Call your child's attention to the phone when it rings. Help her to identify it and go to the ringing phone. Also, prompt your child to identify any other things in the house that make sounds similar to a ringing phone, especially bells.

**C. Answering the Phone**   Once your child has gone to the ringing telephone and has picked up the receiver, she must say "hello," or at least say something. At first she may need considerable prompting to say "hello" to a machine.

If the call is not for her, she must learn to say, "Just a minute, please, I'll go and get [name]"; place the receiver down (but not hang up!); and fetch you or any other family member the caller asks for. To help your child build these skills, you can have friends call and ask for specific family members. Start with requests for people who are in the immediate vicinity of the telephone—even visible from it. Next, she can get family members who are nearby but not visible and finally move on to people in other parts of the house.

What if a caller asks for someone who is not at home? You will probably want to teach your child that if she cannot find the person requested, or knows that he or she is away, she should get someone else who is home. If she is home alone, she must, at the least, return to the telephone and tell the caller, "Bob's not here now." Rehearse these skills with your child on prearranged calls.

**D. Hanging Up the Phone**   When a telephone call is over, it is necessary that your child hang up the receiver squarely on the telephone cradle so that the phone will work for incoming calls. Saying "good-bye" should be your child's cue to hang up the telephone.

**E. Taking a Message**   It is desirable for your child to be able to take a message for someone who is not at home. If she can write, message taking is straightforward. You will only need a notepad and pencil large enough for her to use comfortably or a chalkboard kept within easy reach of the telephone. Frequent callers should be made aware of how long a message your child can handle well. Have them ask your child to repeat the message to them after she has written it down.

You can begin to work on this kind of message taking without the telephone. Once your child does this well, have her practice with actual phone calls that you have arranged. A message heard over the telephone is more difficult to understand than the same message spoken face-to-face. Be sure that she learns to hold the phone and to write at the same time (or to put down the phone, write, and pick up the phone again).

Once your child has noted who called while you were out, you can return the call. However, that may not be necessary with some messages. Frequent callers should be asked to rehearse short, simple messages (e.g.,

"I'll be home late") with your child until she can repeat them without difficulty. Tell them to give her the message and then immediately have her repeat it. ("What are you going to tell Mom?") They should prompt her for any words she has forgotten and praise the completed effort. For practice, and to check on your child's accuracy, you can arrange with friends or family members to call and leave prearranged messages. Be sure to teach your child to hang up if no one answers after two or three "hellos" (to avoid crank calls).

Your child has now learned all of the skills involved in answering the telephone. Frequent practice is necessary if she is to maintain these skills. One strategy you can use is to make your child the family "phone monitor." That is, if she is home and the phone rings, it is her job to answer it. This should give her enough practice to maintain all of the skills taught in this section. If she gets an allowance, you might want to let her earn part of it this way. If you do not use this strategy, you may have to arrange with family members and friends to continue to make calls to your child to give her the practice she needs.

## Using a Name Board

If your child cannot write at all, message taking poses a problem. What is she to do if someone calls when she is alone? In this case, a name board near the phone will be helpful. This is a board with a card (on a hook or in a pocket) for each of your most frequent callers. Each caller's name, and perhaps picture, is placed on one card. (These names can be practiced in the sight word program.) At the top of the board put a hook or a pocket with a picture of the telephone. Teach your child to select the card that matches the caller as soon as that person identifies himself and to put it on the picture of the phone.

Tell your child how to use the board. You can begin to work on this skill without the telephone, but as your child learns, be sure to give her practice with real telephone calls—both calls that you arrange for her and those that just happen. You may want to start with only two or three cards, and gradually increase this number as your child learns how to use the board.

Depending on your child's skills, you can place more than one hook or pocket at the top. For example, you can make a hook for "Will call back," "Be home late," or whatever message your child can understand.

## Procedure II.  Skills for Making a Telephone Call

This section is easiest to teach in deliberate, structured teaching sessions with your child.

    *A.  Placing a Call*   **Note:** If your child is left-handed, reverse the right and left directions given below. If you have a rotary phone, adapt the instructions accordingly.

    Write the numeral "1" on a piece of paper and show it to your child. Ask her to find the "1" on the phone and press it. Show her and guide her, if necessary. Reduce your assistance gradually. Now just show her the number "1" alone, without saying it, until she can press it from just the written numeral. Do this for each numeral separately.

    When your child has learned to press any single number that you show her, write two numerals together on a piece of paper, placing the numerals an inch or so apart. Teach your child to place her left index finger under the first numeral on the paper as she dials with her right finger. When she has finished dialing the first numeral, she must keep her place by moving her left index finger just below the next numeral and keeping it there while she dials that one. Gradually decrease your assistance until she can correctly dial or push any chain of two digits by herself, every time.

    **Note:** If your child has persistent difficulty reading the sequence from left to right, it may be helpful to put a highly noticeable marker such as a green dot to the left of the chain and have her touch this with her finger when she starts. A red dot at the right of the chain will signal her to stop.

    In the same way, teach your child to dial or push a sequence of three, four, five, six, and seven digits. As she learns this skill, write the digits more closely together as they would usually appear in a written phone number.

    **Note:** Your child should practice with many different digit combinations at each step. But, for greater practice, you may want to drill the last three, then four, then five, then six, and then seven digits of her own phone number more often than the other combinations.

    See if your child is able to dial seven-digit numbers from a sheet of paper without holding a finger under each digit in turn. If she can do this correctly by herself every time, you will be able to teach her to dial while holding the telephone receiver. Otherwise, you must teach her to set the receiver aside and continue to use her left hand to mark her place in the chain of numbers while she dials with her right hand.

    *B.  Telephone Signals*   Your child must now learn to tell the difference between the various signals she may hear from the telephone. First, teach her the difference between a dial tone and a "dead" phone. Get a dial tone by simply lifting the receiver; get a "dead" phone by holding down the button on the telephone cradle as you lift the receiver. Teach your child that she must hear a dial tone before she dials.

After your child dials, she may hear a ring, a busy signal, a "dead" phone, or a recorded message.

⊘  Get a "dead" phone by holding down the button on the telephone cradle. Teach your child to hang up and try again at once when she hears this after dialing.

⊘  Get a busy signal by dialing your own number. Teach your child to hang up and try again later when she hears this.

⊘  Get a ring that isn't answered by dialing a place of business (without voice mail) when it is closed. Teach her to count 10 rings and then hang up.

If your child persistently confuses any two signals, have her listen to, identify, and act on both of them in rapid succession. This will help her isolate the difference between them. Give your child as much drill on this exercise as she needs. Have her actually go through the motions of each of the responses, providing help as necessary.

*Voice Mail*    Leaving a message on voice mail is a bit more advanced, but you can teach it as your child masters the steps of placing a phone call. She may need experience in distinguishing between a real person on the line and a recording. Rehearse with your child in advance of the call what she will say. Explain to her the standard answering machine or voice mail greeting, and role play leaving her name, number, and a brief message. Look for opportunities to give her experience with voice mail.

## Procedure III.  Putting It Together: Calling from a Standard Phone

*A.  Calling Home*    Arrange actual practice for your child in calling someone at home from other phones. Teach her to report where she is, what she is doing, when she is coming home, and of course any difficulty she may be having. See that she learns her own phone number, if possible, or that she carries the phone number with her.

If your child has not already memorized her own phone number, the following procedures may be useful. Write your child's telephone number on a piece of paper. Have her practice reading it aloud until she can do so smoothly; also have her practice entering it until she can do so as well. Now cover up the last digit. Have her say and enter the whole number, including the covered digit. Prompt her if necessary, and gradually decrease your assistance until she can do it correctly by herself every time. Now cover up both the last and the next-to-last digits, and repeat the procedure. Continue this way until you have covered up all of the digits in reverse sequence from last to first.

If your child learns to recite and enter her own telephone number from memory, be sure to practice these skills with her frequently at first—several times daily, if possible.

**B. Calling Other Numbers**   You will probably want your child to call a variety of phone numbers: to reach you or other family members at work, to call relatives, or to call her friends. If you have followed this program in order, she has all of the skills to do this. Help her to make a "phone book" that she can carry, with the numbers she is likely to need. Keep the entries far enough apart so she does not confuse them. Print the appropriate name with each number. Show your child how to use the book, and have her practice with it. If she did not learn her own phone number, it should be the first entry in her book.

**C. Emergency**   Teach your child to enter the emergency number in your area (911 or 0) if she is in trouble and cannot reach anyone else. Role play emergency situations with her and have her actually go through the motions. Teach her to say, "This is an emergency," and to say who she is, where she is, and what has happened. You can prevent the calls from being completed by taping down the button on the telephone cradle while you practice.

## Procedure IV.  Calling from a Pay Phone

You can probably teach your child how to make local calls from a pay phone as opportunities present themselves without separate, formal sessions.

Your child must be able to select whatever coin or coin combination is needed in order to use a pay phone. (See the money skills program in this appendix.) Teach your child which slot to put the money in. You can practice on a real pay phone without losing your money by hanging up before a call is completed.

Also teach your child to get her coins from the return slot if the call is incomplete. Call her attention to the sound of the coins dropping into the return.

If you wish, you can teach your child to enter 0, give her name and the number she wants, and ask to reverse the charges for calls outside the local area. This skill, as with all of the others in this program, is best taught through actual practice, with assistance until she can do it reliably by herself. Of course, if your child has completed the money skills program, you can teach her to make long-distance calls in the regular way.

Otherwise, the operation of a pay phone in the United States is exactly like the operation of a standard telephone.

# Telling Time

This telling time program is designed to teach your child to tell time on a standard clock. Even though digital clocks have become very popular, we still recommend teaching with a standard clock. With a clock face, the child can not only tell the correct time but also develop a sense of time. Many children learn to give a rote response to a digital clock without ever developing a sense of what it means. Once your child has mastered time telling with a standard clock, it will not be difficult to generalize the skill to a digital one.

It will take patient teaching on your part to make progress in this area. Yet the reward for you and your child should be well worth the effort. Being able to tell time is a huge step toward independence.

## Entering Skills

Assess entering skills first, unless it is clear that your child knows them. If she does not, it will help greatly to teach them to her before you begin the time program. If you are trying to teach time skills while also teaching how to count from 1 to 12, frustration is bound to result for both of you.

|  |  |
|---|---|
| _____ | Counts from 1 to 12 |
| _____ | Identifies numerals 1–12 |
| _____ | Orders the numerals from 1 to 12 |
| _____ | Places the numerals 1–12 around a clock face |
| _____ | Identifies long (or big) and short (or little) hands |
| _____ | Shows which way the clock moves (clockwise) |
| _____ | Counts to 30 |
| _____ | Counts to 30 by fives |

## Assessment

Take your child through the Time Skills Assessment (p. 359). The sections are arranged in order of difficulty; they correspond point by point with the program sections that follow. Begin teaching in the program section that corresponds to the first assessment section in which your child makes an error.

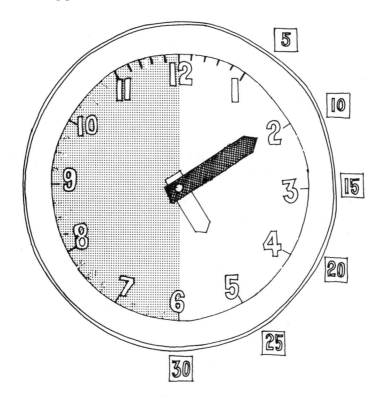

## Materials

You will need a large teaching clock with movable hands. This can be made from a paper plate. First, cut out cardboard hands and attach them with a paper fastener. Make the two hands very different in length, and perhaps color the minute hand. Write in the hours around the outside, and make small marks between the 11 and 12 and the 12 and 1 to signify minutes. Since teaching time is apt to take a long time, you might want to find a commercially made clock in an educational supply store or toy store, as this will be more durable.

## Errorless Teaching

Many children have learned to identify hours correctly, but are quick to guess at other times and are usually wrong. The main teaching rule in this program is not to allow guessing. The procedure we outline is an error-less one. If you are teaching correctly, your child should rarely make a mistake. Encourage her to take her time and to ask for help whenever she doesn't know the answer. If necessary, use a delay procedure; have her

## Time Skills Assessment

Set the teaching clock for each time below. Ask your child "What time is it?"
Put the little hand right on the numeral for the hour, except as noted.
Score the item correct only if your child answers with no help. (But if she can do it with a little help, note this.)
Continue just to the point where she makes several errors in a row.

I. HOURS
____ 2:00
____ 7:00
____ 6:00
____ 11:00
____ 12:00

II. PAST THE HOUR
A. 5 minutes past
____ 8:05
____ 4:05
B. 10–25 minutes past
____ 9:10
____ 6:20
____ 11:25
____ 5:15
C. More difficult:
Hour hand first
____ 2:15
____ 1:20
____ 3:25
Hands on same number
____ 3:15
____ 1:05

III. HALF HOUR (place hour hand a quarter of the way between hours)
____ 10:30
____ 9:30
____ 7:30
____ 1:30

III. (continued)
____ 4:30
____ 5:30
____ 6:30
____ 12:30

IV. BEFORE THE HOUR
A. 5 before
____ 3:55 or 5 before 4
(place little hand on 4)
____ 8:55 or 5 before 9
(place little hand on 9)
B. 10–25 before
____ 6:50
____ 2:40
____ 7:45
____ 2:35
C. More difficult:
Hour hand first
____ 10:45
____ 9:35
____ 11:40
Hands on same number
____ 10:50
____ 7:35

V. "ABOUT"
____ 8:14 (about 15 past 8)
____ 3:42 (about 20 before 4)
____ 6:26 (about 25 past 6)
____ 11:58 (about 12 o'clock)

wait for several seconds before answering your questions instead of quickly guessing an answer.

## Procedure I.  Teaching Hours

Set an hour on your teaching clock—for example, eight o'clock. Ask your child to point to the long hand. "That's right, it's on 12; that's o'clock." Then ask your child to point to the short hand. "Good. What o'clock is it?" (Give the answer if necessary, and then repeat the question.) "What o'clock is it?" (If she tends to guess, have her wait before answering.) "Right, it's eight o'clock. Good."

If necessary, prompt by pointing to the hour number. Progressively fade this pointing cue. You can also write out the word *o'clock* on a piece of tape and place it directly above the 12. Later, when she has mastered this step, remove the tape. Soon fade out, having her point to the long and short hands. You can also change your questions from "What o'clock is it?" to "What time is it?"

◈ Practice by setting a variety of hours. At first, go around the clock in order. Later skip around.
◈ Go through a make-believe day, associating hours with activities.
◈ Play a game. "Is it five o'clock?" Have her answer yes or no, and have her tell the correct time if no.

**Variation**   Have her set the hours you ask for. Hold the minute hand on 12 so she can move only the hour hand (later fade this assistance). If necessary, point at first to the correct number for the short hand, then fade this guidance. Teach twelve o'clock last, only after she gets the other hours regularly with no prompts. She should be able to identify all hours regularly, with infrequent prompts, before moving to Procedure II.

## Procedure II. Teaching 5, 10, 15, 20, and 25 Minutes Past the Hour

  *A. Identify 5 Minutes Past the Hour*   Begin with an hour. ("What time is this?" "Eight o'clock.") Next, have your child count five lines to the "1." You should then place a piece of tape with a small "5" next to the "1" (outside the circle). Say "This is 5 minutes past 8. What time is it?" (Prompt the answer by helping count to the long hand—5 minutes past—and then pointing to the short hand "8.")
  **Note:** Decide if you will say "past" or "after," and then be consistent. The basic procedure to be learned has three steps:

1. Counting from 12 to the long (big) hand (later by fives)
2. Identifying that it is "past" the hour (later she'll have to decide whether it is past or before)
3. Naming the hour from the short hand

For practice, prompt part of the answer. For example,

◈ Begin with 10:00. "What time is it?"
◈ Move to 10:05. "How many minutes past 10:00?"
◈ Repeat with other hours.

*or*

&#11022;   Set at 10:05. "It's 5 minutes past ___ ?" (Point to the hour if necessary.)

Repeat with other hours.

> *Variation   Have your child set the time. For example,*

&#11022;   Begin with 7:00 and ask for 5 minutes past 7:00.

&#11022;   Begin with 5 minutes past 7:00 and ask for 5 minutes past 10:00.
(In each case, she moves only one hand. You can hold the other hand to prevent errors so long as this assistance is necessary.)

Progressively fade out:

&#11022;   Pointing to the correct setting or counting minutes with her

&#11022;   Prompting your child by giving part of the time as you ask the question

&#11022;   Preventing the wrong hand from being moved

&#11022;   Teach 1:05 last (12:05 may be difficult also).

**B.  *Identify 10, 15, 20, and 25 Minutes Past the Hour***   After your child can identify 5 minutes past, fade out counting by ones and begin counting by fives. Write 5, 10, 15, 20, 25, and 30 around the outside of the clock in small numerals. You might want to write these on small pieces of masking tape so they can be removed later.

Using the strategies just presented for 5 minutes past, teach each of these in order until your child has achieved mastery with minimal prompting (e.g., give only occasional guidance about the correct hand to move, or get her started in counting by fives).

Have her count aloud by fives each time she locates the long hand, beginning with the "1" on the clock and pointing to the numbers (e.g., "5, 10, 15, 20, minutes past 8").

State a rule: "Count to the long (big) hand first." If you like, mark the end of this hand with a piece of colored tape to make it distinctive. Later you can remove the tape.

Remember the three-step process:

1. Count to the big (minute) hand by fives.
2. Identify that it is "past" the hour (later deciding if past or before).
3. Name the hour.

Your child will always say: "___ minutes [past or before] [hour]." Have her count by fives even after she has learned some times by rote.

As you set times for her to identify,

☞ Sometimes begin with the hour (e.g., 8:00) and systematically present times by fives as far as she has learned (8:05, 8:10, 8:15).

☞ Sometimes keep the minute hand the same (e.g., 10 minutes past) and change the hour hand (8:10, 3:10, 6:10).

☞ After she can identify times that you systematically change, skip around (8:05, 5:15). You will likely need to prompt more at first when you skip around this way.

*Variation* Have your child set times for you to identify. Tell her to pick times that she knows. When you give your answer, model the three-step process aloud, very distinctly.

**C. When the Hour Hand Comes First** Your child starts at 12, counting by fives to the minute hand. To avoid confusion in the early stages of learning these "past" times, use only times where the long (minute) hand comes first. For example,

As these are mastered, practice times where the hour hand comes first, giving careful prompts to count (past the hour hand) to the long hand. For example,

Save the times when both hands are on the same number (2:10, 5:25) for last. Keep the short (hour) hand right on the hour (rather than placing

it in-between, as it would actually appear). Over time you can gradually move it in between the two hours.

    **Remember:** Don't let her guess. Make her go slowly and follow the counting procedure so that she will not make mistakes.

## Procedure III.  Teaching 30 Minutes Past

First use the same process, counting by fives to the long hand at 30. "It's 30 minutes past 8."

    After some mastery, point out that "You can also say eight-thirty." Each time have her give "30 minutes past \_\_\_\_ and then the equivalent ("Or, \_\_\_\_ -thirty").

    As you drill half-hours, your child may begin to say, " \_\_\_\_ -thirty" each time, without having to count. Don't be surprised, though, when the next day counting by fives is again necessary. Encourage such counting, since *you want to teach her a process for figuring out times*, not just memorization of certain times.

    Place the short hand a quarter of the way between the 2 hours when teaching 30 minutes past. Later you'll fade it to midway between.

    **Note:** Teach your child to associate times with events in the daily routine. Go through a typical day on the clock, and talk about what you do at each of the times.

## Procedure IV.  Teaching 5, 10, 15, 20, and 25 Minutes Before the Hour

Decide if you'll say "before" or "to" and be consistent.

    Proceed as in teaching "past." Use the three-step process:

1.  Count from 12 to the big hand by fives.
2.  Decide whether it's past or before the hour.
3.  Name the hour from the little hand.

    You will need to work now on the decision of *past* or *before*. First, make pieces of tape marked 5, 10, 15, 20, and 25 and place these around the left side of the clock. You might shade in the left side of the clock, or write in big letters *before* and *past* on the two sides, for prompts. In the beginning, you may need to prompt by asking, "Is it before or past?" Then have your child give you the time. You can also drill before and past, even without having her identify the exact time. Make it a game; see how easily she can say "before" or "past" when you set times before and past the hour in a mixed order.

Again, keep the hour hand right on the hour at first. As with past the hour, save for last those times when the hour hand comes before the minute hand (e.g., 15 minutes before 11).

After all of the "before" times have been mastered, practice going around the clock (e.g., from 8:00 to 9:00 by fives.) After your child is identifying most times correctly, remove the pieces of tape marked for 10, 20, and 30 minutes; later, remove the remaining numbers cues (5, 15, and 25).

Practice holding the teaching clock several feet away, so your child cannot touch it while counting out a time. Next, practice on clocks in your home that are large and easy to reach.

Do not have your child wear a watch until Procedures I–IV are basically mastered, with few errors. A brand-new watch can be an excellent reward for a child who learns to tell time.

---

### 🌰 Comments

Some people prefer to teach these times as 35, 40, 45, 50, and 55 minutes past the hour. This method has several advantages: First, it uses just *past* for all times and therefore avoids the *before-past* distinction. Second, times are written this way (e.g., one writes 8:50 rather than 10 minutes before 9:00), and digital clocks display time this way. However, there are several drawbacks as well. This method involves counting by fives to 55, a difficult chore for many children. Also, we tend to think of times as before or past. A child is more likely to understand 10 minutes before 9:00 than 8:50.

We have chosen, for most children, to teach by the before/after method described here. After your child has learned times by this method, you can teach the "digital equivalents" (e.g., that 10 minutes before 9:00 is also 8:50).

---

## Procedure V. Teaching with Long or Short Hand in Between Numerals

We have emphasized errorless teaching in this program. To make the program complete, however, you will have to teach your child to tell times as they actually appear on clocks—with the minute hand and the hour hand in between the numbers on the clock.

Teaching your child to read minutes between the fives may not be worth the effort involved. You may want to teach her to estimate. If so,

☞ Place the long hand between two numerals.

☞ Have her identify which numbers it is between and which it is closer to.

☞ Teach her to say "It's about" when the long hand is 1 or 2 minutes off. For example, 10:14—"It's about 15 minutes past 10"; 10:11—"It's about 10 minutes past 10."

For the short hand: Teach your child that the short hand belongs with the previous number for all past times. Show her on your teaching clock that the short hand has just gone past the 2 when the time is 2:15. This may take some time to learn, so go slowly. Next, teach her that the short hand goes with the next number when it is before the hour. This should only be difficult for 25 minutes before, since for other times the hand will be clearly closer to the next numeral.

## Procedure VI. Teaching Use of Other Clocks and Other Time Concepts

After all times are mastered, practice on the teaching clock with all numbers covered except 3, 6, 9, and 12 (since some clocks and watches look like this). Practice with different clocks around the house. Buy your child a watch and have her wear it; look for opportunities during the day to ask her the time.

Teach equivalents:

1. Half-past eight is the same as eight-thirty or thirty minutes past eight.
2. *After* and *past* are the same; *before, of, to,* and *until* are the same.
3. *Quarter* is the same as 15.
4. Eight ten is the same as ten minutes past eight.
5. Perhaps later teach digital time equivalents (see Procedure IV).

Next, teach A.M., P.M., noon, and midnight. Also teach your child to recognize what time it will be in ___ minutes.

Continue to relate times to important events during the day. Have her tell you the time at various points during the day.

When you reach this point, CONGRATULATIONS! You have taught your child a difficult and useful information skill.

# Money Skills

This money skills program is designed to teach your child basic money skills. These skills include learning the names of coins, determining coin equivalences, counting amounts up to one dollar, and making change for amounts up to one dollar. These skills will provide a firm foundation for teaching more advanced use and management of money.

## Assessment

Complete the Money Skills Assessment (p. 367) with your child. The sections in the assessment parallel those in the program, and generally they gradually increase in difficulty. The assessment should indicate where in the program to start teaching.

## Materials

It's a good idea to put several quarters, dimes, and nickels, along with a number of pennies, in an envelope for your teaching sessions so that you won't have to look for change every day when you want to teach. The only other materials you will need are coin-matching cards. You can make these easily from index cards.

## Errorless Teaching

This program, like the others, is meant to be errorless. If you are teaching correctly, your child should rarely make a mistake. The main rule is: Do not allow guessing. Encourage your child to take his time and say "I don't know" rather than to guess. Encourage him to ask for help when necessary. Reward correct responses no matter how much help you need to give.

## Money Skills Assessment

I. COIN IDENTIFICATION
Can name a:
___ penny
___ nickel
___ dime
___ quarter
___ dollar

II. EQUIVALENCES
Can tell you how many:
___ cents in penny
___ cents in nickel
___ cents in dime
___ cents in quarter
___ cents in dollar
___ nickels in dime
___ nickels in quarter
___ nickels/dimes in quarter
___ dimes in dollar
___ quarters in dollar

III. COUNTING AMOUNTS THROUGH 10¢
___ Can give 1¢–5¢ from pile of pennies
___ Can give 6¢–10¢ from pile of pennies
___ Can give 6¢–10¢ from nickel and pennies

IV. COUNTING 11¢ TO 25¢
___ Can give 11¢–15¢ from dime, nickels, pennies
___ Can give up to 25¢ from dimes, nickels, pennies

V. COUNTING 26¢ TO $1.00
___ Can give amounts up to 50¢ (from array of coins)
___ Can give amounts up to $1.00 (from array of coins)
___ Can give amounts over $1.00 (array of coins/bills)

VI. RELATED SKILLS
*Reading Prices*
Can read:
___ 1¢
___ 5¢
___ 10¢
___ 25¢
___ $1.00
___ 39¢
___ 85¢
___ $.10
___ $.20
___ $.69

*Relative Values (More or Less)*
Can tell which is more:
___ Nickel or penny
___ Dime or nickel
___ Quarter or dime
___ 39¢ or 15¢
___ 75¢ or 29¢
___ $.25 or $.15
___ $.84 or $.79

VII. MAKING CHANGE
Gives back correct change when you:
___ Pay 3¢ with nickel
___ Pay 7¢ with dime
___ Pay 20¢ with quarter
___ Pay 15¢ with quarter
___ Pay 40¢ with two quarters
___ Pay 75¢ with dollar
___ Pay 89¢ with dollar

Counting out money takes time, and there are a number of chances for your child to make an error. Try to anticipate these. If he seems to be getting "off track," stop him, give him some help, or begin again. In later stages, when your child has learned to count money reasonably well, you may want to wait a bit when he begins to make an error to see if he can correct himself. But in the early stages ensure that he will not make an error by moving in to help.

## Procedure I.   Coin Identification

The aim of this section is to teach your child to identify a penny, a nickel, a dime, and a quarter.

***Recognizing***    You can teach your child to tell the difference between coins by their size and, for pennies, color. Begin with just two choices, the quarter and the penny (they differ in both color and size, and therefore are easiest to discriminate between). Place the quarter nearer to your child than the penny and say: "This is the quarter [point] and this is the penny [point]. Show me the QUARTER." When your child points to the correct coin, have him repeat the coin name. "What did you show me? [Quarter] That's right, quarter." Gradually move the penny closer and closer to the quarter, and repeat your questions, asking only for the quarter. Keep the quarter in the same position.

When your child is consistently correct, mix up the order of the coins and repeat until he can point to the quarter each time. Then move the penny closer to him and ask for the penny until he can point to it every time. Finally, mix up both the order of the coins and the kind of coin you ask for until your child can point to the correct one each time.

Then teach discrimination for each of these pairs of coins (going down the list, these become progressively more difficult):

- Nickel and penny
- Dime and penny
- Quarter and dime
- Quarter and nickel
- Dime and nickel

For some children, coin recognition can be taught from the start with three or four coins, especially if they already know some. Otherwise, after two-coin tasks are mastered, move to three and four coins.

---

###  Practicing Coin Discrimination

"More milk? That will be a DIME, please."

LeRoy studied the coins next to his plate. He carefully picked up a dime and handed it to his brother.

"Yeah, that's a dime. Here you go."

> Now that LeRoy could recognize the different coins during the daily teaching session, his brother had found a way to give him more practice at mealtime. LeRoy had to buy everything with coins that Mom gave him at the start of the meal.
> "Hey, LeRoy—you want some ice cream? It's going to cost you a QUARTER!"

***Naming***   Now that your child can recognize coins, teach him to name them. Again, begin with the easy choices (e.g., a quarter and a penny), but instead of asking him to show you the coin, point to each coin and ask, "What's this?"

Go through the same sequence of more and more difficult choices. Remember, go slowly enough that your child makes no—or very few—mistakes.

After your child can name coins when two or more are present, show him just one at a time and ask, "What's this?" (You may have to review by laying down several coins, at least at the beginning of a new session.)

## Procedure II.   Equivalences

This section teaches your child equivalent values of coins. Coin equivalences may be best taught at the same time as you teach counting (see Procedures III, IV, and V). However, some drill of equivalences may speed up later, so you may wish to teach the following now.

*First:*

5 pennies = 1 nickel
2 nickels = 1 dime

*Later:*

2 dimes and 1 nickel = 1 quarter
5 nickels = 1 quarter
2 dimes and 5 pennies = 1 quarter
1 dime and 3 nickels = 1 quarter

In the next sections, as we work on counting out various amounts of change, your child will gradually learn these equivalences. Now, though, the aim is to teach your child by rote.

For the first equivalences take five pennies and stack them slowly, counting out "one, two, three, four, five pennies." Next to the stack place a nickel. Tell your child, "There are five pennies in a nickel." Have him pick up the nickel as you pick up the stack of pennies, and then trade. Count out your five pennies again and repeat, "There are five pennies in a nickel." Perform several more trades and have him state each time, "There are five pennies in a nickel."

This basic procedure can be used to teach the remaining equivalences. Some of the quarter equivalences will be easier to teach after your child has mastered counting at least to 10¢.

## Procedure III. Counting Amounts Through 10¢

There are several basic rules for teaching counting money. *Your child should*

- &#x20db; Separate coins by value (put all pennies together, nickels together, and so on).
- &#x20db; Begin with the highest-value coin (not over the amount needed).
- &#x20db; Move coins left to right as he counts them.
- &#x20db; Count aloud while moving the coins.

*You should* give prompts as needed, count aloud with your child and point to coins if necessary, then fade out your prompts gradually.

**A. Counting 1¢–10¢ with Pennies** This is likely something that your child can already do. If not, drill this systematically. ("Give me 1¢," "Give me 2¢," etc.) If this is still difficult for your child, drop back to having him count amounts that you lay out for him (e.g., you give him 3 pennies and have him count out how much it is).

**B. Counting 6¢–10¢ with a nickel and pennies** This is the first introduction of the idea of starting with the highest-value coin (e.g., a nickel). In teaching these and all higher amounts, use this three-step approach:

1. You lay out an amount and have him count it. When he can do this without help, go to Step 2.
2. Have him count an amount from an array of coins onto a matching card. When he can do this without help, go to Step 3.
3. Have him count an amount from an array of coins without the matching card.

For example, with a child learning to count 6¢, lay out a nickel and penny in front of him (Step 1). Count aloud with him, pointing to each coin: "Bill, start with the nickel. How many cents in the nickel? [Five] OK, let's count. Five cents, six cents. How much? Six cents. Good." After your child can do this with 6¢, 7¢, 8¢, and 9¢, move to Step 2. From an array of nickels and pennies, have him separate them into piles. Then, prompt him to move the appropriate ones onto a matching card. Count aloud together as he moves the coins (remember, the highest-value coins are always moved first).

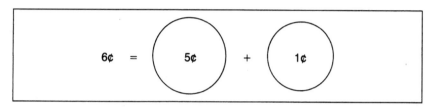

After your child can match the amounts 6¢, 7¢, 8¢, and 9¢ to matching cards, move to Step 3. Have him count out these same amounts without a matching card.

The equivalence of a nickel plus 5 pennies equals a dime, which has been taught by rote, can be reviewed here.

**Note:** Step 2 may not be necessary for your child. If he can go directly from Step 1 to Step 3 with few errors, you can skip Step 2. However, Step 2 is fun for many children and provides good review. You may be able to drop it from your teaching procedure after your child has mastered higher amounts. For now, make up matching cards for other amounts. Simply trace coins onto index cards and remember to begin with the highest-value coin.

## Procedure IV.  Counting 11¢–25¢

Begin with 11¢ through 15¢. Remember to separate coins into piles by value for initial practice; fade out doing so as your child masters the task.

Teach 11¢, 12¢, 13¢, and 14¢ by counting out pennies after saying 10¢ (with a dime or two nickels—vary this). Again, follow the three steps, beginning with laying out amounts for him (Step 1), then having him place amounts on matching cards (Step 2), and finally having him count amounts from the array of coins (Step 3).

Teach equivalences of 15¢ (a nickel plus a dime, three nickels); then teach 16¢ through 20¢, first counting 15¢ with a dime and a nickel and then counting pennies, and finally teach 21¢ through 25¢ in the same way. Review equivalences of a quarter.

Remember to have your child move coins from left to right and count aloud. Give as much help (by pointing or counting with him) as necessary. You should go slowly and not try to do too much in one session. Sessions should be short (10–20 minutes).

## Procedure V. Counting 26¢–$1.00

Remember the counting rules (especially to begin with the highest-value coin). Practice counting the amounts 30¢, then 35¢, 40¢, 45¢, and 50¢ with various combinations of coins, following the three steps (first you lay out the coins, then your child counts onto a matching card, and finally he counts without the card).

Next, practice counting the amounts in-between (say, 33¢, 47¢). Finally, repeat the above process for higher amounts (51¢–$1.00).

In teaching all of these, begin systematically (e.g., 30¢, then 35¢); skip around only after these amounts are essentially mastered in order.

**Variation**  Practice counting by 5s, 10s, and 25s. You can introduce this practice, using coins, at any point in teaching counting. If your child can write, you can also prepare worksheets to be filled in, as follows:

| 5¢ | 10¢ | ___ | ___ | 25¢ | ___ |
|-----|-----|-----|-----|-----|-----|
| 10¢ | ___ | 30¢ | 40¢ | 50¢ | ___ |
| 25¢ | 50¢ | ___ | $1.00 | | |

## Procedure VI.  Related Skills

Two related skills that can be taught as your child masters the basic counting skills are 1) reading prices and 2) the concepts of more and less.

**Reading Prices**  You can begin teaching your child to read prices (e.g., whether written as 9 cents, or $.09) as early as Procedure III, when he is beginning to count amounts. For some children, asking for amounts by writing numbers down and leaving a visual reminder present will be easier.

For children who can read two-digit numbers, teaching them to read prices will be very easy. For other children, assess which numbers they can read, and teach number reading upward from there. Mix these drills in with your coin teaching.

You can later teach your child to read amounts of bills: $1, $2, $5, and $10.

***More and Less***   Your child also needs to learn which of two amounts is more (or less) than the other. Similarly, he needs to learn whether a certain amount of money is enough to buy variously priced items (again, more or less).

You can drill this with both actual coin amounts and written prices (as soon as your child can read them). For example, prepare worksheets on which your child circles the amount in each pair that is more. Begin with amounts that are quite different, such as 25¢ and 3¢. Gradually reduce the difference between amounts as he masters the easier discriminations.

| More or Less Worksheets: Circle which is *more.* | | | | |
|---|---|---|---|---|
| 25¢ | 3¢ | | $.25 | $.03 |
| 20¢ | 5¢ | | $.20 | $.05 |
| | | and | | |
| 15¢ | 25¢ | | $.15 | $.25 |
| 15¢ | 19¢ | | $.15 | $.19 |

## Procedure VII.   Making Change

Learning to make change is more difficult than learning to count out specified amounts. You can begin to teach making change after your child can count amounts from 1¢ to 25¢ from an array of coins and after he knows coin equivalences. In the basic task, you give him an amount and he gives you change. If your child can read numerals, it will help to have price tags written out as a visual reminder.

For example, you say to your child, "I'm going to buy something that costs 5¢." Give him a dime. His task is to count aloud from 5¢ (the item's cost) to 10¢ (what you gave him) and give the appropriate coin(s) to you as he counts. Thus, making change involves the same steps as counting out amounts. The child counts from the amount needed up to the amount given. Practice first with multiples of five, since your child has learned these by rote. For example,

&#x25AB;   Item costs 5¢; you give a dime.
&#x25AB;   Item costs 10¢; you give a quarter.
&#x25AB;   Item costs 15¢; you give two dimes.

Later introduce amounts in between, where your child will first need to count out pennies to the nearest 5¢ or 10¢, and then count nickels and dimes. Stay with amounts up to 25¢ until these are mastered.

---

⌘ **Comments**

In counting out amounts, your child began with the highest-value coin. The order in making change is typically the opposite: Have him begin with the lowest-value coin, counting pennies to the nearest 5¢ or 10¢, then nickels and dimes to the nearest 25¢, and then quarters to a dollar. For example, in counting change from $1.00 for a $.19 item, your child would count 1 penny, 1 nickel, and 3 quarters. This may prove a very difficult idea at first, and it will likely take your child some time to learn to make correct change.

---

***Variation*** Have your child buy an item from you; you give change and your child counts it to see if it is right. Once he's mastered this task, occasionally give him incorrect change to see if he can catch the error.

# Index

MY 22 '02

## DATE DUE

GAYLORD     #3523PI     Printed in USA